ALL OF US OR NONE

ALL OF US OR NONE

Migrant Organizing in an Era of Deportation and Dispossession

MONISHA DAS GUPTA

DUKE UNIVERSITY PRESS
Durham and London   2024

Project Editor: Michael Trudeau
Designed by David Rainey
Typeset in Warnock Pro and Real Head Pro
by Westchester Publishing Services

Library of Congress Cataloging-in-Publication Data
Names: Das Gupta, Monisha, [date] author.
Title: All of us or none : migrant organizing in an era of
depor-tation and dispossession / Monisha Das Gupta.
Description: Durham : Duke University Press, 2024. | Includes
bibliographical references and index.
Identifiers: LCCN 2023053847 (print)
LCCN 2023053848 (ebook)
ISBN 9781478030874 (paperback)
ISBN 9781478026655 (hardcover)
ISBN 9781478059899 (ebook)
Subjects: LCSH: Immigrants—Political activity—United States
—History. | Refugees—Legal status, laws, etc.—United States. |
Deportation—Government policy—United States. | Detention
of persons—United States. | Noncitizens—United States. |
Emigration and immigration law—Social aspects— United
States. | United States—Emigration and immigration—
Government policy.
Classification: LCC JV6477 .D37 2024 (print) | LCC JV6477
(ebook) | DDC 323.3/29120973—DC23/ENG/20240405
LC record available at https://lccn.loc.gov/2023053847
LC ebook record available at https://lccn.loc.gov/2023053848

Cover art: Isaac Barrera, *Let's Get Free*, digital collage, 2016.

To Kieran,

My ray of light

CONTENTS

PREFACE

On October 5, 2017, in an act of civil disobedience, undocumented members of the Los Angeles area Immigrant Youth Coalition (IYC) put their bodies and futures on the line by setting down ten metal prison bed frames to block rush hour traffic in Westwood, Los Angeles. They strategically positioned themselves at the intersection of Wilshire Boulevard and Veterans Avenue across from the Federal Building. Several IYC members, with megaphones in hand, leaped on top of the plywood base of the bunks. Screen-printed logos of the private for-profit prison giants GEO Group and CoreCivic and the data-mining corporation Palantir hung on the rails of the prison beds.[1]

Another group of activists linked to each other with chains stepped off the sidewalk onto the road to surround them. Demonstrators lined the sidewalks. They had marched from California senator Dianne Feinstein's office, holding hand-painted signs declaring, "All of Us or None," "Defend the Criminalized," "Border Patrol Out of Our Communities," and "Black Lives Matter." The day marked the tight deadline for Deferred Action for Childhood Arrivals (DACA) recipients to apply for a two-year renewal of their status.[2] The civil disobedience without a police permit and the prison abolition messages set this demonstration apart from many other pro-DACA marches across the country. The IYC, with undocumented queer youth at the forefront, organized the civil disobedience. The youth were supported by a new coalition, Justice LA, which included activists from the local chapter of Black Lives Matter, and other local organizations working to dismantle correctional control. The coalition was formed to fight the city's new spurt of prison expansion, estimated to cost $3.5 billion, and had used the prison beds in a separate protest against the Los Angeles County proposals.[3] In the tradition of civil disobedience, the IYC activists risked arrest and deportation to expose the violence of the penal and deportation systems in the United States. The main message—"All of Us or None"—telegraphed their solidarity with all those who are fodder for the carceral system.

Predictably, police sirens soon rent the air, as did the blaring horns of enraged commuters stuck in the blockade. The commuters vociferously complained about missing their hospital appointments in Westwood and getting delayed for work. The privilege of their mobility and the temporary inconvenience of a traffic snarl was lost on them. The blockading activists suffer every day from the criminalization of their mobility. They live with the daily fear of arrest because they or their loved ones are forced to drive to work, school, and appointments without a license. They wanted to disrupt business as usual. By confronting cars full of angry commuters and armed police officers amid Donald Trump and Jeff Sessions's war on migrants and people of color, the organizers enacted a common call-and-response, "*Sin Papeles / Sin Miedo*," "No Papers / No Fear." Helmeted Los Angeles Police Department officers wielding their batons announced the assembly unlawful. They arrested nine activists, several of them undocumented, and cleared the intersection within half an hour of the takeover. It was not until the evening that the last of the nine arrested was released from police custody.[4]

A week before the action, Immigration and Customs Enforcement (ICE) had detained 101 individuals in the larger LA area as part of "Operation Safe City," a program endorsed by the Trump administration.[5] The operation targeted sanctuary jurisdictions, which refused to dedicate local law enforcement resources to aid the enforcement of immigration law. These arrests had failed to send the intended chilling message to this group of migrant activists. They were veterans of unpermitted civil disobedience. I had met many of them in previous shutdowns and takeovers of public spaces, and they trained me in civil disobedience. Under Trump, deportable youth continued to test their deportability by exercising the audacious power they built through collective action during the Barack Obama administration, which deported people at record numbers.

Local media reports framed the shutdown as a protest against Trump's rescission of DACA, which it was. But the coverage glossed over IYC's unambiguous resistance against criminalization and carcerality. On the streets, the Westwood protest dramatically linked prison expansion to the expansion of detention centers, the routinization of deportation, and the dangers of data

P.1. Immigrant Youth Coalition organizers shut down traffic in Westwood, LA, on October 5, 2017, by using prison beds to call attention to all forms of incarceration as police advance. Photo credit: Eduardo Lopez. Courtesy of Immigrant Youth Coalition.

collection, algorithmic analyses, and data sharing for criminalized US citizens and noncitizens. The links, however, were neither apparent to the public nor politically expedient to recognize, given the pervasive moral panic over crime. The stark imagery of prison beds did not fit the exceptional DACA narrative. For nearly a decade, advocates and sympathetic lawmakers have biopolitically produced innocent migrant youth as the most viable subjects of proposals to legalize migrants and the most deserving of relief from deportation.

This book tells the story of contemporary antideportation organizing by and for the most indefensible of migrants and refugees—those labeled criminal aliens. The organizers and organizations I write about produce expert knowledge about crimmigration—the convergence of the administrative and civil legal process of immigration enforcement with the criminal legal system. Deportees with criminal charges or convictions, who cannot be represented as the ideal subjects of immigration reform, are the subjects of this book. All four organizing spaces I cover represent a segment of the contemporary immigrant rights movement that demands transformation rather than reform. The coalitions and organizations call for an end to all forms of confinement. They challenge policymakers to look at the root

P.2. Immigrant Youth Coalition organizers, arrested for the October 5, 2017, civil disobedience, and their supporters pose for a group photo with the banner for their action after charges against them were read. Courtesy of Immigrant Youth Coalition.

causes that displace migrants, forcing them to flee economic and physical violence. Queer and feminist politics radicalize these spaces. They cultivate collective care in collective action. They envision the abolition of systems that determine disposability through the lens of gender and sexual justice.

Noncitizens who are branded with the criminal alien label include immigrants and refugees with legal permanent residence, undocumented migrants, and those who enter visa-free from Micronesian nations under a special agreement with the United States. All those charged or convicted of violent and nonviolent crimes are subject to mandatory deportation with few legal avenues to return to the United States. Like citizens under correctional control, they are predominantly people of color. Their loved ones, often left behind in the United States and often US citizens, can remain separated from them for life.

The analyses of these antideportation organizers, rooted in the lived experiences of migrants with criminal records, are unclouded by the settler myths of immigrant success pursued and eventually achieved. The activists' counternarratives, or what I term movement-building stories, reveal the relationship of immigration and crime control to settler colonialism maintained by carceral-security regimes. Their narratives rooted in abolitionist and intersectional organizing depart from the settling stories circulated within the reformist immigrant rights movement. The settling stories represent the United States as a land of immigrants to erase Indigenous presence, politics, and self-determination.

This book frames deportation and crimmigration as technologies of US settler carceral power, which executes gender and sexual violence.[6] By framing deportation as settler carcerality, I mean that the United States maintains control over what is Indigenous land through the expulsion of migrants, a process that increasingly relies on the criminal legal system with its carceral-security infrastructure. As Indigenous feminists have argued, gender and sexual politics are intrinsic to these settler controls.

I offer a way to think about deportation and Indigenous dispossession as thoroughly interdependent processes but not reducible to each other. The antideportation activists' focus on the interior space of the United States (not just the border) in their analyses of crimmigration helps me understand how settler colonial logics course through deportation policies, which rely heavily on criminalization and incarceration—both potent assertions of US sovereignty over a space that in actuality is animated by Indigenous politics of self-governance.

As someone who teaches and writes about migration and organizes for migrant rights in US-occupied Hawai'i, I regularly grapple with the relationships among settler colonialism, the Native Hawaiian sovereignty movement, and the politics of migration. This unsettling process has convinced me that writing about migration as a transnational process to spaces like the United States without engaging Indigenous people, Indigenous politics, and Indigenous studies is no longer possible. Here, I tackle questions about the relationship of migrant rights and Indigenous rights with which I concluded my first book, *Unruly Immigrants*, and have explored in publications since. I write this book as a migration scholar, an activist in the immigrant rights movement, and a settler allied with local Native Hawaiian struggles for sovereignty.

Like all projects, this one evolved, eventually becoming a book about antideportation organizing. I embarked on the project in 2009, inspired by the 2006 immigrant-led mass mobilization to stop federal bills criminalizing undocumented immigrants. In Honolulu, I was mesmerized by images of the mega marches and May Day protests in Los Angeles. I had never witnessed such a massive show of migrant power. In the spring of 2009, I headed to Los Angeles when the election of Barack Obama reenergized the immigrant rights movement. Several veteran immigrant rights activists counseled me to go to Los Angeles. That's where I would find the pulse of the movement, they said. I wanted to be part of this movement at that historic moment. I wanted to understand what ignited the waves of street-level demonstrations, even as I noticed that activist energies were being sucked into the halls of Congress to settle the question of undocumented migration by establishing a plan to legalize those present in the United States. I selected New York City as the other node because immigrant communities there had felt the full brunt of immigration enforcement in the name of national security since 9/11. Soon after 9/11, I documented the backlash against South Asian and Muslim communities with the New York Taxi Workers' Alliance.[7] I wanted to return to the city to examine the response of the immigrant rights movement there to the post-9/11 wave of deportations.

Since 2009, I have participated in marches, vigils, civil disobedience, town halls, strategy meetings, and fundraisers at both sites as an activist and researcher. Between 2009 and 2017, I familiarized myself with twenty-two immigrant rights organizations—fourteen in Los Angeles and eight in New York—and joined many of their activities. I trained with activists and brought back the lessons I learned from the organizers to Honolulu, where I live and work, to contend with the crisis of deportation experienced by migrant communities across our islands.[8]

Over time, I gravitated toward antideportation organizing and away from those heavily invested in comprehensive immigration reform.[9] I have selected to write about four groups. I chose them because their politics best illuminate the massive transformations of immigration enforcement in the interior. They connect the dots between incarceration, immigrant detention, and deportation. I focus on Families For Freedom in New York City, Khmer Girls in Action in Long Beach, the short-term coalition Tod@s Som@s Arizona (Tod@s) in Los Angeles, and the Immigrant Youth Coalition in the Los Angeles area, members of which visited Honolulu to mobilize local migrant youth. My methods of learning about their work went beyond simply eliciting their thoughts through interviews. I use my own involvement and observations as an activist. Sometimes I was a participant-observer, and other times, an observer. As an adult, I at times had to step back altogether in youth-led spaces and learn about the outcomes secondhand. I extensively use activist testimonies, which are underutilized in qualitative (sociological) research. This highly crafted political speech encapsulates the personal cost of detention and deportation to incite social change. I also draw on activist-generated reports, curricula, and handouts produced for political education.

I was introduced to the organizations and individual organizers through the larger network of immigrant rights groups and coalitions. These organizations were part of the exploratory stage of my research. The organizing I detail is influenced by the history of labor, Chicanx, civil rights, Black radical, and reproductive justice movements, even as it challenges many of their methods and styles of leadership to offer new models. Los Angeles is a city of coalitions. I met many of the antideportation organizers through the Southern California Immigration Coalition, whose members have a strong presence in the leadership of the city's Chicano movement and the Multi-ethnic Immigrant Worker Organizing Network, a coalition of immigrant and worker rights organizations, which has led the city's May Day celebration of low-wage workers since 1999. The antideportation organizers crisscross these spaces and have complex relationships with them—some combative, others coalitional. Similarly, there is a constellation of antideportation organizations on the East Coast, including, in New York, Families for Freedom, the Northern Manhattan Coalition for Immigrant Rights, and the Bronx Youth Project for Southeast Asian Youth of the Committee Against Anti-Asian Violence, now the Mekong NYC, PrYSM in Providence, and the now defunct Boston area Deported Diaspora. My interview with Cambodian American organizer Chhaya Chhoum, who then led the Bronx Youth Project, made a deep impression on me. She invited me to think about what a refugee voice and analysis can bring to discussions of immigration reform. That interview eventually turned my steps toward Long Beach and Khmer Girls in Action. I decided to learn more about this organization uniquely dedicated to building the leadership of young Cambodian women from Long Beach's refugee community. In many ways, I was discovering and following the circuits of activism forged over many years across land and ocean.

Who are these pathbreaking activists? This section of the immigrant rights movement is built by those who are directly impacted by deportation, which is often triggered by racially discriminatory policing and a criminal legal system stacked against them. They unapologetically assert their voices, vision, and leadership, parting ways from the reformist agenda pushed by advocacy organizations. They cultivate the leadership of girls, women, queer activists, youth, and the incarcerated. They are people who are immigrants and refugees; who are citizens and noncitizens; who are documented and undocumented; who have violent and nonviolent criminal convictions. They reflect the on-the-ground multiethnic and multiracial makeup of the immigrant rights movement, which is often racialized as "Latino." As an Asian Americanist, I have lifted the voices of Asian Americans, who remain invisible as actors in this struggle. I have also highlighted refugee and legal permanent resident voices that get drowned out in the demand for legalizing those who are undocumented. The activists challenge anti-Blackness, anti-Indigenous racism, homophobia, and transphobia within immigrant communities at the same time that they combat the state-driven war on migrants fed by such violence. The migrant youth activists I feature here express strong and loving relationships with their parents and elders, consciously connecting themselves to their families and communities. They have refused to throw their undocumented or "criminal alien" elders under the bus, so to speak, at a time when every policy proposal that would benefit undocumented youth has portrayed them as unwitting participants in their border-crossing parents' lawlessness, subterfuge, and incompetence.

The activists' courage, militancy, dedication, and tenacity sustain them in the enormously difficult work of fighting deportation. Their campaigns have freed individual deportees from detention, stopped individual deportations, and leveraged Democratic administrations to provide relief for groups like DACA-eligible youth and reduce deportation. Their persistence has sparked and sustained protest politics that today has mainstreamed the call to abolish ICE, which people outside of the movement recognize as a cruel and repressive agency. However, in the words of IYC member Johnathan Perez, antideportation organizing cannot stop at calls to abolish ICE. That generator of human misery, corporate profits, and votes for politicians is part of the massive punishment industry; activists fight to abolish the punishment industry entirely. This is a radical abolitionist implication of the organizing work I document here.[10]

I understand that antideportation activism and the contours of the immigrant rights movement may be quite different in border communities in Texas and Arizona, in a Midwestern metropolis like Chicago, in the New South where the demographics are no longer Black and white, and most certainly, in Hawai'i. The activists recognize this. In their trainings, they account for these specificities to build local capacity for resistance. While the activism I detail emerges from the local ecologies of social movements, the anti- or proimmigrant politics of elected officials, and laws governing crime and corrections, it is connected to US-wide and transnational campaigns such as the Southeast Asian Freedom Network's 1LoveMovement, National Day Laborer Organizing Network's #NotOneMore campaign, and Mijente's #FreeOurFutures actions, to name a few.

The ethnography stretches from the 2009 inauguration of Barack Obama, hailed as the first Black president of the United States, to the first years of the unapologetically white supremacist Trump administration. The policies of the Trump administration in its first years were guided by then attorney general Jeff Sessions, who used his office to implement his career-long anti-civil-rights and anti-immigrant political agenda. Since the arc of the book spans administrations often seen to be as different as day and night, I invite my readers to resist the temptation to cast the Trump administration as an exception to the basic principles of US democracy. Instead, I turn my readers' attention to the enduring strains of violence. The Los Angeles–based veteran immigrant rights activist and prison abolitionist Hamid Khan, who headed South Asian Network in Artesia until 2010 and now leads the Stop LAPD Spying Coalition, repeatedly reminds organizers of the United States' racist, colonial, and capitalist history so that we do not mistake current practices of policing, surveillance, and deportations as a "moment in time."

Overview of the Book

I lay out my framing of deportation as a form of gendered and sexual settler carceral violence in the introduction. To do this, I offer a way to think about migration to the United States, migration policy, and migrant politics in the context of Indigenous politics. The chapter brings the insights of Indigenous studies to bear on the convergence of crime control and deportation. It proposes analytical directions to think across critical migration studies and critical Indigenous studies.

Chapter 1 explains crimmigration from the point of view of antideportation activists. By connecting prisons, detention, and deportation, the activists lay out how and why criminalization has become such an effective method of postentry immigration enforcement. The discussion of the activists' engagement with policies governing crime and immigration serves as a reference for the following chapters.

The activism I cover in the chapters that follow is by and large invisible in the literature on migrant-led social movements. It is marginalized in the mainstream immigrant rights movement as well. The justice work of Tod@s Som@s Arizona, Families for Freedom, Khmer Girls in Action, and the Immigrant Youth Coalition breaks the mold of what can be considered immigrant rights and what is deemed as appropriate methods of struggle. Migrants with criminal convictions, including refugees and immigrants with legal permanent residency, and youth, who experience the daily force of punitive institutions, generate expansive political frameworks, new modes of agitation, and cross-movement visions of justice. Each type of organizing contends with settler carceral power in its own way.

In chapter 2, I focus on unpermitted direct actions in 2010 in Los Angeles led by the collective Tod@s Som@s Arizona. To protest Arizona's anti-immigrant legislation, specifically Senate Bill 1070, the collective targeted the Federal Detention Center and G4S Wackenhut, a for-profit corporation in the business of detention. Feminist and queer activists in Tod@s brought an embodied approach to their civil disobedience, their arrests, and the city's efforts to prosecute them criminally. Their approach exposed the reliance of settler carceral structures on gender-racial-sexual-religious violence. They modeled transformation through caring and creative modes of direct action.

Chapter 3 introduces the New York City–based Families for Freedom, which is among a handful of migrant rights organizations that embraces and involves deportees with criminal convictions. It sheds light on the effects of criminal control on legal permanent residents, who are mostly invisible in immigrant rights advocacy. It demands that all incarcerated people be set free. The FFF members' movement-building stories value criminalized men's care work in their families. By asserting that their families are valuable, FFF parts ways from the settling stories about respectable immigrants who conform to prescribed gender and sexual arrangements. The FFF narratives powerfully intervene in the standard demands of the immigrant rights movement, which seeks inclusion in the settler state.

In chapter 4, I turn to the social justice work of Khmer Girls in Action, which builds the leadership of high school age Cambodian youth in Long Beach. The chapter outlines the distinct demands for gender, economic, racial, and migration justice for refugee communities. These demands, too, are absent from an immigrant rights platform. The organization's political education strips away the benevolent mask of US refugee resettlement. It holds both Cambodia and the United States responsible for genocide and names the deportation of their loved ones, branded as felons, as another phase of deadly state violence. This framing prompts me to think about the deportation of resettled refugees as a form of settler carceral violence and consider KGA's activism in the context of current Tongva struggles for land and cultural rights in Long Beach. Though these struggles remain separate, their juxtaposition invites scholars and activists to think across migration and Indigeneity.

The last chapter looks at abolitionist and decolonial youth organizing across Los Angeles and Hawai'i. It returns us full circle to the Immigrant

Youth Coalition, which distanced itself from the controlling image of the DREAMers—the exceptional undocumented high school students whose human capital and cultural assimilation have come to be cast as the most winnable legalization demand. The IYC conducted a week-long youth empowerment summit in Honolulu. The cross-pollination of movement politics across the ocean led to solidarity efforts between non-Hawaiian Pacific Islander youth and non-Indigenous immigrant youth in Hawai'i. The IYC's undocuqueer political framework, discussions of criminalization, and attention to place encouraged the participants to examine how carceral and settler-imperial power work together. Oceanic decolonial projects emerged from youth-led efforts to raise their voices against their and their community's experiences of criminalization and discrimination.

Each chapter of the book shows how settler structures manifest in deportation. The antideportation organizers' defense of migrants with criminal convictions and their knowledge of crimmigration throws into relief the operation of these structures in distinct ways. Their resistance refuses the promise of legalization and the path to US citizenship. I cast these refusals as avenues to imagine migrant-led movement politics in solidarity with Indigenous people and minoritized groups to dismantle settler arrangements.

ACKNOWLEDGMENTS

The many amazing migrant justice organizers I have met over the years on the East and West Coasts of the United States and in Hawai'i have inspired this book. Their ingenuity and rebellious spirit have transformed the terrain of migration justice in monumental ways.

I owe my knowledge of Los Angeles's complex organizing landscape and the city's rich history of social movements for racial, immigrant, and labor justice to veterans Hamid Khan, Susan Alva, and Shiu-Ming Cheer. They enticed me to fall in love with Los Angeles. The impact of Hamid's razor-sharp intellect and politics is everywhere in this book. He created a beloved community with dal, chawl, and mouthwatering pots of goat or chicken curry simmering in his kitchen. I got to spend time with so many Tod@s Som@s Arizona and Immigrant Youth Coalition organizers over these meals. His home incubated joyful activism.

Johnathan Perez of the Immigrant Youth Coalition has offered his unstinting support to youth in Hawai'i, mentoring and encouraging them to find their voice and path. Their generosity throughout the years has been central. I am deeply grateful to Johnathan, Marcela Hernandez, and Isaac Barrera for working with me on identifying photos from IYC's archive.

In Long Beach, my time at KGA was formative for my political education. Their transformative educational practices made me a better teacher in the classroom. I cherish the time I spent with KGA youths. Lian Cheun, Sophya Chum, Chrissie Sam, Ashley Uyeda, and Joy Yanga offered a warm welcome and have made me feel at home since.

Families for Freedom in New York City has opened their hearts and doors to me. It has been a long-distance relationship and yet so enduring and inspiring. Janay "Jani" Cauthen, Abraham Paulos, Janis Rosheuvel, and

Manisha Vaze have all encouraged me to learn about and document the organization's unique focus on families and those who are criminalized.

The Hawai'i Coalition for Immigrant Rights (HCIR), seeded by the late Stan Bain, became the base for local organizing. I had the opportunity to work with enormously dedicated lawyers Kevin Block, John Egan, Dan Gluck, Clare Hanusz, and Wayne Tanaka, and community-based organizers Amy Agbayani, Susana Arvizu, April Kamilah Bautista, Rose Bautista, Kat Brady, Alan Cota, Gabriela Andrade, Deanna Espinas, Sue Patricia Haglund, Claudia Lara, Leonard Leon, Shingai Masiya, Deja Marie Ostrowski, Paola Rodelas, Darlene Rodriguez, Max Phillip, Doorae Shin, and Carolina Torresvalle. Amy, who calls herself a lobbyist for social justice, astutely counseled and guided us during the campaign for in-state tuition for undocumented students across the University of Hawai'i system. Innocenta Sound-Kikku fostered the oceanic connections in HCIR's work, lending her vision and wisdom. Nancy Aleck's enthusiasm for youth organizing energized us. Clare, whose loss has been heartbreaking, was a fierce and compassionate rebel lawyer who fought deportations and helped countless young migrants with their DACA applications.

In the exploratory years of this project, I benefited enormously from conversations with Mizue Aizeki, Chhaya Chhoum, Nathalie Contreras, Xiomara Corpeno, Heather Cottin, Amy Dalton, Trishala Deb, John Delloro, Jesse Diaz, Bernadette Elorin, Paul Engler, Simi Gandhi, Paulina Gonzalez, Frances Liu, Lolita Andrada Lledo, Nativo Lopez, Soniya Munshi, Suely Ngoy, Mary Ochs, Danny Park, Sandy Plácido, Sam Pullen, Dimple Rana, Robyn Magalit Rodriguez, Odilia Romero, Vivian Rothstein, Greg Simmons, Sandy Wright, and Dae J. Yoon. Thank you for the time you spent with me and your infectious passion for social justice. Mary Kunmi Yu Danico, now my colleague at the university, introduced me to Hamid. Paul Engler and Sam Pullen graciously hosted me at the Center for the Working Poor in Echo Park. We spent many evenings talking about the intersections of labor and immigrant rights. Mary Ochs and I crossed paths again in Honolulu. Her curiosity about the book has been affirming. I spent a precious afternoon with John Delloro looking at his photo albums documenting the many marches and protests that testified to the broad and strong Asian American and Latinx coalitions which took to the streets of LA. We lost John at a very young age. Nativo, whose stamp on LA's immigrant rights movement is indelible, also transitioned.

Just as the collective energy of organizing has sustained me, so too has the support of scholar-activists in the academy. The work of and conversations with Rachel Buff, Jodi Byrd, Linda Carty, Karma Chávez, Bianet Castellenos, Pierette Hondagneu-Sotelo, Grace Hong, Eithne Luibhéid, Joseph Nevins, Bandana Purkayastha, George Sanchez, and Shannon Speed, Becky Thompson, and Khatharya Um have been profoundly influential. Their engagement with my work has been a gift. Workshops on ethnography with Richa Nagar and Kirin Narayan were scintillating. I am grateful to J. Kēhaulani Kauanui for a deep dive into plenary power and to Jodi Byrd for pointing me to scholars working in the intersections of Indigenous studies and migration studies.

A 2017 "Rethinking Transnational Feminisms" University of California Humanities Research Institute Residential Research Group fellowship allowed me to develop the ideas that frame the book. I spent ten pleasurable weeks with brilliant feminist scholars Maylei Blackwell, Rachel Fabian, Grace Hong, Rana Jaleel, Zeynep Korman, Karen Leong, Jessica Millward, and Judy Wu. On returning to Hawai'i, I often leaned on Grace Hong, Karen Leong, and Judy Wu when I needed to untangle my ideas. Thank you, Kevin Escudero, for inviting me to participate in the 2019 Sawyer Seminar on Indigeneity and Diaspora at Brown University and workshop the book's framework with a group of incredible scholars.

I have been lucky to have spaces to write in community, especially during the isolating years of the pandemic. I depended on my writing buddies Rachel Fabian, Kelly Fong, Cynthia Franklin, Naoko Shibusawa, and Richard Rath to keep up my writing practice. Though I am not a historian, Judy Wu generously invited me to write with her lively hui of Asian American women historians Constance Chen, Kelly Fong, Dorothy Fujita-Rony, Jane Hong, Valerie Matsumoto, Isabel Quintana, and Susie Woo. Their feedback and support sharpened my analysis. I am grateful to Dorothy Fujita-Rony for insisting that I needed to give space to the stories of youth organizers in Hawai'i and to the cross-fertilization of political commitments across the ocean. Kelly Fong has been my weekly writing companion. Her encouragement, "You got this," has been comforting, especially when writing amid crisis, loss, and the pressures of pandemic teaching. Thank you, Jani Cauthen, Naazneen Diwan, Marcela Hernandez, Johnathan Perez, Mariela Saba, and the KGA organizers, for carefully reading and commenting on my chapters.

A special word of gratitude to the extraordinary Cynthia Franklin whose friendship and intellectual-political investments have kept me grounded. She has cared for me in countless ways. She has offered incisive comments on my chapters and encouragement throughout. Her sense of humor, generosity, and constant reassurance gave me hope.

My departments, ethnic studies and women, gender, and sexuality studies (WGSS), have steadfastly supported my scholarship and activism. The intellectual ferment in both departments has fed my scholarship. Conversations with Meda Chesney-Lind, Katherine Irwin, Rod Labrador, Jonathan Okamura, Richard Rath, Ayu Saraswati, Kathy Ferguson, and Ty Kāwika Tengan have enriched this project. Both departments played a crucial role in supporting the campaign for in-state tuition for undocumented students. I am grateful for the funding from both my departments for conference travel and editing support.

I found a superb editor in Courtney Berger at Duke University Press. Her steady support has given this project its shape. Courtney offered a rare combination of allowing me to find my focus as I developed the project and offering me gentle guidance when I felt lost, always reminding me of the elements of writing for a broad readership. Her responsiveness, understanding, and kindness have been pivotal. Many thanks to the press's pre- and postproduction team. They kept me on track and provided generous assistance. The book is stronger for the valuable comments I got from the anonymous reviewers.

Paige Rasmussen has helped me develop some of the chapters when they have felt too unwieldy and helped me clarify my arguments.

My family's love and care have buoyed me. My sister Ruchira ensured I had the time and space for research and writing by gracefully shouldering significant caretaking responsibilities. Always a champion, she kept me supplied with treats and lifted my spirits daily with funny photos of the family cats, Tango and Blur. She and my brother-in-law Michael have brought my nephew Kieran into my life. His laughter, playfulness, and creativity have brought such joy. When I stole away to work on the book during the holidays with him, he would lovingly chide me with "Mashi, you're typing a lot of words!" Kieran, this book with all those words is for you.

My father, a venerable academic, often asked me about the progress of this book, though he had lost much of his short-term memory. He would listen intently when I read sections to him. My readers' reports arrived a couple of weeks before I lost him. I cherish the memory of being able to give him the good news. He taught me to love words.

Rich, my coconspirator in life and my sounding board, has plotted this project and this book with me every step of the way. His intellectual and political acumen has reminded me of the stakes. He has been integral to the activism I write about in Los Angeles and Hawai'i. His delight with the life we have built together, his constancy, his laughter, his music, and his adventurousness have given me the heart to live through these tumultuous times.

DEPORTATION AS
SETTLER CARCERALITY

As critical migration scholars, what intellectual and political projects can we imagine to think about the contemporary mass displacement of people in the context of Indigenous sovereignty?[1] What can the juxtaposition of migration justice and Indigenous self-determination reveal about US settler colonialism, an everyday exercise of power I have learned to read in US-occupied Hawai'i? My questions, propelled by antideportation activism that defends "criminal aliens," center on a feminist understanding of deportation as a form of settler carceral power that simultaneously polices gender and sexuality. To theorize deportation as settler carcerality, I examine the expanded use of the criminal legal system to deport people from the United States.

I argue that policing through *ejection* advances settler colonialism even though, on the surface, deporting people may appear to be the opposite of settling migrants on Indigenous lands. A type of territorial control, settler colonialism works by making invisible the appropriation of Indigenous lands and oceanic spaces. It severs the caretaking relations of Indigenous people to land, water, and the elements and eliminates their presence through a range of technologies that relegate them to the past.[2] Settling requires evolving legal regimes that maintain territorial and social control. In this century, the United States consolidates its territorial control through new immigration penalties created to remove undocumented people and legal permanent residents for committing or being charged with deportable crimes. The legal controls reinstall the colonial and normative organization of gender and sexuality folded into racialized social control of migrants. In a nutshell, deportation is one manifestation of racial-gender-sexual violence embedded in US settler power.

Here is how deportation as settler carcerality works. The carceral state appeals to racist-nationalist-heterosexist calls for crime control and continually produces new felonies and felons. The creation of new crimes provides the conditions necessary for mass surveillance and incarceration, which are colonial, transphobic, homophobic, racist, and misogynist. The proliferating felonies are then put in the service of removing migrants, leading to the contemporary wave of mass deportation. This creates nonnormative family forms and kinship. The ejection of "criminal aliens" who live in the United States, in turn, allows the state to rehearse, sharpen, assert, and entrench its sovereignty over Indigenous people—their governance structures, land, and culture. It recruits crime control as part of territorial control, which is justified by liberal antiviolence discourses, strengthening American exceptionalism.[3]

Despite colonization and occupation, Indigenous people exercise sovereignty over the lands, water, and skies the United States claims for itself. As critical ethnic studies scholar Manu Vimalassery points out, the United States reasserts these claims in reactive acts of countersovereignty because "settler invocations of sovereignty require acknowledgment of Indigenous sovereignty . . . in order to maintain any semblance of stability or coherence."[4] Struggles to assert Indigenous self-determination are jurisdictional and territorial, exposing US imperialism and colonialism.[5] Indigenous feminists argue that full-blown Indigenous self-determination must enact decolonial forms of gender and sexuality and end colonial gender-sexual violence on Indigenous bodies—lands, water, and both human and other-than-human life. The territorial, political, and cultural autonomy at the heart of Indigenous self-determination differs fundamentally from civil rights and citizenship-focused struggles of racialized minorities. The latter seeks incorporation in the settler state through legal remedies. American Indian Studies scholar Joanne Barker (Lenape) crystallizes the implications of this distinction for intellectual and political academic formations like ethnic studies and women, gender, and sexuality studies, which are rooted in incorporative civil rights struggles and therefore diverge from the critical Indigenous studies (CIS) attention to "collective rights of Indigenous nations to sovereignty and self-determination in relation *to the state* [rather than within it]."[6] As a scholar who bridges migration, ethnic, and feminist studies, I take the sovereignty of Indigenous peoples over their territories in the present as a point of departure in writing this book. Along with autonomous governance, I want my readers to understand sovereignty articulated in CIS as encompassing Indigenous peoples' ongoing efforts to protect and restore lands and water through undoing colonial and heteropatriarchal extractive practices.

Building on these scholarly and movement insights, I unmask the dual function of US sovereignty, which projects itself as omnipresent by simultaneously managing transnational migration *and* deepening its control over Indigenous people and their governance structures. In explicating the convergence of Indigenous and Asian American experiences, ethnic studies scholars Karen Leong and Myla Vincenti Carpio ask us to look for the linkages among differential state practices of carcerality that result in distinct outcomes of dispossession, displacement, rightlessness, and removal.[7] By intersecting the CIS critiques of the settler politics of US citizenship and civil rights with critical migration studies' insights into the violent securitization of national space, I am able to identify the settler colonial power relations embedded in deportation policies.[8]

To bring CIS into conversation with the migrant-led social justice movement requires me to perform two tasks together. I point out the settler colonial nature of the demands for a pathway to citizenship and civil rights rife in the immigrant rights movement. At the same time, I underscore the migrant-led political stances that call into question the utility of those demands in light of their defense of "criminal aliens." The public questioning of criminality and carcerality sparks the need to address power relations within the organizing spaces. Feminist and queer antideportation activists model collective care to account for the intersecting vulnerabilities they and other organizers experience due to the moral policing of difference. These processes of identifying and addressing internal power relations shape and reshape the public-facing movement-building stories and actions. My twofold task of parsing settler colonial arguments in the mainstream immigrant rights movement and tracing the political visions of dissident migrant justice activists allows me to gauge the extent to which the anticarceral and antideportation alternatives can challenge the settler state. The book presents the transformative promise of migrant-led politics resistant to calls for state-sponsored amelioration.

In this analysis of antideportation activism, I am most interested in tracking the movement-building possibilities of expansive politics that cross immigration and criminal status. I use *migration justice* to signal such political projects. They are informed by the ethos "All of us or none" explicitly articulated by the Immigrant Youth Coalition's (IYC) civil disobedience (see the preface). All the coalitions and organizations covered in this book embrace some form of this ethos because they organize as people who have directly experienced correctional control prior to immigration detention, defend those with criminal charges and convictions, or risk criminal and immigration prosecution when they protest. They refuse to leave behind those who continue to be vulnerable to carceral control. To replace these repressive systems, they commit themselves to imagining and constructing life-affirming alternatives that value sociality. These largely Latinx, Asian, and Pacific Islander organizers forge multiethnic abolitionist frameworks by putting into practice a wide range of philosophies that emerge from Black, Indigenous, and Latin American radical traditions.

The political-ethical orientation of this section of the antideportation movement engenders robust critiques of the racial nation-state with its (empty) promise of inclusion through citizenship, fictitious assertions of US refugee and immigration policies as benevolent, and global-local neoliberal arrangements. The organizers' enactment of migration justice is distinct from immigrant rights organizing, which works within the nation-state and the civil rights framework to press for reform. The immigrant rights organizations' investment in state-sanctioned amelioration leaves no room to discuss the underlying global and national structures of white supremacist, patriarchal, and capitalist structures or question US sovereignty. By contrast, the "structural competency" of migration justice activists allows them to ally with Black Lives Matter and Indigenous struggles to protect their lands and waters against toxification, extraction, and destruction.[9] Thus, I am more interested in the coalitional spaces that antideportation activism opens up because it interrogates the legitimacy of US power, and I am less interested in asking whether displaced migrants are or can be settlers. The antideportation organizing I cover in this book represents dissident activists—many of them feminist, queer, refugee, and prison abolitionist—who, for over a decade, have been arguing that crime control and immigration control rest on the United States' disavowal of structural violence.

The antideportation activists' dissidence holds the key for scholars and social justice actors to recognize and name the connection between settler colonialism and carceral forms of state power. The fieldwork-based chapters mark place-based manifestations of settler carcerality and the ways in which antideportation activists confront them. I show how the activists' understanding of carceral power generates sometimes actualized, other times aspirational, solidarities with Indigenous struggles. I document a spectrum of activist efforts spanning intentional analyses of settler colonialism and those that provide sharp tools to dent settler discourses but do not directly use that political analysis. Some abolitionist organizing efforts, like those of New York City–based Families for Freedom (FFF), focus on deportees with criminal records. Though the organization does not engage with the settler power of deportation, it scripts new discourses that reject American exceptionalism, which is anti-Indigenous and anti-Black, in its very framing (chapter 3). Other efforts, such as those in Long Beach by Khmer Girls in Action (KGA), usefully strip away the benevolent framing of refugee resettlement by foregrounding US wars abroad and at home. But conversations have yet to materialize across two communities in Long Beach, Khmer and Tongva, struggling with the long life of historically specific genocides. On the other end of the spectrum, the Tod@s Som@s Arizona collective (Tod@s), which organized nonviolent direct actions in Los Angeles to protest the anti-immigrant Arizona law SB 1070, directly addresses settler politics (chapter 2). In Hawai'i, an empowerment summit facilitated by members of the IYC–National Immigrant Youth Alliance inspired non-Indigenous and Indigenous Pacific Islander immigrant youth to act in solidarity as they confronted the settler and imperial processes which criminalize Native Hawaiians, Pacific Islanders, and non-Indigenous migrants (chapter 5).

I concentrate on the workings of *interior* enforcement, what legal scholar Daniel Kanstroom calls postentry social control.[10] The interior is a spatiality. As a constructed space, the interior domesticates Indigenous polities and augments immigration enforcement with police power. It obscures the many wars the nation-state fights at home and launches abroad.[11] Police power, immigration enforcement, and imperial projects all nest in this interior space. I illustrate this nesting in my discussions of Long Beach (chapter 4) and Hawai'i (chapter 5). Following antideportation activists in New York, LA, and Hawai'i, I examine how police power has introduced an efficiency to deportation. The activists piece together the protocols, collaborations, and legal instruments used to locally proliferate the power of the Department of Homeland Security in conjunction with police across all the states. The Criminal Alien Program and newer programs like 287(g), Secure Communities, and Operation Community Shield as well as legal instruments like detainers are all part of an elaborate architecture of punishment built to surveil the interior. Activists call the nexus between criminal law and civil immigration enforcement crimmigration. By decoding how crimmigration works, the activists identify pressure points to slow down or halt the smooth operation of the pipeline from jail to prison, to detention, to deportation (see chapter 1). Of course, in the process, they connect crimmigration to a longer history of "foreign" interventions—US imperialism, military actions, and economic policies that have propelled migration.

While I recognize that many of the criminalizing border practices traveled to the interior and set the tone of the national conversations about immigration, as amply demonstrated by immigration scholar Patrisia Macías-Rojas's research on Arizona, I scrutinize what happens away from the US-Mexico border in Los Angeles and New York.[12] The twenty-first-century innovations in immigration enforcement provoke me to stretch myself beyond examining border making or simply calling for "no borders." In this, I find migration justice activist-scholar Harsha Walia's formulation of border imperialism useful. She argues that "while borders are understood as lines demarcating territory, an analysis of border imperialism interrogates modes and networks of governance that determine how bodies will be included within the nation-state, and how territory will be controlled within and in conjunction with the dictates of global empire and transnational capitalism."[13] After all, immigration and deportation are both transnational processes and are densely connected with the policing of the interior space, the full force of which is borne by the subjects of this book.

At the same time, by working with the idea of settler carcerality, I propose that this "domestic" and interior space is also transnational. The interior is animated by Indigenous sovereignty, which, to use Kahnawà:ke Mohawk political anthropologist Audra Simpson's words, "prevail within and apart from settler governance."[14] Deportation policies and practices try to restabilize US power not only at the border but also over the interior. As a transnational feminist scholar, writing this book allows me to rethink the units of analysis and methodologies in our field by conjoining analyses of cross-border flows as circuits welded by imperialism and neoimperialism abroad with settler forms of colonialism. How do we frame settler colonial dispossession of Indigenous lands while accounting for the displacing forces inducing immigration and deportation? I keep the present tense of Indigenous presence and politics in mind even when antideportation activism does not directly engage with Indigenous struggles. When there are no such links, I ask whether the activism produces stories, pedagogies, and actions that destabilize settler colonialism.

As a feminist, I examine deportation through the lens of gender and sexual politics. The carceral settler-imperial state insinuates itself in the most intimate relations of those it punishes. Jails, prisons, and detention centers are organized to maintain the Western, colonial gender binary, lining it up with the binary definition of sexuality (see chapter 2). US settler colonialism eliminates the multiplicity and fluidity of gender identifications and sexual practices in Indigenous cultures to install and yoke binary categorizations of sex to gender.[15] Carceral institutions instantiate the gender and sexual violence of conquest. Deportation also determines legitimate forms of kinship, sexual relations, and the division of household labor (see chapters 3 and 4). Yet, outside of feminist and queer migration scholarship, there is little recognition that deportation constitutes a central site of conflicts over racialized normative (binary) and nonnormative (fluid) gender and sexuality.

The immigrant rights movement widely decries family separation. Incarceration and deportation tear apart loved ones. The call to keep families together, therefore, is ubiquitous. Though this privileging of families can be read as a recourse to monogamous heterosexual conjugal respectability, those antideportation organizations that defend "criminal aliens" throw into relief the state's investment in particular family forms to secure a white or white-identified nationally bounded settler space. These activists' insistence on family unity makes legible the right to kinship and community of noncitizens and their US citizen loved ones, whose lives are structured by the ongoing violence of poverty, crime, and repeated displacement.

The antideportation activism I document converts private grief, shame, and fear into public protest. I frame this type of public speech as movement-building stories. Activists testify to the most intimate aspects of their day-to-day existence to show how correctional control and deportation have turned their lives "upside down." Undocumented youth face their fears of local and immigration enforcement to declare their status publicly (see chapter 5). These public testimonies and the affective space they create help me uncover the intersectional politics embedded in settler carceral power. The testimonies depart from the conventions of the immigrant success story, against which politicians and mainstream media pundits measure all demands for admission, permanent residency, and naturalization. These public forms of storytelling are movement-building because they scramble the discursive divides commonplace in the mainstream immigrant rights movement: innocent versus criminal, families versus felons, violent versus nonviolent, straight versus queer, deserving versus undeserving, documented versus undocumented, migrant versus citizen, and Native versus non-Native. In so doing, they push *against* the settling white supremacist and neoliberal logics embedded in stories of self-making and self-actualization.

In the rest of this chapter, I propose four analytical shifts, organized in pairs, to help critical migration and ethnic studies scholars think across migrancy and Indigeneity; dispossession and deportation; settler power and incarceration; and intimacy and publicity. I pair the concepts to explore their interrelations. The pairs are in generative tension. I draw out their distinctions, but I also dwell on the parallels and overlaps between them. In the last section, on intimacy and publicity, I break down the opposition between what is intimate and what can be public. The affective field created by the public circulation of intimacy lends power and vibrancy to movement-building and solidarities. Even when it is tempting to draw equivalencies, I avoid conflating struggles, and instead, identify the grounds for coalitions, which depend on the politics of difference or what feminist theorists Roderick Ferguson and Grace Hong evocatively term "strange affinities."[16] The analytical shifts fleshed out here inform the subsequent chapters.

Migrancy and Indigeneity

Indigenous people become legible to migration scholars when ongoing processes of land dispossession, essential to capitalist accumulation, force them to move. A significant body of literature covers Indigenous people migrating from Central and Latin America and crucially situates their dispossession and subsequent displacement in neoliberal economic policies such as the North American Free Trade Agreement (NAFTA), and outright war, all of which are structured through racialized geopolitical hierarchies or, in the case of Native Americans, through US colonial policies such as termination in the 1930s, which created urban Indians. The conclusion drawn by migration scholars from these processes is that "Indigenous people are also migrants." The structural conversion of Indigenous people into migrants brackets off the particularities of their struggles over land, culture, language, and political autonomy. It is as if the displacement endows Indigenous people with mobility. Otherwise, they are seen as fixed in place because their politics revolve around land rights to counter the centuries-long processes of dispossession. Indigenous and performance studies scholar Nohelani Teves (Kanaka Maoli) undoes the assumption that Indigenous peoples' relations to land necessarily fix them in place in the context of the Native Hawaiian diaspora by arguing that the connections to and love for land and culture are not severed on migration.[17]

Critical approaches to Latinx Indigeneities to understand the migration of Indigenous peoples across the Americas also serve to correct migration studies' overdetermination of mobility. Writing about Indigenous women escaping from Honduras, Guatemala, and Mexico and making their way to the US-Mexico border, Native American studies scholar and anthropologist Shannon Speed (Chickasaw) profoundly challenges the compartmentalization of Indigenous and migration studies. As they flee, these women are in motion and then in a state of suspension as they find themselves in detention when they reach the US border and seek asylum. The women's vulnerabilities, she argues, are rooted simultaneously in their migration and the violence they experience from settler and neoliberal structures they encounter across national spaces. In this way, she also sutures together Indigenous studies in North American and Indigenous Latin American studies.

A hemispheric framework allows for analyses grounded in Indigenous migrants' reconceptions of their ties to land and culture, and their layered relationship to variations in colonial, postcolonial, and settler state indigenist policies as they traverse the Americas.[18] Building on this hemispheric-transnational approach, Latinx studies scholar Maylei Blackwell has argued that antimigrant racism and class discrimination directed at Indigenous migrants who live in the United States are enmeshed with their encounters with multiple colonialities, which erase, absorb, and dispossess them in Central and Latin America.[19] A similar dynamic of racialization in US-occupied Hawai'i combined with US military-imperial control over Micronesia plays out for migrants from the freely associated states in that region. Indigeneity remains a constitutive element of the exclusions the migrants face, as well as of their modes of communal resistance to erasure and dispossession.

The assertion of Indigenous peoples' ties to ancestral land as part and parcel of Indigenous sovereignty often gets lost in our efforts to understand states of displacement, vagrancy, and exile in which subjectivity and territoriality do not line up. Cultural studies scholar Laura Lyons notes the routine evacuation of the materiality of land in the literature on deterritorialization—a concept useful to critical migration scholars.[20] This evacuation deepens the occlusion of Indigenous people's genealogical (not metaphorical or proprietary) relationship to land. Indigenous self-determination hinges on tending to relations between land and all life. People's genealogical ties to place intimately link culture and identity to land, bodies of water, the sky, and other elements. This dynamic constellation constitutes Indigenous politics.

Migration scholars Nandita Sharma and Cynthia Wright have identified claims to Indigeneity as a dangerous political project of fixing people in place to imagine a space, which is cordoned off ethnically. According to them, the right to land and culture is necessarily autochthonous because they base "principles of justice and allocation of resources (especially land) on notions of their *natural* connections to those places."[21] Sharma and Wright reduce the political emphasis in Indigenous sovereignty movements on a land base to "natural" ties. This line of analysis relies on equating Indigenous struggles for land rights with fixity, signaled by their use of the word "autochthony." They see Indigenous nationhood to be no different from modern nation-states founded on Westphalian notions of autochthony or the invention of sovereignty as uniform territorial control, which determines questions of belonging. As legal scholar Leti Volpp astutely points out, the autochthonous nature of the Westphalian nation-state "turns the settler into native" and has to establish "some relationship to the soil" to reinvent itself as a "nation of immigrants."[22] This recognition invites careful attention to the relationship among place, land, space, and people.

Indigenous conceptualizations of sovereignty are wide-ranging.[23] My research as a migration scholar has been deeply influenced by cis frameworks advanced by feminist Indigenous scholars and scholars who have theorized settler colonialism.[24] They all part ways with the exclusive, coercive, and anthropocentric notions of the modern nation-state and the sovereign citizen-subject who underwrites it. The realities of Indigenous self-governance spark settler anxieties about new displacements, especially for people of color, who, in reality, bear the brunt of exclusionary US (*not Indigenous*) nationalism. At worst, this argumentation has cast Indigenous sovereignty, which insists on land rights and place-based governance and knowledge, as "neoracist"—a repetition of the place-bound logic of modern nationalism. The forms that the decolonial Indigenous theories and practices take are not for us as migration scholars to foreclose in our anxiety to know what sort of nation is being constructed and imagined through Indigenous politics. Nor should we comfort ourselves with the thought that Indigenous epistemologies of collective accountability, mutuality, and interconnection will eliminate the question of the participation of racialized and sexual minorities in settler colonial structures and processes. A more interesting line of inquiry opens up when we consider Indigeneity as a disruption of the uniform US territorial power consolidated through deportation. This shift in focus on processes goes well beyond questions about the production of illegal and legal and settler and Indigenous subjecthoods.

The present tense of Indigenous politics and what Barker calls the "polity of the indigenous" is crucial to understanding the stakes of migration politics—their enactment and narration.[25] To think of Indigenous politics in the present tense—axiomatic in Indigenous studies—means that Native American and Native Hawaiian self-determination have to be treated as forces in the present. Immigration controls cannot be conceived as yet another phase of settler colonialism enabling a resurgence of xenophobia and anti-Blackness against minoritized peoples. Such a framing relegates settler politics vis-à-vis Indigenous assertions of sovereignty as a chapter in the past. Considering the ongoing exercise of Indigenous sovereignty and the United States as a transnational space can help migration scholars move toward interweaving theorizations of sovereignty, rights, and US imperial-colonial power.[26]

To analytically traverse deportability, criminality, settler colonialism, and Indigeneity, we must grasp that Indigenous people cannot be reduced to racial minorities in the search for a common ground to bridge Indigenous and migrant politics. Indigenous political projects aim at the restoration of their lands and self-governance. This project is unique to Indigenous people. It cannot be equated with migration justice, which targets racialized policing of space through immigration laws and their enforcement, restricting the rest from the West. The migration justice movement demands safe and dignified residence, currently denied to those migrants who get absorbed into US racial-class-gender-sexual hierarchies as minorities. Putting pressure on this difference does not preclude recognizing that both projects share similar targets in the form of white supremacist US countersovereignty and the oppressive structures the United States maintains globally. Land dispossession displaces Indigenous migrants; when they try to cross into the United States, they are most often denied asylum and deported.[27] Deportable Indigenous and non-Indigenous migrants share the common experience of displacement, but the root causes of the displacement are different for the two groups. This difference invites coalitions.[28]

Attending to migrant and Indigenous politics illuminates a common object of analysis—the production of US sovereignty to naturalize borders and obscure the presence of sovereign Indigenous polities within and across those borders. Both migrant and Indigenous struggles reveal how seemingly liberatory vehicles such as universal citizenship and civil rights are implicated in the distinct processes of the ejection of noncitizen migrants through deportation and the erosion of Indigenous sovereignty, to which land is central. It is important to remember that civil rights have not served racialized minorities at risk of deportation because, as Macías-Rojas argues, the punitive turn of immigration enforcement is consistent with, not antithetical to, the expansion of civil rights.[29]

As critical migration scholars, we adopt the insights of the theory of racial formation to scrutinize the relationship between race and space.[30] We ask who can enter certain national spaces, under what conditions, and who is ejected in order to secure whiteness. However, the autonomy of Indigeneity, and its implications for the central place of land rights and self-governance, escapes the theory of racial formation.[31] Race remains the master category in understanding the treatment of Indigenous people and the production of white nationalism, eliding questions of settler colonialism. Literary scholar Mark Rifkin shows how US Indian policy is designed to supplant the political substance of Indigeneity with racialized and culturalized discourses of "Indianness."[32] To take the Indigenous sovereignty claims seriously means moving away from treating Indigenous peoples as racial minorities. It also means recognizing that racial minorities and their mobilization of ethnic nationalism since the 1960s have been absorbed into an internal colonization framework without regard to the fact that racial minorities, unlike members of Indigenous Nations, do not exercise the right to political self-determination and they do not have Indigenous polities' nation-to-nation relationship with the US state.[33]

Furthermore, the race-class-gender framework that has developed out of women of color and Third World feminism continues to refract the political difference marked by Indigeneity as racial-imperial. It has not fully taken up the challenge of contending with the distinctive demands of Indigenous feminist politics that contend with settler colonialism. Indigenous feminist analyses, which have unmasked the violence of colonial control in the form of normative gender, sexual, and kinship arrangements and the accompanying disruption of Indigenous governance and cultures, have been subsumed under the sign of Third World and women of color feminism.[34] In other words, this framework too relies on a shared and indistinguishable sisterhood between Third World and Indigenous women on the grounds that Third World women in the United States experience the violence of US imperialism abroad and internal colonization at home.

Instead, I call on migration scholars, who work from a critical and feminist perspective, to question the United States in particular, and the modern nation-state in general, as the legitimate and normative form around which people are expected to organize political power. The demystification of the nation-state and the goal of full membership expose their colonial origins and their new forms in the present. Kanaka ʻŌiwi scholar and nationalist Haunani-Kay Trask argues that the effects of these settler modes of governance on Indigenous people and land dispossession cannot be addressed with race-based remedies.[35] Trask conceptualizes civil rights as a contract between white settlers and racialized minorities. I keep this sobering insight in mind to critique the turn to civil rights in the legislation-driven immigrant rights movements. Instead of getting caught up in which racialized minorities count as settlers, I have followed scholars who have built on Trask's call for accountability from racial minorities for advancing settler colonialism; I look carefully at the methods of migrant resistance.[36] These methods sometimes lead racial minorities to bargain for power within the settler colonial system and at other times lead them to resist settler ideologies and structures and, going a step further, to connect their struggles to those of Indigenous people. This book tracks the enticements of settler colonial practices and discourses to stave off deportation. It also marks the points of connection when migrants, legally present immigrants, and refugees refuse the "gifts" of civil rights and US citizenship.[37]

Dispossession and Displacement

My discussion above of the distinctions between Indigenous and migrant political projects lays the groundwork to understand why the removal of Native Americans from their Nations is not equivalent to the removal of migrants from the United States through deportation, even though the Department of Homeland Security uses the term "removal" to describe the administrative process of deportation. There has been a move in legal scholarship on immigration to compare the US policy to remove Native Americans from their land (dispossession) starting in 1830 with the evolution of late nineteenth-century policies to remove immigrants (deportation). Kanstroom traces the development of policies to remove aliens to the legal precedence set by Cherokee removal.[38] Though such a comparison offers an example of putting the legal treatment of Indigenous Nations and immigrants in conversation, it suffers from the tendency in legal scholarship to treat Indigenous people as aliens, to use Volpp's astute observation about the field.[39]

For my argument, dispossession works through the alienation and privatization of land held in common by an Indigenous Nation, whether it is federally recognized or not. Dispossession is wrapped in the settling of Indigenous *lands*. Settler colonialism is land-based, and it produces settlers as natives, who claim control over land and waters, backed by nativist ideologies and a political economy that privatizes land and holds large swathes of it in trust for the settler state's abuse. Settler power often dispossesses *and* dislocates Indigenous people from their ancestral homes on Turtle Island and the United States' insular empire in the Pacific.

I use displacement, not settler-colonialism-induced dispossession, to describe the mechanisms driving the movement of non-Indigenous people across nation-state-bounded spaces. Not all such migrants to the United States come from settler colonial nation-states and, therefore, are not dispossessed through land-devouring settler processes. This does not mean that the loss of land rights is not part of their migration stories. Their loss of land and livelihoods is often caused by displacement as a result of imperial wars, civil wars, gender- and sexuality-based violence, political persecution, and neoliberal economic policies in their nation-states. When they arrive in the United States, they are racialized as minorities.[40] Deportation, as a transnational US settler state act, displaces them to another nation-state yet again.

Keeping in place these critical distinctions between Indigenous people and racial minorities, and between dispossession and displacement, to understand removal, I follow all the ways in which the state's claim on the right to deport is bound up with the continuous effort to dispossess Indigenous people of their material and cultural base. Settler colonialism, then, undermines Indigenous sovereignty *and* determines deportability. It is a two-in-one deal.

The invention and evolution of the legal doctrine of US plenary power has been taken up by Kanstroom in his work on postentry social control and removals as a point of contact between the treatment of Indigenous people and migrants. Plenary power extends unlimited congressional authority over domestic space invoking primary and uniform control over that territory. Though Kanstroom dates its invention as a legal doctrine in the context of Cherokee removal in the 1830s, legal scholars David Wilkins (Lumbee) and K. Tsianina Lomawaima (Mvskoke/Creek) trace its consolidation as unlimited and absolute in the latter part of the nineteenth century. This version of plenary power continues to diminish Native treaty, land, and water rights. It clears the way for the federal government to keep encroaching on Native lands to exploit and militarize them.[41] This process is ongoing. Indigenous studies scholar and poet Margo Tamez (Dene Ndé) exposes the impunity with which the US federal government appropriated unceded Ndé lands after 9/11 to build a border wall in Big Water Country (Lower Río Grande River, Texas) in an exertion of "settler military masculinity." She characterizes this type of necropolitical US territorial control as "soveryempty," a force that attempts to drain life from the land, the elements, and people. However, Ndé women's legal, embodied, storied resistance locally, at the US federal level, and in international arenas of human rights produces subversive and "difficult knowledge" from this very space of confinement to foster vitality.[42]

The doctrine of plenary power was extended to immigrants in three late nineteenth-century US Supreme Court rulings on the racial-exclusion-based deportation of Chinese and Japanese aliens. As Volpp points out, these cases are foundational to legal discussions of the evolution of immigration controls in a way that disappears Indigeneity.[43] In a dangerous slippage between recounting an earlier phase of the legal history of plenary power and analyzing it, Kanstroom conflates the deportation of racialized migrants with Cherokee removal. He equates the work of plenary power in obfuscating Cherokee self-determination to remove them from their ancestral lands with the exclusion and expulsion of individual Chinese citizens based on their race and national origin.

Indian removal and Chinese exclusion, however, are not the same in substance or effect. Even though the courts debate this, Cherokees are not foreign nationals in the same way Chinese migrants to the United States were in the late nineteenth century. The United States has developed a nation-within-the nation Indian policy in a way that differentiates it from US foreign relations. Glossing over the differences, Kanstroom claims, "The forced removal *from U.S. territory* [sic] was a central feature of Indian law long before it became such for immigrants."[44] This erases Cherokee sovereignty and the implications of the legal construction of the "domestic dependent nation" in the 1831 *Cherokee Nation v. Georgia* case. The misguided analogy between the deportation of foreign nationals and the subjection of the Cherokee Nation to removal is a legal sleight of hand that converts the Indigenous into the alien.

In the case of aliens, congressional plenary power operates with almost no judicial constraint, repeatedly throwing into crisis the question of deportable noncitizens' entitlement to due process. The US Supreme Court continues to debate the limits of plenary power when determining the indefinite detention of immigrants. These questions are not likely to rein in the operation of plenary power imposed over Native Nations. Nonetheless,

I find useful Manu Vimalassery's casting of US sovereignty as "counter-sovereignty . . . a perpetual reaction to the prior and primary claims of Native peoples on the territories that the United States claims as its own."[45] The term "counter-sovereignty" reminds us that the United States' plenary power is not absolute. The United States constantly attempts to stabilize its power to project internal coherence to manage the very real presence of sovereignty within sovereignty, Simpson's first signpost.[46] The comparativism encouraged by the critical turn in ethnic studies can open up these investigations by paying close attention to the distinctions among anti-immigrant racism, anti-Indigenous policies, and anti-Blackness while seeking the veins of structural violence coursing through them.[47]

Settler Power and Incarceration

The United States simultaneously operates as a settler colonial, imperial, neoliberal, carceral, white supremacist, and heteropatriarchal state. But each mode does a particular type of ideological and material work. In this section, I show how the connective tissues of settler colonialism attach Indigenous dispossession through dislocation, confinement, and imprisonment to anti-Blackness encoded in mass incarceration and to immigrant detention and deportation. Several Indigenous scholars have theorized the fundamentally carceral nature of the United States' power. Writing about the seventy-five-mile militarized border wall in Texas that suffocates her Big Water Country community, Tamez encapsulates the carceral nature of the settler state when she says that "in the walled Ndé world, walls, detention, the carceral and non-recognition are fused."[48] Similarly, Nick Estes (Kul Wicasa) and his coauthors remind us that settler power is carceral and punitive. Many reservations started as concentration camps. Since "borders exist everywhere settler order confronts Native order," they argue that settler power contains, surveils, and kills, marking Indigenous people living outside of reservations as interlopers.[49]

Here, I correct the near absence of discussions of crime control as a form of settler power in the extensive scholarship about mass incarceration that followed the end of legalized racial segregation in the 1960s. The framing of mass incarceration as the New Jim Crow, a reference to the reincarnation of legalized discrimination against African Americans in the post–civil rights era, has considerable appeal for antideportation activists.

Even as the activists connect their criminalization to racism, they are critically conscious of the alien status of deportees with criminal charges or convictions. This immigration status sets the legal treatment of "criminal aliens" apart from the criminal legal system's relegation of African Americans to second-class citizenship. Methodologically, the two communities' points of contact with the US carceral state require a precise examination of the state processes of criminalization and prosecution so as not to flatten out significant differences while identifying the grounds for coalitions.

Scholars have written extensively and powerfully about the foundational connection between anti-Black racism and carcerality, tracing its reincarnations from the enslavement of Africans and African Americans to their mass incarceration today.[50] The intersections between the sites and practices of migrant detention and the prison system, developed to dehumanize African Americans, are being increasingly explored by those who study immigrant communities.[51] However, far less attention has been paid to settler power in the literature on incarceration, with a few exceptions that have inspired me.[52] Leong and Carpio urge scholars studying carceral practices to recognize that "the erasures of colonization as a process and genocide as a colonial technology from discussions of slavery and the carceral state manifest the settler state at work even in critiques of the carceral state."[53] Their call to focus analytically and methodologically on state practices as the link is an important reminder of how to uncover the tracks of crime control without equating the types of subjugation.

Crime control serves as one conduit of power over Indian country. Criminal jurisdiction deepened US federal control over Indian tribal governments with a series of legal-juridical measures in the late nineteenth century. An absolute version of congressional plenary power beyond judicial review was invented during this period to govern intratribal crime on Indian reservations. This version was then applied in the trilogy of US Supreme Court rulings between 1889 and 1893 on the exclusion of Chinese and Japanese immigrants, setting a precedent operative today for the US government's authority to deport non-US-citizen immigrants. Wilkins and Lomawaima have shown that between 1880 and 1920, the extension of federal jurisdiction over federally defined criminal acts started to erode tribal sovereignty as part of a slew of assimilation policies. The measures were spurred by the 1884 victory in the US Supreme Court of Brulé leader, Crow Dog, who successfully contested his death sentence imposed by federal agents in violation of the Lakota adjudication of intratribal homicide. In reaction, Congress passed the Major Crimes Act (MCA) in 1885 establishing overriding federal authority in prosecuting violent and nonviolent crimes. The very next year, Kagama unsuccessfully challenged the MCA's authority in the Supreme Court, which upheld his indictment by the US attorney of Northern California for a murder on California's Hoopa Valley reservation.[54]

The MCA, a settler colonial tool, imposes Euro-American protocols of prosecution and punishment to impair tribal self-determination. Though the term "plenary power" was not used in the Kagama ruling, it introduced the notion of absolute and unlimited congressional fiat beyond the exclusive power of Congress to govern interstate and foreign commerce with Native Nations defined by the commerce clause and the preemptive federal power over states in matters relating to Indian affairs.[55] The ruling rationalized the lack of a constitutional basis for the exercise of this type of power at the expense of tribal sovereignty by trotting out the well-worn arguments about Native American incompetence and weakness and their need for tutelage and protection as "wards" of the United States. Wilkins and Lomawaima argue that this version of congressional plenary power, unrestrained by constitutional checks and developed in the context of contestations over Indian tribal jurisdiction over crime, was used to great effect in the 1903 Supreme Court case *Lone Wolf v. Hitchcock* to dispossess two million acres of Kiowa, Comanche, and Apache land.[56] Thus, US sovereign power exercised in deportation cases is founded on dispossessing Indigenous people of their landbase, deepening colonial political control.

The twentieth- and twenty-first-century criminal legal effects of federal Indian law are aggravated by the termination era Public Law 280, which transferred criminal jurisdiction to certain states. In 1978, a Supreme Court ruling further weakened the jurisdiction of tribal governments by stripping them of the power to prosecute crimes committed by non-Indians on Indian reservations and further entrenching racial and reprosexual notions of Indianness at the expense of their recognition as political, self-governing entities.[57] Muscogee legal scholar Sarah Deer has mapped the vulnerability to sexual violence of Native American women and their lack of access to justice produced by this long series of federal actions.[58] This settler colonial form of power that encodes assaults on Native American sovereignty, land dispossession, and sexual violence is then transmuted and transferred to govern immigrants. The frequent invocation by courts in deportation cases today of judicial deference to congressional plenary power, the rationalization of the lack of judicial review, and the constant effort to deny due process to migrants derive from this settler carceral genealogy, which, however, is rarely traced.

More evident to activists and scholars are the links between the enduring control of the criminal legal system over African American communities and the incarceration of Black, Latinx, and Asian noncitizens. Socially marginalized citizens and noncitizens of color and Black immigrants, who often live in the same impoverished and hyperpoliced neighborhoods, equally feel the impacts of correctional control, accelerated by the 1980s war on crime. In response, the antideportation activists spell out how this system, built to decimate African American communities, also devours other minoritized groups, including Black immigrants. They see the reflections of the carceral tactics deployed by local law enforcement in immigration enforcement. They recognize, analyze, and reject the anti-Black and anti-Muslim racism encoded in the constant refrains in the immigrant rights movement that "We Are Not Criminal" and "We Are Not Terrorists."

Crimmigration represents some key differences, despite the overlaps in migrant and African American experiences with policing. "Criminal aliens" living in the United States often face the consequence of permanent deportation, setting them apart from citizens. The demands of such migrants to stop the criminalization of Black people and people of color exceed the bounds of a civil rights framing of mass incarceration. Legal scholar Michelle Alexander has forcefully argued that today the "New Jim Crow," or the new ways to legally exclude African Americans with criminal convictions from voting, jury service, jobs, public housing, other forms of public assistance, and federal college loans have created a monumental, and yet invisible, crisis in civil rights. This present-day second-class citizenship for African Americans requires, in her view, a new civil rights movement focused on the effects of a prison-oriented and racially-tinged moral panic about crime.[59]

The formulation of the "New Jim Crow" resonates with antideportation activists.[60] They used this language when many governments and states started to pass copycat bills modeled after Arizona's SB 1070. The Arizona law attempted to deploy state and local law enforcement to police the immigration status of the state's residents and criminalize a host of daily activities of undocumented migrants and their citizen allies. The activists use the analogy of the "New Jim Crow" to specify an apartheid system that uses immigration status to legally deny migrants their basic human rights to rentals, public education, health care, public assistance, day laborer jobs, and driver's licenses. Simultaneously, they argue that legalization is unlikely to help those groups of migrants at risk of criminalization and subsequent deportation. The points of contact between prison abolition and anti-deportation organizing, then, cannot take the form of a new civil rights movement. Tod@s, FFF, KGA, the IYC, and youth in Hawai'i demonstrate their acute awareness of the distinct impacts of criminalization, paving the way for alliances with Black and Indigenous organizing against policing.

I extend my critique of a civil rights approach by heeding Deer's reminder that the Indian Civil Rights Act of 1968 was used to discipline tribal courts rather than addressing the concerns about police brutality raised in the late 1960s by American Indian activists. It made tribal courts responsible for enforcing individual rights under the US Constitution in a way that subjected the tribal process to US federal review. It circumscribed the powers of tribal courts to misdemeanor-level sentencing.[61] The nation-state-bound civil rights framework also impedes understanding the proliferating types and sites of confinement across borders as the global lockdown, a formulation put forth by transnational feminist and ethnic studies scholar Julia Chinyere Oparah in collaboration with former prisoners and prison abolitionist activists.[62] If those struggling for prison abolition want to confront settler colonialism, they need to realize that the "individualism of rights claims and rights discourse at large mirrors the logic of the prison industrial complex that argues that violence is only and always locatable on the level of the individual," as Eric Stanley puts it in reflecting on the mainstream LGBT movement's investment civil rights gains.[63] The antideportation activists' turn toward abolitionist and transformative justice moves away from state-centered and nationally insulated responses. The activists bear witness to the intimate impacts of the coming together of crime and immigration control in the context of neoliberal and colonial-imperial policies, giving them the fluency in the workings of crimmigration.

Intimacy and Publicity

"We want your labor, not your lives." In the *Karma of Brown Folk*, Vijay Prashad distills the expediency of US immigration laws in opening and closing the doors to labor from the Global South.[64] He diagnoses the United States' unquenchable thirst for cheapened and flexible labor, made pliable through the threat of exclusion or expulsion, at the expense of the migrants' lives. Even after the abolition of racial quotas in the 1965 amendment to the

Immigration and Nationality Act and its stated preference for family reunification, the reduction of migrants to their labor market functions limits the debates over migration. Labor is compartmentalized from life. Anti-deportation migrant justice activists, who are the subjects of this book, insert their lives and the intimate into public protest. They publicly recount the disruption to their intimate relations without appealing to settler and racialized discourses of heteronormative respectability. Simultaneously, the activists engage in internal decolonial work, with feminist and queer activists taking the lead.

Mass deportation may seem to run counter to the market principle of utilizing migrants as laborers. But detention is big business, with 70 percent of these facilities run by private for-profit corporations.[65] These facilities need migrants to fill beds and perform the labor of cleaning, serving food, and providing full-time childcare. The biopolitical project produces an unlawful population—aliens whose very existence must be imagined through racial-gender ideologies. This project potently converges with the political economy of incarceration (see chapters 1, 2, and 5). Drawing on Angela Davis's insight into the prison industrial complex, incarceration "utilizes punishment as a source of potentially stupendous profits" while devouring social wealth.[66] Like other forms of incarceration, detention profits from severing people from their loved ones and community.

The contemporary immigrant rights movement navigates the split between labor and life in its fight against illegalization and deportation. On the one hand, immigrant rights activists send a powerful message about the indispensability of migrant labor through such actions as "A Day without an Immigrant" in the wake of the 2006 mega marches and after the election of Donald Trump.[67] DREAMers have had to project themselves as untapped economic actors in their fight to pass legislation that would give undocumented youth a path to legalization. On the other hand, we see the ubiquity of banners declaring "Keep Families Together! / Stop Deportation," "Stop Tearing Families Apart," or "Broken Hearts / Broken Families" at every immigrant rights march, vigil, and action. Coming out publicly as undocumented, DREAMers modeled public storytelling that lays bare their despair and fragile hopes. The movement as a whole publicizes the impact of restrictive immigration policies on the lives of migrants. But what gets revealed and for what purpose differs within the movement.

The migrant justice activists collapse the distance between intimacy and publicity and labor and lives to deploy transformative political methods. They craft narrative strategies to produce movement-building stories. The activists' critical approach to organizing reveals much about gender and sexuality inscribed in immigration control, settler colonialism, and anti-Black racism or what feminist scholar Andrea Smith frames as the three pillars of heteropatriarchal white supremacy.[68] Queer and feminist antideportation activists produce intimate knowledge of policing and incarceration through their bodily encounters with them (see chapters 2 and 5). For example, those arrested for their direct actions staged by Tod@s show that the very act of jailing begins with stabilizing the colonial gender binary and its conflation with sex by designating them as "male" or "female." Poet and literary scholar Deborah Miranda (Ohlone-Costanoan Esselen and Chumash) has termed the punishment and extermination of third gender and Two-Spirit people during the Spanish colonization of California *gendercide*, "the killing of a particular gender because of their gender."[69] Today, all jails, prisons, and detention centers are constructed around binary sex. Straight and colonial imaginations of predatory and pathological heterosexuality and homosexuality underwrite these homosocially organized spaces.[70] The activists' methods of protest expose the structural violence and aim to transform these dehumanizing social arrangements.

The activists' public-facing work is accompanied by the labor of feminist and queer activists *within* their organizations and coalitions to foster a political culture that can address the internal replication of dominant power relations. Throughout the book, I mark the engagements with what Blackwell calls the "internalities of power." In the context of the Chicano movement, Blackwell shows the importance of recovering insurgent feminist consciousness away from the public arena of protest to understand the full scope of Chicana power.[71] In abolition antideportation organizing, feminist and queer activists hold space for those movement actors who are multiply nonconforming and confined ideologically and physically. They use the principles of transformative justice to reduce harm and create safety internally.[72] They address masculinist modes of organizing by folding in care and critical reflection. They continually contest the anti-Black politics of respectability by dismantling the deserving-undeserving divide constructed along the lines of criminality. They spell out the ways in which immigration regulations and militarization undercut Indigenous sovereignty. Most significantly, they assert their voices and visions in those left movement spaces dominated by cis heterosexual or homonationalist agendas. Together, this type of organizing demonstrates the many ways in which intimacy becomes a means to build the movement to stop deportation.

The activists bring their privatized experiences of violence, loss, shame, and fear into public spaces to demand public accountability. Such public acts require trust, support, and radical care modeled by the queer and feminist antideportation organizers.[73] To prepare for the vulnerability of activists engaged in direct action to the public's anger and to arrest, caretaking becomes essential. Queer and feminist activists infuse these highly charged public spaces with an ethic of care. In doing so, they challenge and transform masculinist cultures within their organizing spaces.

During direct action, a sense of common cause, love, trust, and courage ripples through those gathered. Caretakers get to know those who risk arrest intimately from head to toe; they learn about their likes and dislikes and their physical and mental health. Sips of water, bites of food, shade, touch, and chants give strength and courage to those who use lockboxes to chain themselves to each other. Activists talk about feeling enveloped with love from their community when they step off the curb to stop traffic. A sizzle of energy electrifies the air at a Coming Out of the Shadows event, organized by undocumented youth, when one of them steps up to say with a quiver in their voice, "I am surrounded here by you in this loving circle but also by police officers who are watching us and listening to us. I am really afraid to say this. I got into trouble and am deportable. There, I have said it!" Such acts that I have witnessed mobilize public feelings to build a movement as they draw people together in that moment or for the long haul.[74]

Those labeled criminals and their loved ones seize a collective space of protest to talk publicly about their lives before and after the deportation of a loved one branded as a criminal alien. Kinship ties and community formation have become the bullseye of immigration enforcement. The principle of attrition through enforcement targets social reproduction of families and communities and their economic survival with surgical precision. The principle was the explicitly stated objective of Arizona's 2010 anti-immigrant SB 1070, which created state-level crimes related to a person's immigration status and invested state and local police with the power to enforce immigration law.[75] Though many parts of SB 1070 have been struck down by courts, county-level agreements formalize collaboration between police and Immigration and Customs Enforcement (ICE).

Antideportation activists testify to the intimate ravages of attrition through enforcement—their pain, trauma, and rage of having loved ones ripped apart from their families. They talk about their relationships to their children, parents, siblings, cousins, aunts, and uncles as well as the dead, the ancestors in need of ministering. They invite those who bear witness to their stories into a world that cannot be reduced to cost-benefit analyses. In speaking of this world, they put a shape to the fine grain of their intimate lives, usually shrouded in shame and isolation—feelings that are common among those who suffer from mass incarceration. To embrace felons as family publicly scrambles settler narratives of the ideal immigrant. Undocumented youth who have broken away from the DREAMers have directly intervened in the portrayal of childhood arrivals as innocent victims of their parents' criminalized action of crossing borders. They have generated new modes of storytelling that affirm intergenerational bonds by recognizing their parents' acts of courage. The didactic power of *testimonios*, which speak of the "personal impact of structural subordination," stimulate solidarity.[76] Social scientists often treat testimonial speech or writing skeptically, but feminist scholars have underlined the value of self-representation in testimonies precisely because they are political and produce theory through their emotional impact.[77] The affective power of narratives and actions led by deportees and their allies connects them to each other.

The migrants' expressions of sociality threaten the atomizing intent of neoliberal governance encoded in inducing self-deportation through an attack on families and communities and the gutting of publicly funded programs. The intimacy expressed by the deportees and their loved ones generates a broad sense of collectivity encapsulated in the radical call "All of Us or None." The affective production of a collectivity asserts itself against the routine devaluation of migrant lives. This internal movement-building work of affect mobilized through *testimonios*, vigils, and direct action becomes just as important as drawing all those untouched by criminalization and deportation into the movement.[78] In my own act of bearing witness, I have come to understand that storytelling is a strategy to talk across consequential differences in immigration status, criminal convictions, gender, class, race, sexuality, and family arrangements.

This book joins a body of migration scholarship that examines the constitutive work of gender and sexuality in contemporary immigration enforcement and deportation policies.[79] I argue that crimmigration-sensitive antideportation activism provides an aperture into the state's regulation of settler constructions of gender, sexuality, and kinship through immigration policies more than fifty years after the de jure color and gender blindness of 1965 Immigration and Nationality Act and its amendments.[80] I highlight critical discussions of the policing of gender and sexuality in antideportation organizing to shed light on feminist and queer interventions within the movement. I document activists' reflections on gender and sexuality enabled by an interrogation of criminalization and criminality. I also push our own organizing efforts to frame our resistance as a direct response to the disciplining language of gender, sexual, and settler respectability coded into deportation policies and in the immigrant rights movement.

Conclusion

My orientation to this work—both as scholar and activist—has been that of a transnational feminist. In the years I have done this work, I have challenged myself to extend the investigative and political terrain of transnational feminism. I have had to rethink my writing practice. In the following chapters, I have committed myself to my desire, which has surfaced while protesting, discussing, mulling, teaching, and writing, for feminist and queer pro-migrant politics rising at the intersection of resisting US settler colonialism and imperialism. As a transnational feminist, I consciously turn my attention to the interior space of the United States (not just the geopolitical constitution of borders and the imperial flows across them). The activists I write about have taught me to examine interior enforcement and its relationship to correctional control. The focus on the interior challenges me to account for a domestic territory animated by Indigenous sovereignty. Second, I strive to impart the present tense of Indigenous politics. I ask myself what it means to write about one type of immigration enforcement—deportation from the interior—by keeping in mind the present tense of Indigenous sovereignty over a space, which the United States claims for itself. Last, the book furthers the wealth of transnational feminist analyses about solidarity building and the inflection of solidarity work with all types of power relations. In capturing and suggesting solidarities between migrant and Indigenous communities, I keep in mind that land rights and self-determination are central to Indigenous politics, and these struggles are distinct from the struggles of migrants and refugees. Here, I dwell on the words of Joanne Barker, who, in her entry on "Indigenous Feminism" says, "Indigenous feminism has asserted the polity of the Indigenous: the unique governance, territory, and culture of an Indigenous people in a system of (non)human relationships and responsibilities to one another. In doing so, Indigenous feminisms rearticulate the futurity of Indigeneity in *political coalition* with non-Indigenous peoples against the ongoing social forces of US imperialism, racism, and sexism."[81] In telling the story of a radical strand of antideportation activism, I signpost its coalitional possibilities.

1

"ALL OF US OR NONE"

At a November 2017 Youth Empowerment Summit organized by the San Gabriel Valley Immigrant Youth Coalition (IYC) and held at a Baldwin Park high school, the seventy-odd participants, including me, pondered an alternative budget for the California Department of Corrections and Rehabilitation, which had requested $11 billion in general funds.[1] We engaged in a "Care Not Cages" exercise, considering how part of that budget could be used to build 280 youth centers, 2,152 single-family homes, 240 assisted living facilities for those with mental health needs, and 1,792 transitional apartments for the houseless. The summit organizers provoked us to think concretely about peoples' economic, bodily, and psychological safety outside of law-and-order approaches such as surveillance, arrests, lockdowns, and lockups—the brunt of which is borne by youth who are Black, Indigenous, and people of color (BIPOC), many of them immigrants, many living in poverty. Workshops like this one draw on a long organizing tradition of inviting communities to make a people's budget to imagine, present, and implement safety and security as they define them, beyond policing and incarceration. Such calls to shift taxpayer monies away from agencies that police and punish have started to gain mainstream media coverage with widespread calls in 2018 to abolish Immigration and Customs Enforcement (ICE) and calls to defund the police in the summer of 2020 following renewed public outrage at yet another wave of police and vigilante killings of Black people. As the summit taught us, demands to dismantle arms of law and immigration enforcement must be paired with reallocating funds for life-sustaining projects.

Although correctional practices and anti-Black racism are often extraneous to the conventional immigrant rights discussions, the IYC's empowerment summits reformulate the migrant justice project through coalitional visions of abolition (see chapter 5). Their analysis of crimmigration reflects a clear understanding of the anti-Black, anti-Indigenous, anti-immigrant, homophobic, and transphobic function of criminalization. Broadly, the undocumented, legal permanent resident, Indigenous migrant, feminist, and queer organizers featured in the book arrive at notions of justice, which recognize the harm caused by policing and incarceration. Based on their experiences, they also understand carceral policies deploy what Dean Spade terms "routine administrative violence."[2] Such violence manifests in the link between immigration status and access to health care, jobs, federal college loans, and driver's licenses, as well as in overt carceral practices of school suspensions, gang injunctions, prisons, immigrant detention centers, and the shackling of deportees on flights. They take to heart the abolitionist insight that "alienation, punishment, or State violence, such as policing and incarceration" cannot address interpersonal and structural harm. These state practices do not ensure safety or accountability.[3]

This chapter explains the architecture of "crimmigration" from the perspective of antideportation activists. It examines the entrenchment of settler carcerality through the evolution of postentry enforcement. How have these legal innovations deepened the United States' territorial control and fortified the "homeland" in the name of public safety and national security? How have they rendered migrants and refugees residing in the interior space vulnerable to surveillance and police-immigration enforcement? Postentry, migrants continue to be brutalized by these arms of the state. To explain crimmigration, I draw on activist-produced curricula, educational materials, and policy reports. Together these sources of knowledge reveal the making and treatment of "criminal aliens." They show how criminality introduces efficiency into interior immigration enforcement. The documents unpack how immigration enforcement builds on and mimics developments in the criminal legal system that have enabled mass incarceration. Like mass incarceration, crimmigration is driven by discriminatory practices structured along the lines of race, age, class, religion, gender, and sexuality. In the chapters that follow, I flesh out the racialized gender and sexual politics of crimmigration by grounding them in the specific analyses arising from the justice work of Tod@s Som@s Arizona (Tod@s), Families for Freedom (FFF), Khmer Girls in Action (KGA), the IYC, and youth organizers in Hawai'i.

By 2010, the antideportation activists featured in this book began using the neologism "crimmigration" for deportation tactics that depend on migrants' encounters with local law enforcement and subjection to local, state, and federal correctional control. That year, with the nationwide mobilization against Arizona law SB 1070, migrant justice activists started to address the dangers of local police involvement in immigration enforcement. The direct action and popular education by the Los Angeles–based collective Tod@s Som@s Arizona effectively exposed the mechanisms of interior enforcement, which piped people from their schools and neighborhoods into juvenile detention centers, jails, or prisons—and then to immigration prisons for deportation (chapter 2).

In excavating the connections between the criminal legal system and the civil and administrative procedures of deportation, several binary oppositions disappear, such as civil versus criminal law, criminal (undeserving) versus innocent (deserving) deportees, violent versus nonviolent offenders, and feminine versus masculine gender identity. This strand of antideportation activism complicates the bright line many proimmigration advocates draw to distinguish between immigration violations as civil offenses and those under the purview of the criminal legal system. Such advocates argue that civil offenses are being criminalized, but they have little to say about immigrants with criminal charges or convictions targeted for removal. By contrast, the organizers covered in this book pay unflinching attention to the criminal legal system and have developed alternatives to the comprehensive immigration reform (CIR) platform. Every CIR legislative proposal backed by the mainstream immigrant rights movement has attached legalization to intensified settler colonial practices of interior enforcement and border militarization. Congress already lavishly funds border security, severely impacting the homelands of Indigenous peoples living across the US-Mexico border alongside migrants attempting to cross that border. Margo Tamez (Dene Ndé) characterizes the border wall built by force in Big Water Country (Lower Río Grande River) in Texas and the drones that surveil it in the face of the land protectors' sustained refusal as emblematic of the settler state's "colossal carceral architecture."[4]

While supporters of comprehensive immigration reform have been willing, since 2018, to discuss the misuse of resources in deporting people with low-level offenses, such as a broken taillight, they remain silent about "criminal aliens" who have felonies for gang affiliation, drug possession, assault, domestic violence, or suspected ties with terrorist groups. The stance "All of Us or None," the central message of the IYC 2017 civil disobedience detailed in the preface, crystallizes the activists' refusal to prioritize decriminalizing some groups over others. Instead, the movement against deportation recognizes carceral responses to crime as forms of racial and colonial control. By presenting the organizers' dissection of crimmigration, I highlight the ongoing insurgency of those who are directly impacted.[5]

The Making of the "Criminal Alien"

The passage of the 1996 Illegal Immigration Reform and Immigrant Responsibility Act (IIRAIRA) and the Antiterrorism and Effective Death Penalty Act (AEDPA) marks a watershed for interior enforcement. The acts recategorized a variety of offenses, including misdemeanors, as aggravated felonies to expand deportable crimes. The retroactive application of aggravated felonies meant that immigrants who had already served time or fulfilled their court-ordered penalties and community service for an offense were now at risk of deportation. Detention and deportation became mandatory minimums for those charged with or convicted of these new felonies. Though mandatory detention of specific categories of immigrants was legislated in 1988, it exploded with the passage of the 1996 laws, and the pace of deportation accelerated.[6] Those detained were to be removed from the United States within ninety days instead of six months. Before 1996, immigration judges had discretionary power to grant relief from deportation to long-term legal permanent residents (LPRs) with criminal records if they had family and could establish that their deportation would cause them hardship.[7] The Immigration and Naturalization Act waiver that granted judges the discretion was eliminated in 1996. Congress established a statutory structure to identify and expel "criminal aliens" efficiently. Not surprisingly, racially discriminatory policing has led to an overrepresentation of Black and Latinx migrants in prison. However, East Asians, South Asians, and Southeast Asians are also distinctively racialized, charged with crimes stereotypically associated with their racial-ethnic identities, incarcerated, and marked for deportation. As I will explain, LPR Southeast Asian refugees from Vietnam, Cambodia, and Laos become deportable because of their criminalization as gang involved.[8]

These 1996 developments governing criminal aliens tightened US imperial-settler carceral control over large swaths of the Pacific. Yet, immigration scholarship rarely comments on this.[9] The 1996 laws extended deportability for criminal charges and convictions to the citizens of three Pacific nations, the Federated States of Micronesia, the Republic of Marshall Islands, and the Republic of Palau, even though they have a special immigration status. These Indigenous islanders migrate and live legally in the United States visa-free under international agreements, the Compacts of Free Association (COFA), which classified COFA citizens as "qualified aliens" between 1986 and 1996. In 1996, they were stripped of this classification. To date, compacts give the United States complete and exclusive military control over this region's land, airspace, and waters, where the United States conducted sixty-seven hydrogen and atomic bomb tests between 1946 and 1958. The US imperial control continues to be devastating for COFA citizens, who have poor access to jobs, health care, and education on their islands.[10] US-occupied Hawai'i is COFA migrants' top destination, and here they face intense discrimination and criminalization under settler laws. Zero tolerance criminal laws have made COFA citizen youth and adults vulnerable to deportation since the 1996 laws (see chapter 5).

Settler carcerality and US imperialism work together. To borrow from Grace Hong, structures of disavowal, which distribute state violence unevenly across populations, become necessary for the United States to perpetuate the criminalization and deportation of COFA residents, who are literally poisoned by radiation and dispossessed by the United States.[11] The treatment of COFA residents as LPRs, even though they fall under a very different immigration regime, bears out Shannon Speed's argument about the sleight of hand through which the US laws convert dispossessed and displaced Indigenous people into immigrants to criminalize and incarcerate them.[12]

Immigration Enforcement in Prisons

While 1996 constitutes a watershed, as antideportation activists show, the groundwork for crimmigration and postentry social control of immigrants was already laid by the late 1980s. I learned about the 1988 Alien Criminal Apprehension Program (CAP) through FFF's "Deportation 101" curriculum. Since the late 1980s, CAP has permitted immigration agents to enter jails and prisons to identify incarcerated noncitizens and initiate deportation proceedings while they are incarcerated. This program taps into the carceral system that has been built since Richard Nixon was the president in the name of the war on drugs and crime, reflecting racial injustice in sentencing and incarceration. CAP was launched in the wake of the 1986 Immigration Reform and Control Act (IRCA), best known for granting one-time asylum for undocumented immigrants and imposing antilabor employer sanctions. Less known are the efforts to involve the Immigration and Naturalization Services (INS) in drug enforcement at the US-Mexico border and the utilization of CAP to ease the pressure on prisons overflowing with people who were casualties of the Ronald Reagan administration's war on drugs by deporting residents designated criminal aliens.[13]

In the interior, immigration agents may visit prisons or have stations where they may profile noncitizens through access to prison databases and interview those identified to establish their immigration status. Since the 1980s, correctional facilities have become an entry point for the INS to identify and remove migrants, documented and undocumented. After 9/11, the newly created Immigration and Customs Enforcement (ICE) adopted, expanded, and refined these practices. Over time, the data sharing environment among enforcement agencies has become far more sophisticated with fusion centers and data surveillance, leading to greater precision in identifying noncitizens in prisons.[14] The collaboration between the corrections departments and immigration enables the direct transfer of prison inmates to immigration detention centers on the completion of their sentence. A former organizer for FFF, Manisha Vaze, pointed out the inhumanity of profiling incarcerated people to determine their immigration status.[15] Although prisons are not bound to give access to ICE, the law-and-order platform incentivizes the cooperation of the corrections departments with federal immigration authorities.

Police stations and jails also use CAP. When noncitizens are arrested, their personal data, including their place of birth, are passed on to immigration agents. Police, ICE, and the Customs and Border Protection (CBP) work closely at the booking stage.[16] Agents from ICE or CBP can interview the arrested person in police custody without formal agreements between local law enforcement and immigration enforcement like 287(g) and the Secure Communities program. A noncitizen in jail risks an immigration hold or a detainer for an additional forty-eight hours after being released from criminal custody. Even though a detainer for immigration enforcement is a non-binding request, most police precincts comply. The detainer can result in removal to a detention center, where the person may be served with a notice to appear before an immigration judge, an order for expedited removal, or a referral for illegal entry. It can lead the judge to deny bond or raise the amount. Most notably, the outcome of the criminal case—even a dismissal—does not impede immigration violation charges and puts deportation in motion.[17] This is how crimmigration works.

Antideportation activists have identified detainers as the key carceral instrument allowing prisons and jails to transfer noncitizens to ICE. Many of their campaigns introduce city- and state-level legislation to eliminate detainers. City council members in New York have introduced reforms since 2014 to limit the New York Police Department's use of detainers, except for those with prior convictions for "violent and serious crimes."[18] Undeterred, FFF, featured in chapter 3, and its allies continue to address how ICE and immigration prosecution practices criminalize immigrants. Such efforts connect the widespread patterns of racially discriminatory policing and imprisonment to the deportation of "criminal aliens," leading FFF to build strong coalitions with racial justice groups working on issues of police brutality, mass incarceration, and bail justice. It organized against the New York Police Department's (NYPD) stop-and-frisk practices, which disproportionately targeted people of color.[19] A 2014 FFF infographic illustrates that NYPD stopped and arrested people of color at nearly nine times the rate of white people. Since more than 80 percent of immigrants in the city are people of color, "it is no surprise that many immigrants have been deported after contact with the city's criminal justice system."[20] With the election of Donald Trump and mounting concerns expressed by the city's immigrant organizers and advocates, the New York attorney general's office issued guidelines in 2017 barring local law enforcement from arresting persons with civil immigration violations without a judicial warrant.[21] A New York appellate court upheld the bar in 2018.[22] The California legislature passed the TRUST Act (AB 4) in 2013, under which county jails can no longer hold noncitizens with misdemeanors for immigration purposes.[23] The IYC pushed hard for this legislation as part of the "ICE Out of California" campaign (see chapter 5). Similarly, FFF continues to organize to get "ICE Out of New York" in a broad coalition as part of its "Release Not Transfer" campaign.

For antideportation activists in New York and LA, postconviction relief and contesting wrongful convictions have emerged as crucial issues in community education and organizing.[24] These activists educate people about available legal avenues to vacate convictions and have them expunged from their records. They are pressuring the governors' offices to push for clemency. Their campaigns engage directly with criminal law to train ordinary people without legal backgrounds to build their cases against deportation, despite the poverty of due process rights for immigrants. The FFF's "Deportation 101" curriculum states, "We all know that the legal system doesn't provide us with the remedies we need. And as people who are directly affected by the deportation system, we have firsthand knowledge and experience about how the system tears families apart."[25] One fight for postconviction relief has involved asserting the right of a noncitizen

1.1. Families for Freedom and its allies organized an "ICE out of NY / Release Not Transfer" emergency rally outside 26 Federal Plaza in Manhattan on July 29, 2022. The action followed the sudden transfer of over seventy immigrant New Yorkers detained in the state's Orange County Correctional Facility to a jail in Adams County, Mississippi. Courtesy of Families for Freedom.

charged with a crime to be informed of the immigration consequences (i.e., deportation) by the court-appointed legal counsel before entering a plea bargain. These challenges to deportation strike at the heart of plea bargaining that has been routinized in the criminal legal system since the 1980s war on drugs. Plea bargaining has been a significant driver in putting Black people and people of color behind bars.[26] In documenting detainee stories, organizers learn to identify the vulnerabilities of the criminal legal system by scrutinizing the routine rights violations. When fighting individual cases, the organizations try to stop or reverse deportations by leveraging ICE's and consulates' failures to follow their own procedures. To make policy changes, they put pressure on local, state, and national politicians.

Today, CAP is ICE's largest deportation program, responsible for three-fourths of all postentry removals.[27] CAP's efficacy is attributable to a series of federal and state laws, which have been analyzed exhaustively by scholars who have provided a mountain of evidence for the systematic policing and incarceration of Black, Asian, Latinx, gay, lesbian, transgender, and economically precarious people.[28] "Get tough on crime" policing strategies driven by a zero tolerance approach—like "broken windows," gang injunctions, trying and sentencing minors as adults, draconian laws governing drug possession and use, and three-strikes laws—have converged to provide a resource-efficient way to catch migrants in the interior, strip them of their status (if they had legal status) and put them into deportation proceedings.

At the border, CAP has spawned another type of relationship between immigration and law enforcement. As sociologist Patrisia Macías-Rojas has revealed, in Arizona's border towns, the border patrol is increasingly performing the job of local law enforcement. The convergence of crime control and border security has taken the form of CBP agents charging border residents—US citizens, legal permanent residents, and members of tribal nations—with drug trafficking and, increasingly, human trafficking, the definition of which Arizona has broadened since 2005. Macías-Rojas points out that these "criminalizing processes . . . brand residents as criminal through prosecution, sentencing, imprisonment, and even wrongful deportation."[29] At the border, migrants and asylum seekers are transferred to prisons from detention centers.

While practices at the border and the interior differ, they both rely on yoking crime control to immigration control. Unauthorized entry has been criminalized under US Code Section 1325 since 1911 with a first-time unauthorized entry categorized as a federal misdemeanor and unauthorized reentry a federal felony. The code's enforcement accelerated under the Barack Obama administration and became even more draconian under Donald Trump. In 2018, the Trump administration ordered that all unauthorized adult entrants be charged criminally and taken into criminal custody under its "zero tolerance policy," which targeted parents crossing with children and separated them by putting the adults in criminal custody.[30] Under the Biden administration, the zero tolerance policy has been scrapped, but the entry and reentry prosecution of migrants at the border continues, as do a variety of deterrence protocols, reinforcing the reliance of immigration enforcement across administrations on the notion of "criminal aliens" to justify inhumane policies.[31]

Gang Control and Criminalizing Youth

Starting in the late 1980s, California introduced a slew of civil and criminal penalties to punish gang-involved juveniles, overwhelmingly young men, in the name of controlling gang activity. The federal government followed suit with harsh penalties for this group. Immigrant youth from socioeconomically depressed neighborhoods started to be racialized as crime-prone,

1.2. A Khmer Girls in Action diorama of their Long Beach neighborhood asking for an end to the school-to-prison pipeline and an investment in schooling and wellness. The diorama was part of KGA's 2018 "Show Youth the Love" campaign showcased at its Yellow Lounge event. The art lead for the diorama was Jennefer Heng. Photo credit: Joy Yanga. Courtesy of Khmer Girls in Action.

gang-involved, and, therefore, incurably violent. The laws and regulations cemented the relationship between crime and race through the policing of the immigrant youth's neighborhoods and the spaces they traversed.[32] Youth members of the IYC and KGA resist an array of policies put in place to police BIPOC youth who are siphoned into the school-to-prison pipeline (see chapters 4 and 5). Both organizations break the silence around the vulnerability of migrant Asian youth to crime control in impoverished urban neighborhoods.

Tracing the genesis of gang injunctions to 1987, legal scholar Ana Muñiz lays out how her working-class Black and Latinx neighborhood of Cadillac-Corning, bordering affluent West Los Angeles, became a laboratory for testing out this policing tool.[33] Gang injunctions are civil orders against a neighborhood, which sanction behavior and activities that are considered harmless when engaged in or performed by affluent and white youth. Though ostensibly colorblind, gang injunctions conjoin race, economic standing, and space to put Black, Latinx, and Asian youth at risk of being labeled and policed (see chapter 4). The injunctions start defining gangs as unincorporated associations, and those considered to be members are by association subject to suspicion and containment. Gang injunctions allowed the Los Angeles Police Department (LAPD) to use the civil court system, thereby denying those subjected to the injunctions the right to legal counsel and jury. Muñiz argues, "Thus gang injunctions provide police and prosecutors with the legal discretion to carry out extralegal control and repression."[34] She made this point about the injunctions forcefully in person at a March 19, 2016, Human Rights Commission hearing that I attended in Sylmar, California, by emphasizing how the legal construction of gangs controls youth of color, their families, and friends.

In 1988, California passed the Street Terrorism Enforcement and Prevention (STEP) Act. This act categorized participation in a street gang as a substantive crime, and it permitted enhanced sentencing for felonies committed by gang members. A precursor of the infamous CalGangs database was initiated to label and track youth.[35] Under the California Welfare and Institutions Code Section 707(b), minors between age fourteen and age seventeen could be tried as adults if they were alleged to have committed certain categories of crime, including gang-related offenses. Anthropologist Elena Zilberg, who devoted many years as a community advocate at the venerable Central American Resource Center (CARECEN) in LA's Pico Union neighborhood, noticed the criminalization of Salvadoran refugee youth as gang members. The 1992 LA uprisings compounded the racialized criminalization and deportation of Latinx immigrants.[36] The moral panic over lawlessness birthed California's 1994 three-strikes law, which doubled the sentences of those with prior felonies. That same year, Congress passed the Violent Crime Control and Law Enforcement Act, which included a Criminal Street Gangs Statute that legislated sentence enhancement for those who had committed "an act of juvenile delinquency involving a violent or controlled substances felony." This piece of legislation is colloquially referred to as "The Beast."[37]

In conjunction with the 1994 federal legislation, the INS launched the Violent Gang Task Force to deport immigrant youth, many of them legal permanent residents with criminal records.[38] Despite legislation creating these contact points between the criminal legal system and immigration enforcement, Zilberg astutely notes that "many immigrant rights organizations considered it [the criminalization of inner city youth] a 'boutique' issue."[39] Once the carceral effects of the 1996 IIRIRA and AEDPA became evident, the immigrant rights movement began to see the connection between immigration enforcement and criminalization. The call "Fix 96," now a hashtag, started to circulate. However, in most cases, advocacy was limited to those who were considered to have committed minor and nonviolent crimes.

At the start of this century, California instituted even harsher penalties for gang-related crimes and more grounds to impose adult penalties on juveniles. In 2000, Proposition 21 added to the STEP Act.[40] To be prosecuted for gang-related offenses, one did not need to be a gang member; an alleged association was enough to be charged with coconspiracy. With the post-9/11 emergence of a reconstituted Department of Homeland Security (DHS), ICE became responsible for interior enforcement. Its National Gang Unit inaugurated Operation Community Shield (OCS) in 2005.[41] The unit collects intelligence; shares data with local, state, federal, and foreign law enforcement agencies; and designs operations to conduct raids with the cooperation of local police departments. OCS sweeps pick up not only those suspected of gang involvement but also those with other types of criminal records or outstanding deportation orders.

Like refugee youth from El Salvador, Guatemala, and Nicaragua, youth from Vietnam, Cambodia, and Laos also became vulnerable to deportation because of being relentlessly policed and incarcerated for gang involvement. In this context, the Long Beach–based KGA develops its campaigns to address the criminalization of youth and participates in national and transnational efforts for fair repatriation (see chapter 4). By 1992, the Long Beach police instituted gang injunctions, which trapped Cambodian youth resettling in the city in the criminal legal system. This trend was not unique to California. In cities across the nation, Southeast Asian youth were facing the same types of policing techniques that piped them into prisons. In fact, my very first antideportation community meeting dealt with the aftermath of raids and arrests authorized by OCS in 2008 in Lowell, Massachusetts, which is home to a large Cambodian community. Deported Diaspora, a community-based organization in the greater Boston area, had called the meeting to respond to the fear, panic, and needs of the community after twelve Southeast Asian community members were arrested and removed overnight to out-of-state detention centers to be deported.[42]

In Seattle, the court battle of Kim Ho Ma, a Cambodian refugee, Seattle resident, and detainee with a final order of removal, instructs us on the connections among immigration status, gang control laws, international relations, and US plenary power. The intricacies of Ma's case illuminate two points. First, the prospect of Ma's indefinite detention rekindles debates over the limits of US plenary power. Exercised by Congress, this type of power is exempt from judicial review. These debates are managed by containing questions about plenary power within a civil rights framework.

Courts narrowly adjudicate whether civil rights protect immigrants. Since courts had already determined that aliens like Ma who resided within US borders, unlike those seeking admission, were entitled to the due process clause of the Fifth Amendment, the point of contention revolved around habeas corpus. Could the attorney general continue to detain Ma beyond the statutory period because Cambodia refused to accept deportees? Second, the particularities of repatriation for Southeast Asian refugees have implications for movement building. The efforts of Southeast Asian activists to deploy human rights regimes exceeds civil rights, opening up a discursive space for other rights regimes.

For Southeast Asian activists, Ma, who tells his story in the documentary *Sentenced Home*, is a person (not just a court case) who pays the price of an unjust legal system and unequal international relations. As a Cambodian refugee, Ma was a legal permanent resident of the United States. He was arrested at age seventeen for what was determined to be a 1995 gang-related shooting. He was tried and convicted as an adult because he was considered to be a gang member.[43] As soon as he completed his prison sentence in June 1997, he was directly transferred into the custody of the INS because of his criminal conviction. By this time, the 1996 laws were in effect. The following month, an immigration judge ruled that Ma was deportable and ineligible for any form of immigration relief because he was involved in gang activity and convicted of a serious crime (first-degree manslaughter) for which he had served the maximum sentence. Ma remained in detention because immigration prosecutors argued that he posed a serious risk to public safety, and by the end of 1997, he was served with his final deportation order. However, at the time, Cambodia did not have a repatriation agreement with the United States, and thus, Ma could not be deported. As a result, ICE continued to detain Ma beyond the allowable ninety-day period triggered by the final order of removal.

In February 1999, Ma filed a writ of habeas corpus, arguing that he would likely be detained indefinitely because Cambodia did not accept deportees. In the western district of Washington alone, at least one hundred immigrants faced indefinite detention. Ma's case, filed with the US District Court of the Western District of Washington in 1999, worked its way up to the US Court of Appeals Ninth Circuit, which upheld the district court's decision to grant Ma the writ of habeas corpus. As his case traveled up to the US Supreme Court, it was consolidated in the landmark US Supreme Court case *Zadvydas v. Davis* in 2001. The US Supreme Court's writ focused on the constitutionality of indefinite detention beyond the statutory period of an alien present in the United States. In its determination, the Supreme Court did not deny that Congress had plenary power in regulating immigration. However, it could not establish any "clear indication of congressional intent to grant the Attorney General the power to hold indefinitely in confinement an alien ordered removed."[44] Though Ma successfully challenged his indefinite detention without review beyond the statutory ninety-day period, he was among the first ten Cambodians marked as criminal aliens and deported once the United States and Cambodia reached a repatriation agreement in 2002.[45]

Legal arguments over immigrant detention show that plenary power is not immune to challenges. At the same time, the legality of the doctrine is not called into question, only its limits. Furthermore, its limits valorize civil rights, absorbing immigrants into that regime. Immigrant rights remain confined to arguments over noncitizens' entitlements to civil rights at the expense of other recognizable legal regimes, such as human rights or tribal jurisprudence, that challenge US plenary power. The "victories" for deportable immigrants, in reality fragile, can become legible only through the language of civil rights. As a result, the legal defense of civil rights against flagrant violations of human rights, such as indefinite detention, shores up settler colonial control over territory, discourse, and bodies.

Ma's case also reveals that Congress and the laws it passes are not the only determinants of deportation. Southeast Asian activist organizations engage with the State Department and the United Nations to seek redress. This is instructive for all those building a movement for migrant justice. In the case of deportable Cambodian refugees, the State Department emerges as one pillar of the massive legal architecture of criminal and civil laws governing noncitizens who are vulnerable to law-and-order policies. The task of engineering a repatriation agreement with Cambodia lay with the State Department (not Congress), which means Southeast Asian antideportation organizing tackles foreign policy. To date, Southeast Asian refugees become deportable through their contact with the criminal legal system. Immigration reform advocates target Congress.[46] In cases where the State Department is authorized to negotiate and renegotiate nation-to-nation repatriation agreements, demands for legislative action need to be paired with negotiations with the executive branch of the US government.

This context is essential to understand why two Southeast Asian coalitions, the Southeast Asian Freedom Network (SEAFN) and the 1Love Movement, demand a revised and fair repatriation agreement from the State Department and the United Nations. They stress the importance of community input. Indeed, the 1999 district court case involving Ma cites evidence presented by the INS that the State Department was already in negotiations with Cambodia.[47] This documentation bears out SEAFN's contention that the State Department was negotiating the 2002 US-Cambodia agreement (currently in force) without the knowledge of, let alone consultation with, advocates in the Cambodian refugee community.

The Southeast Asian activist-led 2015 Fair Repatriation campaign demands protection from deportation for those who entered the United States with refugee status before the 1993 normalization of US-Cambodia diplomatic relations. Addressing the plight of those already deported, the platform introduced language to defend refugees removed to Cambodia, allowing them to return. The proposed revisions aim to align the US-Cambodia repatriation agreement with international standards and the 2008 US-Vietnam repatriation agreement.

In 2015 testimony before the Human Rights Council during the Universal Periodic Review of the United States, SEAFN, citing US violation of several articles in the Universal Declaration of Human Rights, clearly stated:

> Most Southeast Asian refugees were resettled into inhumane conditions in impoverished neighborhoods, making us vulnerable to poverty, crime, violence, structural disadvantage, racism, discrimination and profiling. Many young people fell through the cracks in an under-resourced education system unfit to meet their needs, leaving only 65 percent of Cambodian-American youth graduating from high school. Many enter into a highly functional and highly funded School-to-Prison Pipeline. Law enforcement agencies in cities across the country began coding Cambodian communities as "gang infested" and we were surveilled and profiled for arrest and incarceration. Over-policing of our community led to racial profiling, police brutality, and high incarceration rates, higher than any other Asian ethnic group in relation to the size of our population.[48]

These demands foreground the human rights of Southeast Asians refugees. The SEAFN representatives link the failure of resettlement to youth languishing in prisons and detention centers. They recognize the continuation of oppressive foreign policies in the expulsion of refugee youth to the very spaces from which they had been displaced by US-engineered war. As I show in chapter 5, US-foreign-policy-driven military interests in the Pacific are also fundamental to understanding the intersections among US imperialism, settler colonialism, and carcerality in antideportation struggles in Hawai'i. Our challenge as scholars and activists is to explore what happens when we combine this sort of transnational acumen with analyses of settler colonial power.

Immigration Control as National Security

By the close of the twentieth century, public policy and public opinion explicitly defined immigration as a national security issue. The federal government heightened immigration enforcement in the interior and at ports of entry. The 9/11 attacks further justified surveillance, raids, detention, and removal.[49] This political environment cleared the way to purge noncitizens with criminal records from the settled-space-turned-"homeland" in the name of national security. The Federal Bureau of Investigation (FBI) conducted raids targeting South Asian and other Muslim communities. As the documentary *The Feeling of Being Watched* and its accompanying discussion guide demonstrate, the FBI had already instituted an extensive surveillance apparatus in the 1980s as a counterterrorism operation.[50] After 9/11, under the guise of fighting terrorism, the FBI and the DHS refined racial and religious profiling. Mosques, nonprofits, and entire neighborhoods came under fresh surveillance. The National Security Entry-Exit Registration System (2002–11), popularly known as Special Registration, targeted men over age sixteen from twenty-four Muslim-majority countries and blatantly criminalized people based on gender, national origin, and religion. Public safety and national security became public policy wisdom in all discussions about controlling immigration and migrant communities in the United States.

The post-9/11 deportation crisis gave birth to organizations like Families for Freedom in New York and new campaigns in existing organizations like the LA area South Asian Network (SAN). The activists in the more critical antideportation organizations developed a structural analysis to emphasize the use of counterterrorism operations for immigration enforcement. At a time when signs declaring "We Are Not Criminals" and "We Are Not Terrorists" were ubiquitous at proimmigrant rallies, these organizations questioned the mechanisms through which people were branded criminals and terrorists. They quickly recognized that programs ostensibly initiated to secure the nation against "terrorists" were being used routinely to deport migrants.[51]

Many of the testimonies collected during FFF's first years document the travails of Muslim men in New York who complied with Special Registration only to be detained for an immigration violation and then removed. On the Pacific coast, between January and April 2003, SAN conducted seven hundred intakes of men who reported to register at the federal building in downtown Los Angeles. SAN's data analysis of the intakes revealed that a quarter of those who registered with DHS were arrested. SAN also tracked those who were disappeared and those who were served with a notice to appear for their deportation. It noted that some of the registrants it assisted had to wait for a long time to adjust their status with the US Citizenship and Immigration Services (USCIS), and characterized the waiting period as a state strategy of forced legal liminality, increasing the risks of detention and deportation.[52] Reflecting on the experience, Hamid Khan, then executive director of SAN, perceptively noted that Special Registration was a "report to deport program" designed explicitly to profile Muslims.[53] On the national level, the advocacy group South Asian Americans Leading Together reported that thirteen thousand of eighty-three thousand men who had registered were in deportation proceedings.[54] Even as Special Registration was terminated in 2011, the surveillance of immigrant communities for the purpose of deportation continues. ICE agents conducting home raids use the same terrifying "knock-and-talk" tactics as the FBI.

In response to the deployment of national security rhetoric and policies to heighten immigrant communities' vulnerability to deportation, six Southern Californian grassroots groups and Tucson, Arizona's Coalicion de Derechos Humanos (hereafter referred to as the Allies) issued a statement in 2007 laying out core principles and proposals that radically departed from the Comprehensive Immigration Reform (CIR) platform.[55] The Allies, which included KGA and SAN, refused to stand behind "racist and unjust immigration proposals" that further criminalized and impoverished immigrants, communities of color, and Indigenous people. They exposed the willingness of advocacy groups based in Washington, DC, as well as several local immigrant rights groups, to support a limited legalization plan in exchange for massively funded border enforcement measures and a skills-based guest-worker program in a 2007 immigration reform effort, which ultimately failed to pass because of right-wing opposition.[56] In their statement, the Allies demanded the demilitarization of the border and a redistribution of resources "away from prison-building, policing and criminalization to social, health and education services, family reunification, ending the backlog in visas and applications for permanent residency and citizenship, and full civil and labor rights protections for all persons." A decade before the IYC summit described at the beginning of the chapter, the Allies were already laying the groundwork for abolition and alternatives to carceral responses to migration.

The 2007 statement, remarkable for its political analysis and vision, identifies the "inward creep" of enhanced and militarized enforcement practices to secure the southern border. It calls out the collaborations between police and immigration to deport migrants, develop data sharing protocols among government agencies, and deepen control over hyperpoliced communities. The statement enumerates the ways immigration reform proposals continue to materially cement the perception that migration, unless punitively controlled, constitutes a national security threat. The Allies chart a direction in activism that recognizes that the crisis in migration is actually a crisis in human rights. Their statement takes a clear abolitionist stance that situates migration within vast neoimperial inequalities that drive people to the United States where they find an "American nightmare" rather than the "American Dream."[57]

Police-Immigration Collaborations

Immigration enforcement at the local level, permitted by Congress since 1996, has been crucial for crimmigration. With the reorganization of the federal agencies responsible for immigration enforcement, ICE now has thirteen programs under the umbrella of ICE Agreements of Cooperation in Communities to Enhance Safety and Security (ICE ACCESS) allowing local-federal partnerships to enforce immigration law. DHS has developed newer instruments like Secure Communities (S-Comm) in addition to the 287(g) programs included in ICE ACCESS.[58]

These programs secure local law enforcement buy-in to assist with "catching" deportable migrants. During the George W. Bush and Barack Obama years, ICE began to incentivize the cooperation of local police and sheriff's departments in immigration enforcement activities. The 287(g) programs, authorized by the 1996 IIRIRA, allowed (previously prohibited) agreements between the federal government and local and state jurisdictions permitting law enforcement officers to arrest or screen those in their custody for civil immigration law violations. The law enforcement officers are supposed to be trained in immigration enforcement with federal funds and are cross deputized "under the color of Federal authority."[59] Activists have pointed out that even in counties like Los Angeles, where the police department is prohibited from excessive immigration enforcement by Special Order 40, county jails are authorized by 287(g) to identify the immigration status of noncitizens in their custody. Data sharing across agencies has further facilitated LAPD's access to information about residents' immigration status. Importantly, activist and legal scholar Pooja Gehi observes that although the Supreme Court struck down several parts of Arizona law SB 1070, the nexus it enshrined between policing and immigration enforcement has survived and the criminalizing elements of the law continue to be legally perpetuated.[60]

The effectiveness of programs that permit local-federal cooperation has been enhanced through the use the technology-intensive data sharing program Secure Communities (S-Comm), inaugurated by the federal government in 2008—hence the spotlight on Palantir during the 2017 IYC-Justice LA direct action (see the preface). A tech company, Palantir has developed the Integrative Case Management tool for the DHS.[61] The new technologies allow participating precincts and jails to match the fingerprints of those in custody with DHS's Automated Biometric Identification System and the FBI's vast database of criminal records to identify whether a person has a civil, immigration-related infraction. If a person is identified for deportation through DHS databases, the participating local police department places a forty-eight-hour detainer, discussed above, so that ICE agents can pick up the individual. Counties initiate these agreements between ICE and state identification bureaus without inviting public comment. At a 2012 IYC training for youth in Honolulu, activist Jonathan Perez pinpointed the chilling nature of S-Comm, saying that the use of biometrics and data sharing across different government agencies meant "your fingerprint does all the talking" even when one invokes their Fifth Amendment right to remain silent.

According to ICE, it had implemented S-Comm in 3,181 jurisdictions nationwide by 2013, including three counties in Hawai'i. In 2014, the Obama administration replaced S-Comm with a Priority Enforcement Program (PEP) to ostensibly shift the focus to deporting persons with felonies. Under the Trump administration, S-Comm was reactivated, and ICE boasts of using the program to remove 363,400 criminal aliens since it started in 2008.[62] Even though the Trump administration instituted an executive order that dismantled priority categories, putting all removable migrants at risk of deportation, and the Biden administration revoked it, the biometric data sharing environment remains intact, and the federal-local cooperation to remove deportable migrants, under construction since the 1980s, continues.[63]

S-Comm-type programs became the battlegrounds in antideportation activism. The organizing pioneered by those fighting deportation has gained broader support within the immigrant rights movement a decade after the introduction of biometric data sharing at police precincts. Organizers compiled and widely shared toolkits to educate their membership about how these programs work. They mobilized their constituencies and allies to generate political pressure at the local level. The antideportation campaigns have demanded that local jurisdictions not enter into agreements with ICE or opt out of existing agreements. Such pressure was successful in New York, where the New York State Working Group against Deportation, a broad coalition that included FFF, convinced Governor Andrew Cuomo to suspend the implementation of S-Comm in 2011, only to be thwarted in 2012 by a federal decision to make S-Comm mandatory for all jurisdictions.

Just as the Allies on the West Coast critically examined the CIR legal agenda to build an expansive racial and migrant justice platform, the Antiviolence Advocates (AVA) subcommittee of New York State Working Group against Deportation worked on "Points of Unity."[64] These unity points gathered different social justice constituencies, not just immigrant rights activists, to articulate a stance based on a clearsighted analysis of criminalization and profiling outside conventional binary oppositions such as victim versus perpetrator and deserving versus undeserving. Feminist and queer intersectional discussions within AVA interrogated the reliance of antiviolence advocates on carceral and reactive responses rather than preventive ones. The subcommittee provoked immigrant rights advocates to consider the structural roots of gender- and sexuality-based violence and invited those working with survivors of interpersonal violence to take a searching look at carceral feminism, which depends on policing, prosecution, and prison terms to punish perpetrators.[65]

As Immigrant Defense Project organizer Mizue Aizeki documents, these discussions pushed many participants of AVA to attend to the voices of gender nonconforming and trans people of color, who are daily criminalized and brutalized by police for survival activities deemed in immigration law as crimes of moral turpitude or drug offenses.[66] A rare occurrence in immigrant rights activism, advocates examined broken windows policing as experienced by LGBTQ+, gender nonconforming, and homeless people. This type of policing criminalizes their very presence in public spaces and targets their livelihoods. The subcommittee participants dissected antidomestic-violence laws to reveal how these measures, informed by carceral logics, put immigrant women at risk of criminal charges. Advocates recognized the vulnerability of Black women, low-income LGBTQ+, and gender nonconforming people to police brutality when trying to report intimate partner violence.[67]

The AVA discussions clearly demonstrated that immigrants transferred to ICE were likely to experience racist, sexist, homophobic, and transphobic policing. Reframing social justice work by putting survivors at the center unravels the simplistic distinction between victims and perpetrators.[68] Such discussions across movements cultivate an abolitionist imagination and promote actions that pose transformative alternatives to carceral solutions, creating a political ecology for prison abolition and transformative justice.

Political Economy of Detention

Although there have been local and national policy conversations about decarceration, they do not line up with the continued expansion of detention centers for immigrants. During the Great Recession of 2007–9, when California's state and local governments were cutting corrections budgets and were willing to revisit the draconian Rockefeller drug laws, $55.2 million in federal money was pumped into the state coffers as contractual payments for housing immigrant detainees in local jails and state prisons.[69] On the national level, in the summer of 2015, Congress expressed a fleeting bipartisan will to roll back the harsh sentencing laws for nonviolent crimes and review the probation system after President Obama's highly publicized visit to a medium-security federal prison. The gestures came in the wake of longer-term pressure from a broad coalition of actors in favor of reforming prison policies.[70] At the same time that there was hand wringing over mass incarceration and oversentencing, President Obama, as Mizue Aizeki of the Immigrant Defense Project observes, "turbocharged the DHS" by targeting "criminal aliens" for removal, expanding local-federal cooperation in immigration enforcement and overseeing the record number of annual deportations in immigration history.[71] Moreover, both the House and Senate were introducing a rash of legislation to institute a five-year minimum for the mandatory imprisonment of migrants who attempted to reenter the United States and to punish state and local governments that resisted entering agreements allowing police-ICE cooperation.[72]

Antideportation activists have painstakingly pieced together the political economy of detention to identify its economic incentives. As of February 2024, 38,258 persons were in ICE custody.[73] Since 2009, the congressional budget for DHS has formally required the agency to maintain thirty-four thousand beds to hold deportable migrants. While requesting tax dollars to increase bed capacity has been tied to the effectiveness of immigration enforcement since the 1980s, the requirement by Congress was new.[74] The expansion guaranteed profits for the private prison industry. By 2015, 73 percent of all detainees in 205 facilities were housed in private for-profit detention centers, up from 49 percent in 2009. This share has remained around 70 percent. The GEO Group and the Corrections Corporation of America (CCA, rebranded as CoreCivic in 2016), which lobby Congress and make campaign contributions, have been at the forefront of these developments. Even as immigration enforcement dollars for the guaranteed minimum beds are appropriated at the federal level, local and state governments become active partners in contracting with ICE to rent out space and then subcontracting with corporate entities that run the facilities.[75]

The business of detention requires crimmigration. The pressure to fill the bed quota intensifies immigration enforcement and its need to work with local law enforcement to detain those who come in contact with police or are already under correctional control. Activists' fight against detainers at police precincts challenges the business of detention. In a significant win in 2017, a broad coalition of activists and advocates was successful in getting rid of the detention center bed quotas in DHS appropriations at the national level. However, guaranteed minimums continue to be written into local government subcontracting agreements with private prisons.[76] Since the private companies get paid for the beds, ICE agents are under pressure to fill them.

Numerous antideportation demonstrations have spotlighted the GEO Group and CoreCivic, previously known as CCA. The second LA civil disobedience in July 2010 against Arizona's SB 1070, which I analyze in chapter 2, was staged in front of the GEO Group's headquarters to draw attention to the corporatization of detention. Antideportation activists argue that the business of detention puts immigrants "on sale" and estimate that corporations make $150 per day per incarcerated person. By investigating corporate practices and their relationship with governments, they have uncovered these corporations' multiscalar influence in shaping local, national, and international prison policy. Activists used prison beds in the October 5, 2017, Westwood civil disobedience to dramatize the profit-driven "perverse incentives" driving deportation.[77] In 2019, California governor Gavin Newsom signed a bill to phase out contracts to incarcerate immigrants in private for-profit detention centers. However, this will not translate into less incarceration, only a transfer of detainees to centers out of state if they cannot be held at the state-run centers.[78]

Testimonies of deportees and their loved ones bear witness to predatory practices and reveal the double jeopardy of civil sanctions for time-for-crime built into the pipeline connecting prisons to detention centers.[79] Antideportation campaigns like "ICE out of Rikers" represent one type of effort to break the link between the criminal legal system and immigration enforcement (see chapter 3). Antideportation activists have also identified the dangers of deportation for migrants who are no longer under correctional control posed by contacts with agencies such as the USCIS, an arm of DHS with no enforcement function. This lesson has made them cautious of any program that subjects an immigrant to a background check to adjust their status. Across the United States, activists launched the "End Detention Week of Action" to publicly protest the growth of for-profit detention and the drive to prosecute immigration-related infractions as crimes. When California senator Dianne Feinstein backed a 2015 bill for a tighter relationship between ICE and local police, antideportation activists chained themselves and occupied the lobby of the senator's San Francisco office in an act of civil disobedience.[80]

Migrants waiting to be deported continue to be economically valuable when incarcerated. Economic value is produced not just when migrants

1.3. A multiethnic group of undocumented youth block a bus carrying community members to be processed for deportation in front of San Francisco offices of Immigration and Customs Enforcement on October 17, 2013. Among those who took part in the civil disobedience was an undocuqueer activist with the East Bay chapter of the Immigrant Youth Coalition. The action was organized by #Not1More. Credit for filming and editing: Jesús Iñiguez. Courtesy of Dreamers Adrift and #Not1More.

labor in the workforce, as proimmigration advocates vociferously argue. Unlike the labor of impoverished African Americans, who have been relegated to economic blight and forced unemployment since the 1970s when the US economy started to restructure, migrant labor is regularly framed as "desirable" by advocates. To counter the perception that immigrants are burdens, advocates have amassed and circulated data on the economic contributions of immigrants and the economic power of DACA youth.[81] Understood this way, locking up and, in most cases, permanently removing such workers on a mass scale seems senseless. While detention centers, like prisons, may seem like wastelands (a common settler colonial trope for appropriating and toxifying Indigenous land), filling detention center beds and achieving cost efficiency by ensuring a steady, though quickly changing, stream of detainees ensures profits for corporations that are in the business of physical imprisonment and virtual surveillance. The facilities generate local jobs in corrections, construction, and service-providing industries. Furthermore, those incarcerated in for-profit detention centers perform upkeep, food service, and childcare tasks for as little as $1 per shift.[82] Like prisons, detention centers result from the decades-long economic restructuring of racial capitalism, which has followed deindustrialization.[83] Abolitionist Angela Davis called out the prison industrial complex for devouring social wealth while generating massive profits for private corporations.[84] Deporting cheapened and exploitable labor may hurt one economic sector while incentivizing another rapidly expanding one, explaining why deportation makes economic sense.

With 2018 federal budget allocations under the Trump administration further fueling immigration enforcement, detention, and deportation, social justice workers pressed for sanctuary cities by adopting and escalating existing sanctuary practices. The new sanctuary movement takes inspiration from the 1980s history of churches and synagogues declaring themselves sanctuaries for those escaping the violence of the civil wars in El Salvador and Guatemala, where the United States covertly supported repressive regimes and death squads. During the Trump years, large civil society coalitions have pressured city councils to pass policies that refuse to divert local resources to cooperate with immigration enforcement as one way to stop feeding immigrants into detention centers.

While many organizers have welcomed the current mobilization to demand that cities protect their immigrant residents, those like Hamid Khan, who is now with the Stop LAPD Spying Coalition, and Jennicet Gutiérrez of the LA area–based La Familia Trans Queer Liberation Movement question the notion of sanctuary for immigrant, queer, and trans urban communities impacted by policing and gentrification. They ask, what is a sanctuary with jails and a vast apparatus of virtual surveillance enabled by data mining?[85] Instead, such politics envision rebel or freedom cities. Organizations like BYP 100, Mijente, and Black Alliance for Just Immigration are pushing activists to "dream bigger and to do more" to end "all policing and immigration enforcement practices that target Black and Brown communities, immigrant and US born . . . , to envision and build communities we want, through reinvestment of resources away from surveillance, punishment and exclusion and toward addressing community needs."[86] The shift to the language of rebellion spurs visions of freedom emerging at the cusp of movements fighting the many forms of punishment and confinement, creating new spaces for solidarity.[87]

Conclusion

The attachment of illegality to undocumented migrants has most certainly fed fears about lawlessness in the service of presenting deportation as a defense of national security. Kelly Lytle Hernández has traced the confinement of deportable immigrants to the Geary Act of 1892, which targeted Chinese laborers in the United States for removal if they did not register with the federal government.[88] The act and the challenge to its constitutionality mounted by Chinese Americans, she argues, represent the founding moment when deportation "resulted in the invention of immigrant detentions as a strange new sector of human confinement."[89] It was strange because these detention centers were separated from criminal confinement, and detainees were forced into a year of hard labor before being deported. Over the twentieth century, we see a different development: the suturing of criminal and civil mechanisms. Accounts of deportation remain partial without the story of crimmigration, which subjects noncitizens to criminalization to put them behind prison bars.

My account above, drawn from activist-generated educational materials and policy papers, reveals that many immigration enforcement practices come straight out of the law enforcement playbook. Police pretext stops and searches for drugs, successful in driving countless African Americans into prisons,[90] have been adapted by programs like S-Comm to identify deportable migrants. The pretext of traffic violations, such as the oft-cited broken taillight, leads police officers to check for a valid driver's license, book the vehicle operator, and, sometimes (illegally), detain their passengers to check their immigration status and turn them over to immigration agents.[91] The language of zero tolerance, used to cage children and imprison their adult caregivers separately at the border, was introduced into policing in the 1980s and 1990s to aggressively punish low-level street offenses, which police started to define as harming a residential community's quality of life and as seeding serious crimes.[92]

The principle of mandatory minimum prison sentences engineered in the 1980s war on drugs and mandatory arrests for certain types of crimes have migrated to immigration law in the form of mandatory detention and deportation of "criminal aliens." As with criminal law, these policies reduce the discretionary power of judges, placing the power in the hands of the immigration enforcement agents, who exercise prosecutorial discretion in their encounters with immigrants. Immigration enforcement mimics law enforcement, making crimmigration effective. As I demonstrate in this chapter, settling logics arise out of not only the federal government's defense of deportation but also reform-oriented immigrant rights advocacy.

This chapter laid out the architecture of crimmigration. The following chapters about organizing expose the layers of racialized gender-sexual policing embedded in crimmigration. The activists throw into relief the central but often invisible function of crimmigration, and indeed of all policing, to enforce racial, gender, sexual, and class hierarchies. These hierarchies are necessary to represent activists and those they care about as deserving the punishment of separation through incarceration, detention, and deportation. Together, the organizers' political analyses demonstrate that crimmigration-dependent deportation policies produce both normalizing power (the criminal alien) and biopower (a population that has to be managed to secure the nation-state built on settler colonialism and white supremacy). These forms of power reconstitute normative and nonnormative racialized gender and sexuality across space and time. Deportation policies attempt to align the settler nation-state's territoriality and racialized gender-sexual forms of national belonging to determine legitimate forms of kinship, sexual relations, and social reproduction of migrant communities.[93]

Activists who take apart the processes of crimmigration arrive organically at abolition. They shed light on the dehumanizing and profit-making functions of criminalization. Each of the following chapters unfolds how the organizers explicate the carceral logic that informs deportation in their particular political contexts. They also underline how abolitionist commitments disrupt the reform-oriented immigrant rights strategies and discourses. Because this radical part of the movement takes on carceral systems of domination, it builds alliances with those articulating the foundational anti-Blackness of policing and those who bear the disproportionate burden of policing on their bodies because they do not conform to binary gender and sexuality. The abolitionist and antioppression incitement—"All of Us or None"—opens up this space of engagement.

However, the framing of crimmigration as a settler colonial practice needs clearer and consistent articulation with abolitionist migrant rights politics. Diné scholar and abolitionist Melanie Yazzie speaks extensively about the urgent need to decolonize and queer the immigrant rights movement along the southwest border.[94] In *Red Nation Rising*, Yazzie and her coauthors teach us that settler power cannot be understood outside of policing and incarceration. The violence that pervades the United States is a defense against the undeniable presence of Native peoples and their social-political order in the entire settled space.[95] Thus, anticarceral migrant justice must engage with the present tense of Indigenous politics. This challenge is taken up by coalitions in LA like the Allies and Tod@s, which name the impact of punitive and militarized border enforcement on cross-border Diné (Navajo), O'odham, Yaqui, Kumeyaay, Kikapoo tribal nations, reservations, and pueblos. In a still rare example, undocumented IYC trainers incorporated the stories and predicaments of COFA youth who are neither undocumented nor "qualified aliens" in the organizing they seeded in Hawai'i. As I narrate the visions of abolition and the dreams of community security outside of punitive arms of the state in the following chapters, I think through the cozy relationship between settler colonialism and imperialism, racial capitalism and labor migration, policing, heteropatriarchy, and immigration enforcement.

2

"IT IS OUR MORAL RESPONSIBILITY TO DISOBEY UNJUST LAWS"

Jacaranda trees billow purple all over Los Angeles, Tovaangar, the land and waters of Gabrielino/Tongva, and Tataviam. It is July 2010. I am visiting the city to resume my ethnographic research after an exploratory foray the previous year. That month is linked in my mind with the fever pitch of agitation against Arizona's blatantly racist and anti-immigrant Senate Bill 1070 (SB 1070), the brilliant jacaranda petals curling in the Southern California heat, and the cooling taste of cucumber paletas (ice pops) from a bodega in Atwater Village. On my arrival, Hamid Khan, then executive director of the Artesia-based South Asian Network, told me about a new collective, Todos Somos Arizona (TsAZ). Later, TsAZ would be renamed Tod@s Som@s Arizona to move away from the masculine pronouns.[1] It coalesced in LA as soon as Arizona Governor Jan Brewer signed SB 1070 into law in April. Tod@s offered an organizing space to contend with the dangerous precedent set by SB 1070—crimmigration, a legal innovation I explain in the previous chapter. The coalition anticipated the ways in which the Department of Homeland Security would continue to formalize the practice of involving and relying on local law enforcement to criminalize migrants or identify those with prior charges and convictions to deport them. Tod@s's peaceful direct actions to stand up to unjust laws were deliberately criminalized by the city of Los Angeles, making plain its use of the criminal legal system to try (unsuccessfully) to stamp out resistance.

The collective drew activists and artists from different walks of life who were generationally, ethnically, and racially diverse and embraced a range of radical political ideologies. Hamid invited me to a July 18 community townhall Tod@s hosted at a city-run recreation center in downtown

Los Angeles. The townhall attracted more than a hundred participants. I was greeted at the door by an activist whom I would grow to know well, Naazneen Diwan. She handed me a ball of yarn and pins to trace my migration on a large hand-painted world map already crisscrossed with multi-colored yarn in a vivid representation of mobility and displacement. This icebreaker facilitated the townhall's interactive format and primed us for a discussion of racial profiling and criminalization of immigrant communities. That meeting became a springboard to organize fresh direct actions in anticipation of sb 1070 coming into force in Arizona at the end of the month. The provisions looming over Arizona did not seem distant for those living in Southern California, where many jurisdictions permitted trained local police to enforce immigration law under the 287(g) program. Immigration and Customs Enforcement (ice) was already collaborating with police and sheriff departments in San Bernardino and Riverside counties and Costa Mesa and LA County–run jails.[2]

The purpose of Tod@s from its early days was to engage in direct action to protest sb 1070 without the permission of the Los Angeles Police Department (henceforth referred to as unpermitted civil disobedience). The collective organized two nonviolent direct actions: one on May 6 at the downtown ice detention center run by the Federal Bureau of Prisons and the second targeting the private multinational security corporation g4s Wackenhut on July 29, the day sb 1070 went into effect.[3] By shutting down the streets, Tod@s intended to halt "the flow of the way in which immigration does its business in LA" and create "a public moment of solidarity with Black and brown, and Native folks in Arizona," to quote Patricia Torres, who participated in both actions.[4] The city arrested and brought criminal charges against twenty-four Tod@s activists for the two actions.[5]

The collective clearly understood sb 1070's intent to create a range of crimes, from misdemeanors to felonies, to target the day-to-day activities of immigrants. Its long-term vision did not stop with a demand for a moratorium on raids and detention. It demanded an *abolition* of these practices. The collective recognized that the bill would produce a steady flow of criminalized and deportable migrants into jails and then detention centers.[6] This flow would be achieved by empowering local law enforcement to check whether residents were carrying documents that authorized their presence in the United States. In fact, in 2012, the US Supreme Court let stand the authority of law enforcement to verify a person's immigration status at stops while striking down most provisions of sb 1070. Tod@s foresaw the consolidation of crimmigration.

Tod@s pooled the passion and talents of organizers in Los Angeles's dense social justice networks. I met amazing organizers in Tod@s, and together, they made the collective into a force to be reckoned with by the city and the Los Angeles Police Department (LAPD) through direct actions and education. Those who seeded the collective in April brought in other seasoned activists who organized immigrant and undocumented youth, fought for day laborers and unionized service sector workers, and demanded racial justice and housing equity in the city. The summer of 2010 sizzled with the emerging power of undocumented youth. They, too, engaged in direct action and risked arrest and deportation, escalating their demand that the Senate hold a hearing on the federal Development, Relief and Education of Alien Minors (DREAM) Act. Other activists came from abolitionist spaces like Critical Resistance, radical Black, Indigenous, and people of color (BIPOC) feminist and queer spaces to end all forms of state violence like INCITE!, and the Boycott Divestment Sanctions (BDS) movement for Palestinian liberation. Many had ties to organizations serving LA's Chican@, Latinx, and Asian American immigrants.

However, in Tod@s, they came together as individuals committed to nonviolent direct action, not as representatives of their organizations. The activists were immersed in local Black, Latinx, and Asian American protest traditions as well as the revolutionary ideas incubated in Latin America and Mexico. I quickly discovered that many of these core members had training in civil disobedience, which continues to be part of Los Angeles's activist culture, as evidenced by the 2017 Westwood shutdown with which I open the book.

This chapter focuses on 2010 as a moment that pried open a space for direct action and unpermitted civil disobedience in the migration justice movement.[7] Among the types of contemporary antideportation activism I discuss, LA's Tod@s represents an early activist analysis of SB 1070 as settler carceral power. The protests illuminated settler carcerality as the combustion of domestic carceral power, immigration control, and private profit-driven interests fueled by racial, gender, and sexual violence. Tod@s's efforts moved the needle toward imagining a future without policing, detentions, and deportation outside of liberal appeals to the state for recognition and rights.

While SB 1070 was widely decried as an anti-immigrant law that opened the door wide for legitimized racial profiling, Tod@s members were attuned to the Tohono O'odham Nation's jurisdictional arguments against the law. The collective stood in solidarity with the Nation. The Tohono O'odham

Nation Legislative Council's Resolution on SB 1070 asserted the Nation's jurisdiction over civil and criminal laws governing persons residing within it and its authority to negotiate with state and federal governments on laws that impacted it. The resolution pointed out SB 1070's illegitimate exercise of US power over the Nation, though this crucial point received no media attention.[8] For its part, Tod@s saw SB 1070 as a racist, anti-immigrant, and anti-Indigenous piece of legislation. The collective's understanding of settler colonialism also stemmed from some members' involvement with the BDS movement. Tod@s connected two settler carceral states, the United States and Israel, by excavating how private security firms secure US tax dollars in government contracts and profit from human misery at the US border, in the interior space settled by the United States, and in Palestine.[9]

Remarkably, feminist and queer politics in Tod@s refracted the question of criminalizing immigrants through the lens of ongoing US colonial violence that installs and enforces gender binaries and criminalizes queer sexualities. The politics, emerging in the context of resisting crimmigration, brought to the surface the gender and sexual violence of settler governance imposed on Indigenous people in North America. Such an analysis of settler power lies at the core of queer and feminist Indigenous studies, which demonstrates that this type of power punishes and attempts to eliminate Nation-specific plurality of gender, sexual, familial, and communal arrangements and connection to land.[10] When the Tod@s members introduced this Indigenous analysis, usually missing from struggles for migration justice, the move demanded a feminist engagement with settler colonialism.

Furthermore, in a revolutionary move, feminist and queer activists introduced the ethic of collective care to the coalition.[11] The feminist and queer activists' embodied approach to civil disobedience challenged the cisgender, straight citizen body as the default for such protests. They presented radical alternatives to masculinist modes of analysis and action, which are more easily read as civil disobedience or more easily recognized as immigrant rights. Naazneen and Patricia, both arrested during the May 6 action, wanted to "shed queer insight on the dominant tropes composing immigrant rights organizing and discourses."[12] The dominant tropes and discourses in the mainstream movement did not recognize sexual and gender justice as integral to social justice. Immigrant rights organizers rarely acknowledged care as part of their justice work. They remained silent about the labor of women, queer, and nonbinary comrades in providing this care.

Queer and feminist activists in Tod@s practiced care in the coalition as they prepared for the direct actions, during the actions, and in their aftermath. Consequently, I am able to document a rare moment in which these activists introduced two types of praxis. Internally, they enacted the world they wanted to create by introducing the transformative power of performing and valuing otherwise feminized and invisible care work as essential to activism. In their public-facing work, they explicitly and directly linked the normalized gender and sexual violation of nonconforming bodies to ongoing settler colonial-carceral arrangements.[13] In my account of the protest against SB 1070, I privilege the analyses advanced by the queer and feminist Tod@s members.

This chapter is based on in-person immersion in Tod@s for a month before, during, and after the July 29 action. On returning to Honolulu, I followed Tod@s's struggle against the city through our listserv and social media. To understand why collective members were attracted to direct action, I draw on interviews I conducted with a diverse range of LA's (im)migrant rights activists between 2009 and 2016.[14] As the shape of this book became clear, I reached out to several activists involved in the summer of 2010 action: Mariella Saba, Naazneen, and Patricia generously agreed to be interviewed in 2016 when I visited Los Angeles.[15] All three activists were arrested and charged with breaking the law by the city attorney's office—Naazneen and Patricia for the May 6 Tod@s action and Mariella for a May 20 direct action with the Wilshire 9 in support of the DREAM Act. In several places, I present Naazneen and Patricia's voices as interwoven (as they were in a 2011 article they wrote about Tod@s) because that's how they spoke during the interview. I met with them during another wave of civil disobedience in LA, this time for Black lives and for Central American refugees at the US-Mexico border. With all three activists, I coreconstructed our participation as activists in the collective, and we reflected on our activism together.

I begin with why radical migration justice activists gravitated toward nonviolent direct action. The rest of the chapter is organized around temporal units: "Prep Time," "Direct Action," "Jail Time," and "Wait Time." I present the sections, "Prep Time" and "Direct Action," through my eyes as a participant in the collective's July action. These two sections emphasize the crystallization of prison abolitionist politics in understanding detentions and deportations. They highlight the affective labor of feminist and queer activists as a counterweight to masculinist versions of civil disobedience protest. "Jail Time" focuses on queer and feminist revelations of gender policing as part of jailing. "Wait Time" documents why and how queer and feminist Tod@s members initiated a creative and joyful type of direct action in the form of street theater to counteract the toll of the drawn-out legal battle with the city, which sought to bring criminal action against those who were arrested for the 2010 summer civil disobedience. Each section links the SB 1070 fight to the broader discussion of for-profit carcerality, racism, and settler colonialism through a queer of color framework.

Throughout, I track two generative internal flashpoints.[16] Tod@s feminists pressured the collective to queer the movement for immigrant rights by attending to the many forms of systemic violence expressed through carceral power to contain bodies and land.[17] Also, undocumented youth and their allies within Tod@s started to voice their autonomy and insisted on their own analysis of the DREAM Act, a development I return to in chapter 5. They challenged Tod@s's discomfort with many provisions of the bill.[18] The differences in ideologies, approaches, and styles in Tod@s, I argue, generated new and underattended methods in the struggles against deportation.

Why Civil Disobedience?

Why did Tod@s engage in unpermitted civil disobedience, which they knew would result in arrests and charges? In LA, a section of immigrant rights activists wanted to channel their activism into transformative analyses and actions in a clean break from reformist demands. These fractures appeared during the 2006 mega marches, when the We Are America coalition made up of LA's organized labor, some of the city's major immigrant-serving nonprofits, and the Catholic Church's leadership opposed LA's March 25 Coalition's direct action plan to stage a nationwide work stoppage and economic boycott on May Day.[19] Resisting the We Are America coalition's pressure to domesticate the immigrant rights movement with signs of Americanization (US flags and white T-shirts) and protestations of innocence ("We are not criminals"), the militant voices urged for the need to recognize criminalization as a fundamental process of social control directed at Black and brown people.

Arizona's law allowed the activists to spotlight the state's criminalizing mechanisms and escalate the protests to nonviolent direct action. Tod@s activists developed positions that contrasted sharply with the widespread condemnation of SB 1070 on the grounds that it violated civil liberties. This mainstream framing of SB 1070 contains migration justice within a civil rights framework and restricts demands on the state to liberal and reformist measures. Tod@s pointed out that such a containment allowed the Barack Obama administration to battle SB 1070 while requiring police-immigration cooperation in the form of Secure Communities. The opposition to SB 1070 also did not tackle the routine criminalization of low-income nonbinary, trans, and intersex immigrants of color.[20]

In considering why civil disobedience was a primary tactic, I focus on the confluence of three streams—queer and feminist abolitionism, undocumented youth activism, and labor organizing. Civil disobedience offered a chance for activists like Naazneen and Patricia to experiment with feminist and queer antiviolence responses publicly and within the coalition. Nonviolent civil disobedience is first and foremost embodied. It requires protesting state power with one's body, which absorbs the violent acts of policing and caging.

Naazneen and Patricia organized from the flesh by connecting the interpersonal violence they have experienced to structural violence.[21] They tested their commitment to abolition by exploring ways to address the interpersonal harm they have experienced without relying on the dehumanizing structures of state power. The continual criminalization of immigrants forced into carceral spaces became an entry point into abolitionist feminist and queer politics.[22] Reflecting on their decision to engage in civil disobedience and get arrested, Naazneen and Patricia said: "This way, with my body, I can support the immigrant community but also use it as a strategy to say, 'This is my analysis of violence, which is state violence coming through on my body and in everyday ways.' . . . [The civil disobedience] was fueled by a desire to explore what it is like to bring feminist bodies into the space . . . [and] the capacity to join a very mainstream civil disobedience act, a very masculine sort of action."[23] In the process of contending with carcerality in the public act of civil disobedience, they, along with other feminist, queer, and nonbinary Tod@s members, started to internally address what feminist critical legal scholar and activist Kimberlé Crenshaw calls intersectional failures in social justice movements. These failures stem from privileging one type of injustice over others. These Tod@s activists intentionally attended to the vulnerabilities among members arising from the entangled experiences of their race, nationality, gender, sexuality, and disability and the resultant trauma locked in their bodies. They painstakingly built a culture of care. This network of care offered an alternative to state-reliant correctives to these traumas. The attention to bodies counteracted masculinist single-issue approach to justice, which excised gender and sexuality from political analysis. Instead of the masculinist valorization of bravado in civil disobedience, the culture of care made space for vulnerability. These shifts instigated by queer and feminist Tod@s activists were worldmaking, calling into being new ways of relating before they could be structurally achieved.

Many undocumented youth in Tod@s identified as queer and feminist. Their self-conscious resistance to their devaluation in every institutional encounter fed their appetite for civil disobedience in the summer of 2010.[24] Among them were Neidi Dominguez Zamorano (who would later drive the campaign for Deferred Action for Childhood Arrivals) and Mariella Saba, a citizen ally. They brought their experiences as organizers in Students Informing Now (S.I.N.) at the University of California, Santa Cruz. Founders of S.I.N. forged their organizing "in the intersection of two emerging movements: for educational justice and greater immigrant rights."[25] The members, *SINistas*, cut their teeth in building nonhierarchical spaces informed by Latina feminists who taught them that personal transformation and collective resistance go together. As undergraduates, they developed the voices of students who were eligible for resident tuition to attend the state university under California's AB 540 but found themselves with little institutional support after enrolling. To fight for equity in education, they put the principle of *sin vergüenza* (without shame) at the center. When *SINistas* returned to their hometown—Los Angeles—in the summer of 2010, they straddled agitations around the DREAM Act and SB 1070, exercising their power as migrant youth organizers. Mariella was among the documented allies (later named "the Wilshire 9") arrested for blocking traffic with a sit-in at the Westwood Federal Building on May 20. They had risen to support the two million undocumented youth and the DREAM Act.

Last, Tod@s attracted organizers who worked at the intersections of immigrant and labor rights and trained intensively in civil disobedience in 2008.[26] Paulina Gonzalez, who joined Tod@s as soon as it was formed, had encouraged the labor and immigrant rights activists to participate in these trainings.[27] Many, including labor organizer Sam Pullen, attended training sessions conducted by the International Center for Nonviolent Conflict to learn the philosophical underpinnings of nonviolent struggle and strategies to recruit people into the movement, identify targets, create a compelling message, and marshal resources. Sam said the training taught the organizers to "create [the] sharpest and [the most] difficult moral dilemma for the target in order to pressure a political change." Sam noted that "radical measures require radical sacrifices." He was a core Center for the Working Poor member and had quit his job with a union to fully dedicate himself to the RISE Movement, a 2008 LA coalition that emerged from the training.[28]

On Oct 15, 2008, RISE, "a new non-violent wing of the immigrant rights movement" launched a three-week hunger strike, Fast for Our Future, involving immigrants and allies in a massive effort at an encampment set up in La Placita Olvera, the oldest plaza in LA.[29] By the time of the hunger strike, RISE's focus had shifted to radicalizing the immigrant rights movement itself from its initial goal of pressuring presidential candidates, in particular Arizona's John McCain, to take a stand on immigration reform.[30] The coalition aimed to reignite the movement and "keep a steady and unrelenting focus on the unjust immigrant system."[31] While RISE was not able to sustain subsequent waves of civil disobedience as initially planned, the demands of the 2008 hunger strikers ("Stop the Raids" / "¡Alto a las redadas!") became a clarion call in the spring and summer marches of 2009. Sam observed in 2009 that "it's going to take another phase of non-violent direct action, mobilizing and sacrifice, ultimately dramatizing the horrors of being an undocumented immigrant, exploited in this economy."[32] And, indeed, it did. In 2010, several strands of direct action intertwined, drawing in activists agitating about budget cuts in California's state schools, bus fare and rent hikes, SB 1070, and the DREAM Act. Activists gravitated to civil disobedience to test antiviolence methodologies or to express their power as directly and publicly as possible. Whatever the motivation, Shiu-Ming Cheer, a veteran migrant rights activist and lawyer who was key to Tod@s, reminded me that "the form of activism and action people take are determined by their social condition."[33]

Prep Time

We organized ourselves at lightning speed in the ten days between the townhall on July 18 and the action on July 29. We needed to paint banners, conduct research, contact the press (including Spanish language and other ethnic media), plan social media campaigns, and train in civil disobedience. Such careful planning and attention to detail are not always obvious to the public. A civil disobedience action is intentionally staged to appear spontaneous—a bolt out of the blue. My partner Rich, who is involved with the movements for data justice and labor rights, and I became fully involved in the July 29 action. Below, I detail the collective's preparatory process. I mark the interventions made by queer, feminist, and undocumented activists. These interventions sparked tensions *and* shaped our preparation.

Given the unpermitted nature of the action, Tod@s, which held open meetings, asked all attendees to share who brought them to Tod@s. The friend-of-a-friend vouching created relative safety for members to share sensitive information, such as immigration status, police records, or details about employment or health. At all times, at least seventy of us were in the room. At the meetings, the feminist and queer members asked us to recognize that legal status and cis, male-bodied, able-bodied, heterosexual privileges divided us. This continual process made space for those who did not have some of those privileges.

Our first task for the July 29 action was to identify a target. It took considerable research and education over several meetings to land on G4S Wackenhut. In discussing the legislative intention of SB 1070, we started to take apart all the pieces of the prison industrial complex that criminalize BIPOC communities and immigrants. The Corrections Corporation of America and Wackenhut made our list as two of the most profitable in the business. Constructing what Purnima Bose and Laura Lyons have called "corporate genealogies," the activist-researchers unearthed the buyout of the prison arm of Wackenhut Corrections Corporation by a multinational security firm, GEO Group, in 2000 and the merger of the rest of the corporation with a Danish security conglomerate, Group 4 Flack, in 2004. G4S Wackenhut, which transported detainees and deportees, was one head of the hydra, and their offices were located in Los Angeles in a skyscraper at the intersection of Wilshire Boulevard and Highland Avenue.[34]

We wanted people to see that SB 1070 monetized our communities' suffering by escalating criminalization, detention, and deportation.[35] Hamid helped us connect the virulently anti-immigrant and racist legislative agenda of politicians like Kansas's Kris Kobach and Arizona's Russell Pearce to the for-profit prison and detention industry. The Tod@s research team discovered that G4S Wackenhut started contracting with the Department of Homeland Security in 2006. The contract was renewed in 2009. In that year alone, the corporation received $56.9 million in ICE contracts and another $52.3 million in a transportation contract with the US Customs and Border Protection. Wackenhut saw a 10 percent increase in its profits in 2009.[36] The prison profit motive behind SB 1070 was vindicated in a two-part October 2010 National Public Radio investigative report.[37] Furthermore, Naazneen and others in the BDS movement were researching Israel's contracts with G4S. These members made us aware of how private corporations bolster the policing work of settler states, including dispossessing and brutalizing Palestinians.[38] The information was designed into a handout that was widely distributed on the day of the action.[39]

All this research about G4S Wackenhut had the internal function of educating those of us in Tod@s who were new to abolitionist politics. As I explain below, Tod@s members held in the women's jail for the May action started to reflect on the connection between gender policing and other punitive forms of social control. We started to piece together the many manifestations of settler colonialism; racial-, gender-, and sexuality-based violence; and anti-immigrant legislation in the form of policing and incarceration. It helped us make sense of the choice of a private corporation obscured in a skyscraper.

The other big decision was the form that the direct action would take. Paulina, who had been arrested on May 6 and had intensive training in civil disobedience, invited our collective to brainstorm the kinds of action we wanted to stage. Initially, participants proposed many creative direct action ideas, with feminist, queer, and undocumented Tod@s comrades taking the lead. We suggested stopping people and asking for documentation of their identity and legal status at different locations in the city; making guerrilla art; creating temporary autonomous zones across the city to instigate the public to imagine a world without borders, misogyny, transphobia, and homophobia; shutting down a police garage, which impounded the cars of undocumented persons taken into detention; and dropping banners at the LA city hall where we would also construct a human border and jam the entrances. All of these would be public and disruptive actions for which we would not seek a permit from the LAPD.

At one point, a participant arrested in the May 6 action tossed out this idea: "If this is about disobeying unjust laws, I want to ask who in this room is willing to be arrested." Were people willing to risk arrest in taking over the Wilshire Boulevard and Highland Avenue intersection where the G4S Wackenhut office was housed? Since I was new to the collective and civil disobedience, I was unprepared for the question. I could feel the moral pressure build up in the room. To me, it sounded like a dare—a masculinist way of doing things. All the other ideas evaporated. Three persons in the room raised their hands without a qualm. Several others put their names forward after some thought. My status at that time as a legal permanent resident and my out-of-state location gave me pause. Above all, the idea of being in the LAPD's custody terrified me. Was there a place for terror or misgivings? The LAPD is notorious for using force and deploying urban combat equipment and SWAT teams against migrant-led nonviolent demonstrations. The police brutality against the activists, vendors, and the unhoused during the 2007 May Day MacArthur Park left many, including Hamid, with serious injuries from rubber bullets, beatings, and tear gas. The feminist and queer members who had experienced the brutality, arrest, and jailing activated the collective ethics of care as a counterweight to the internal dynamic of projecting brash masculinity.

While no one explained in detail until later what an arrest would entail, Tod@s members insisted that certain risks be considered in-depth. Immigration status was one such deciding factor. Some undocumented members expressed their reservations about the strong impulse in the collective to protect them from direct encounters with police by discouraging them from risking arrest. In 2010, documented people were still representing those who were undocumented. Yet, right at that moment, undocumented youth were risking arrest and deportation. As Tod@s was planning the July 29 action, undocumented students and their allies were hunger striking at Senator Dianne Feinstein's Westwood office, demanding that the DREAM Act be moved out of the Senate judiciary committee. This action followed undocumented youth getting arrested for sit-ins staged at Senator John McCain's office on May 17 in Tucson, Arizona, and at the Westwood Federal Building in LA on May 20. In LA, undocumented youth organizers like Neidi Dominguez Zamorano and Johnathan Perez and allies like Mariella Saba were moving between these actions and passionately calling on Tod@s to support the students on hunger strike. Our protest against SB 1070 grazed against what would manifest as a new wave of organizing, "Undocumented and Unafraid," in which undocumented activists represented themselves and escalated their direct action (see chapter 5).

Within twenty-four hours of these discussions, Tod@s had a list of ten members, all documented, who committed to risking arrest. As with the earlier action, no one who risked arrest would carry identification documents. In the context of SB 1070, it was a direct refusal to carry and produce their "papers" for law enforcement. We self-organized into nonhierarchal affinity groups as soon as the action took form. Collective members, including undocumented youth, could join the tactical team or serve as medics and caregivers, media coordinators, legal observers, police liaisons, or crowd coordinators and chanters. The feminist and queer members spread themselves across all the affinity groups. They taught us crucial and caring ways to support the action and be present at it without risking arrest.

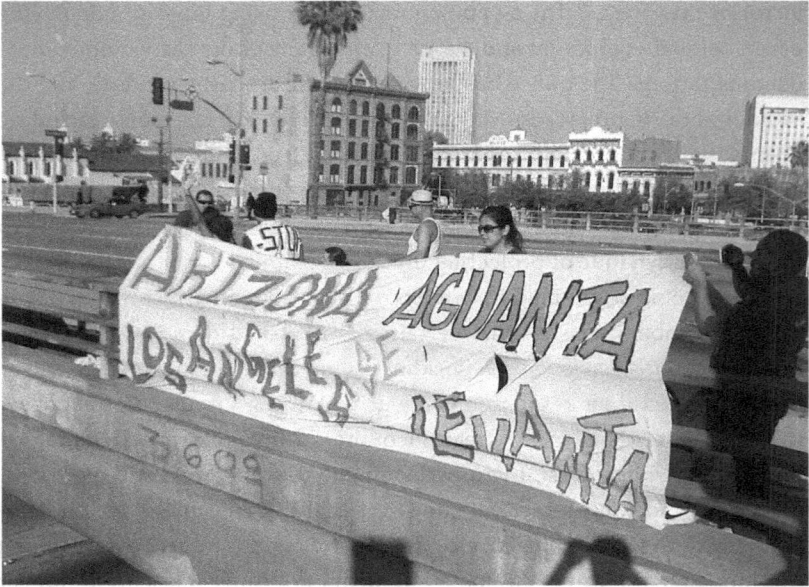

2.1. Tod@s Som@s Arizona members dropping a banner over Freeway 101 in downtown LA to protest SB 1070 on July 26, 2010. Photo credit: Rich Rath.

Building up to July 29, we dropped huge hand-painted banners downtown over the 101 Freeway during the morning and evening rush hour on July 26 and 27. The actions attracted positive commuter and media attention. On the evening before the July 29 action, those of us volunteering as crowd coordinators went through a de-escalation and peacekeeping training with Neidi, who split her time between the Tod@s meetings and the DREAMer hunger strike at Dianne Feinstein's office.[40] She taught us how to hold our bodies, plant our feet, and defuse incendiary situations with angry commuters as well as provocateurs. I felt a rush of relief as Neidi started the training by explicitly stating that most of us had experienced some form of bodily trauma and asked us to honor the experience as we used our bodies for nonviolence.

Direct Action: ¡Arizona Aguanta! ¡Los Angeles se Levanta!

On the morning of July 29, Rich and I met with a cluster of Tod@s activists who would walk across Wilshire Boulevard to stop oncoming traffic. Others were doing the same at the three other corners of the intersection. The air still had a touch of desert coolness. At around 7:30 a.m., the van carrying those risking arrest arrived, and we stepped out into the intersection at the head of our group as the traffic light turned red. The other three groups did the same. About fifty of us had effectively taken over the intersection and stopped all traffic. Several others worked quickly to spread the massive fifty-foot canvas with the message "End Deportation." We had painted it in the yard of Self Help Graphics & Art, a venerable East LA artivism institution.[41] Ten of our Tod@s comrades nimbly arranged themselves in a daisy chain and lay down on the canvas in a perfect circle with their arms locked with a device nicknamed the sleeping dragon lockbox. Their choreographed precision was breathtaking.

Standing in the intersection, we guarded that space in the middle. Our group held a large banner that stretched across the breadth of Wilshire Avenue with the message, "honk to END racist laws." Drivers honked loudly and persistently, not always in support of our opposition to SB 1070. They wanted us to get out of their way. One driver almost hit the blockaders at the right turn from Highland to Wilshire. We stood our ground and chanted with conviction, "It is our moral responsibility to disobey unjust laws." We breathed life into Dr. Martin Luther King Jr.'s words from Birmingham jail in another time and place. By blocking the intersection with our bodies, Tod@s initiated the unpermitted civil disobedience to protest SB 1070.

Soon, the sound of sirens filled the air, and we were surrounded by banks of police. By 8 a.m., Tod@s's social media posts, shared at lightning speed, announced, "People have locked down in the streets and the police have arrived but our protestors stand fast and their supporters stand strong. We aren't going anywhere!!" Police diverted the stalled cars and all oncoming traffic. During this time, crowd coordinators could leave our positions and walk in circles around the ten Tod@s activists. As the news of the blockade spread by social media, supporters poured in from different parts of Los Angeles. Soon, the Bus Riders Union members joined us and led us in spirited chants.[42] Percussionists from Instituto de Educación Popular del Sur de California (IDEPSCA) and Koreatown Immigrant Workers Alliance injected a shot of energy with their beats. Tod@s members installed a "Notice of Termination," a huge neon pink poster board on the street in front of the skyscraper that housed the G4S Wackenhut office, announcing that the corporation was fired for abusing incarcerated people, separating families, and profiting from criminalizing immigrants.

Imagine lying on the street in the middle of a busy intersection on a late July morning in Los Angeles. By 8:30 a.m., the day's heat was rising from

2.2. Tod@s Som@s Arizona members lying down at the intersection of Wilshire Boulevard and Highland Avenue on July 29, 2010, the day SB 1070 went into effect in Arizona. Photo credit: Rich Rath.

below, and the sun was beating down. Those who had locked themselves to each other were lying with their faces turned up to the trees, the sky, and the skyscraper that housed G4S Wackenhut. They looked vulnerable and incredibly courageous at the same time. Their arms outstretched, they touched each other's fingers inside the tubes. Peripherally, they could see the edges of the sidewalk and people's feet—ours and those of bystanders. They had to reorient their senses and attune themselves to the sounds around them—infuriated drivers on their way to work honking their horns, our chanting and drumming, and sirens. Looking at our comrades on the ground, I grasped why members like Patricia had talked so much about trust, love, and vulnerability in the fast-paced days leading up to our action. Solidarity sizzled off the road into the air ringing with our chants. We took turns shading those lying down. Tod@s caretakers and medics bent over the prone figures, tenderly swabbing their lips and applying chapsticks, rubbing in sunscreen, giving them sips of water or a section of an orange, murmuring words of encouragement, and describing what was happening all around us.

Our feminist and queer comrades had integrated caretaking into the civil disobedience action. They were enacting radical care, the labor so essential to sustaining movements and yet so undervalued. Explaining why this ethics of care was as important as legal observation, Mariella said, "The steady presence of the caregivers in the midst of the chaos of the action sends the message to those risking arrest, 'You are not alone in this, and I am not going to leave your side, and whatever you need, you can express it.'"[43] She pointed out that the caretakers needed to anticipate every need of the person for whom they were caring from head to toe and ask each person about their likes and dislikes. As caretakers, they also needed an extra layer of training because they too were risking arrest because they were present right next to those taking direct action.

The legal observers coordinated between those risking arrest and the LAPD officers, walking back and forth to inform the activists of the negotiations. One of the legal observers, Shiu-Ming, later explained that the back and forth safeguarded the rights of those lying in the intersection and those blocking traffic. The legal observers consulted with each person risking arrest to convey their wishes to the police officers.[44] Tactically, the back-and-forth process prolonged the disruption to ensure that the protest had the intended impact of drawing supporters to the spot and attracting media attention. As we stalled, we held the crowd's attention with short speeches and a press conference to explain the protest.

The LAPD issued its dispersal order around 10:30 a.m. As crowd coordinators, we had been trained to clear the intersection when asked to disperse, gather on the sidewalks with our signs, and continue chanting. By that time, the crowds had swelled. We had to ensure that members of the public who joined us understood that they needed to follow our commitment to nonviolence. Our chants grew louder as the officers got to work on our comrades, with the legal observers and our media team watching every move. We hooted the first few lines of KRS-One's "Sound of Da Police" with glee, along with whoops of "No Justice / No Peace / No Racist Police" while looking straight into the eyes of the officers, many of them officers of color, as they corralled us on to sidewalk. We were so tense! It took over an hour for the officers to separate the activists locked to each other. They used electric saws to cut the tubes and chains. Each handcuffed protestor nonviolently resisted their arrest. As the police dragged them to the vans, we again chanted, our voices rising together in a crescendo, "It is our moral responsibility to disobey unjust laws." As part of the media and support team, Rich recorded the soundscape of the action and created a sound art piece to which readers can listen and sense the action.[45]

Police separated the ten arrested into two groups. One group was booked at the Wilshire Community Police Station on Venice Boulevard, where I headed with several Tod@s members. The other group was taken to the Jesse Brewer Regional Headquarters, also known as the 77th Precinct on South Broadway. At each station, police booked those they arrested as John and Jane Does, until they traced their identities. Once the Wilshire station processed and released those arrested, we made our way to the 77th Precinct. A stark contrast to the Wilshire station, the 77th Precinct, located in a heavily surveilled area of LA, exuded human misery. The people going in and out of the building were primarily Black and brown. The station was surrounded by storefronts with signs blinking "Bail Bonds," evidencing another crossing of commercial interests with incarceration. Since bail must be paid in cash or a cashier's check, a method peculiar to the US criminal legal system, poor people of color, unable to post cash bail in full, depend on commercial bail bonds for which they pay a nonrefundable fee and often put up a collateral.[46] Evidence of how the system worked to conjoin profit and prisons surrounded us. As we waited on the precinct steps, we flipped through each other's photographs of the action on our phones, offering our own angle of vision. It was dark out before the 77th Precinct released our comrades. We hugged each other in joy and heaved a collective sigh of relief, allowing ourselves to absorb the success of our action. After the action, I had to head back to Honolulu, following Tod@s's continued efforts to educate people about the ramifications of SB 1070 and their legal fight with the city through our email list and social media posts.

Jail Time

Unlike those arrested for the earlier May 6 civil disobedience, those arrested on July 29 were released the same day from jail. In this section, I focus on the queer and feminist activists arrested in May and their reflections on carcerality and abolition. In the absence of identification, the arresting officers classified the eight as female. They were detained in the women's jail at Parker Center downtown—a gleaming steel and tempered glass structure without window bars built as a state-of-the-art jail in the 1950s and later demolished in 2019. Immediately, the Tod@s members grasped the gender policing function of carceral spaces. Those who had participated in the prison abolition organization Critical Resistance evaluated the alternatives to carceral responses as they sat in jail. During this time, they also wrestled with the contrast between themselves and those who had been jailed and charged with various crimes, which said more about the everyday policing of Los Angeles's Black and brown neighborhoods than about the lawlessness in these spaces. Tod@s members, who had intentionally broken the law, left jail knowing their companions for those twenty-four hours may spend many more days in jail because they could not afford cash bail and had no legal or jail support team looking out for them. These jail time reflections convinced Naazneen, Patricia, and like-minded Tod@s comrades that their queer and feminist analysis needed to be fully incorporated into the anticarceral politics for migrant rights. They continually raised their perspective at Tod@s meetings in the months that followed the civil disobedience actions.

Since Tod@s members were not carrying identification, the police explicitly engaged in assigning their sex and gender, firmly binding the two together. The very first questions the police officers asked Tod@s members when booking them aimed at identifying their sex. Having just used their bodies, as Naazneen said, to "block the state from carrying out its mission of violence against undesirables," the state's need at the police station to reduce their bodies to male or female to start the work of jailing reminded them that prisons and jails, like so many other institutions, reproduced and enforced sex and gender normativity. Adding to Naazneen's voice, Patricia said, "I just don't love the gender binary. But that's the first question they asked. *So those questions* [about one's sex] *were pretty hard for me to answer.*"[47] Eight of the fourteen Tod@s members brought to the Parker Center were classified as Jane Does, until the police established their state-issued identities.

Naazneen and Patricia, charting the feminist and queer thought and action in Tod@s in a coauthored article, critically reflected on the everyday colonial containment of bodies through sex assignment. The glass and concrete of the Parker Center instantiated that violence. Inspired by Qwo-li Driskell (Cherokee), who restories decolonization and Native nationhood through complex Two-Spirit critiques, Naazneen and Patricia connected carceral spaces to a form of settler control over expressions of gender and sexuality. They also drew on their involvement with the LA chapter of INCITE!, which puts BIPOC survivors at the center of the movement to end gender-based violence. Naazneen and Patricia's different stories of dislocation to the United States and their relationship to distinct colonial legacies sharpened the politics that link the gender and sexual violence inherent in dispossessing Indigenous people of their land and culture to the enforcement of binary sex and gender through incarceration.

The two Tod@s activists used their visceral experience of getting booked to reflect on a fellow activist, Sriram, who identified as a queer brown transgender man. Queer and brown bodies amplified the contingency of citizenship. Two intertwined suspicions about Sriram's gender expression and terrorism would be attached to his body, making civil disobedience particularly dangerous for him.[48] Naazneen and Patricia retold Sriram's story to provoke Tod@s to consider who could put their bodies on the line. Sriram could not participate in the type of civil disobedience Tod@s staged to protest SB 1070.

Relatedly, Naazneen and Patricia called into question the hyperlegibility in Tod@s and the broader immigrant rights movement of certain types of gender-based traumas. At a Tod@s meeting on the night before they engaged in the May civil disobedience, they questioned the symbolic deployment of the "tragic" figure of a migrant woman subjected to rape during her journey to the US-Mexico border. They protested the appeal to one kind of violence. Whose bodily violence becomes important enough to energize activists to engage in civil disobedience and risk arrest? Where was an analysis of "heterosexual, heteropatriarchal, and colonial violence" that did not end at the border or with cisgender women, they asked. Marking the discursive exclusion of queer and trans bodies from the migration justice agenda because of a limited understanding of gender-based violence, they demanded that radical activists stop participating in such dehumanizing practices.[49] Jail time generated the reflection and critique of the vein of heteronormativity in organizing the protest. In the months that followed, an enormous amount of labor was done by queer and feminist activists like Naazneen, Patricia, Johnathan, and the *SINistas* in an attempt to transform Tod@s, as I detail below.

Several "Jane Does" had survived trauma. In jail, they investigated their understanding of prison abolition as persons who had suffered harm. As Naazneen and Patricia recalled in their interview,

NAAZNEEN: One of the most interesting conversations we had in jail was around abolitionist work and being survivors of childhood sexual assault, not believing in the prison industrial complex and, at the same time, [having] the real need for some kind of accountability but not retaliation . . . just being and feeling safe. And there were some of us, including me at that point, that were just coming into that politics, grappling with it. . . . It was like, "I don't know how I would feel about a blanket sort of pass [for the abuser]. Does it mean no one goes to jail?" Abolitionist work when it's done right . . .

PATRICIA: Yeah, yeah, [it creates a sense of] feeling safe . . . it is trying to check patriarchal power that has . . .

NAAZNEEN: . . . led to a lot of assault on female-bodied children, particularly, genderqueer.[50]

Tod@s members simultaneously affirmed the need for survivors to find a resolution to their sexual and gender-based violations *and* the need to interrogate the utility of a criminal legal response to such trauma. They tested their commitment to prison abolition starting with their bodies, trapped at one time by abusers and at that moment by an institution—the jail.

Equally important, jail time reminded the Tod@s activists of their privilege as people arrested for political protest. During the twenty-four hours the activists spent in the women's jail, their paths crossed with others locked up not for their moral objection to an unjust law but because of the LAPD's routine predatory sweeps through impoverished Black communities and communities of color. The contrast between why the two groups were sharing the jail space and how they were treated became inescapable. In their conversations, the activists learned about the person who was waiting at a bus stop and got swept into jail during a police raid in the neighborhood; about another person who was arrested for wearing brass knuckles; and about others who were locked up for self-defense. The activists bore witness to the criminalization of the everyday survival activities of Black people and people of color as a part of policing, a process that SB 1070 made part and parcel of immigration enforcement.

The other cell mates asked why the Tod@s activists were in jail. In the "Jane Doe / Personal Narrative" section of their article, Naazneen and Patricia say, "*Some wonder why the hell we would lay down on our bodies, inconvenience our locations of privilege for others. Others nod, hear my explanation of en lak ech, and they need no explanation.*"[51] Many activists I met through Tod@s said they were guided in their civil disobedience by the K'iche' Code of Conduct, *En lak ech* (translated in the movement as "I am you / you are me" or "I am another you"), circulated by Delano-born cofounder of Teatro Campesino, Luis Valdez.[52] The activists adopted this code of recognizing one's self in the other to defy dehumanization that justified violent laws to punish BIPOC communities. This K'iche' code was also a diasporic adaptation of a fundamental principle of nonviolent civil disobedience—to confront those who enforce unjust laws with their humanity. That recognition imbues civil disobedience with its ethical call. Practicing this principle in a jail space made the experience both "hellish and healing," to use Naazneen and Patricia's words.[53]

The hardest part for Tod@s members was leaving behind those who would travel through various parts of the prison industrial complex without relief. In contrast to their companions in jail, the Parker Center officers wanted to get the Tod@s activists processed as quickly as possible. They perceived the Tod@s members as wasting cell space meant for the "real criminals." The LAPD officers at the Parker Center, Wilshire Community Jail, and the 77th Precinct, by and large, saw Tod@s members as idealists, "do-gooders," an inconvenience, because of the time-consuming process of establishing their identities and the interruption of LAPD's "real" work of crime control.[54] Tod@s members jailed in the two actions were released on their own recognizance. The activists had been prepared for much worse. However, their relief was short-lived once the city attorney's office decided to throw the book at them.

Wait Time

The city attorney's office decided to criminally prosecute thirty-three activists altogether.[55] The office initiated charges against the twenty-four Tod@s members arrested for the May 6 and July 29 actions and the Wilshire 9 arrested in a separate action in support of the DREAM Act. In doing this, the then city attorney Carmen Trutanich departed from his predecessors. That office usually offered protestors a diversion program instead of pressing charges. In the eight months that followed the July 29 protest, Tod@s fought the charges until they were dropped.[56] In the following months, at least sixty-odd members remained active and the coalition drew new members.

Wait time characterizes the long, drawn-out, sometimes enervating uncertainty that haunted the collective. The tried-and-tested state tactics of exhausting vibrant movements with protracted legal battles and sowing dissension by offering individuals the chance to lessen charges or get charges dismissed certainly took a toll on Tod@s. I see the city's tactics as another expression of "attrition through enforcement," the stated intent of SB 1070 and, in this case, the effort to alienate activists from the movement. The need to develop a legal strategy for a trial started to dominate the collective's work even as it continued to educate the public and organize multiple demonstrations to keep the focus on SB 1070 and copycat bills.

I first examine Tod@s's confrontation with the city and then the internal frictions. On the one hand, the city's tough stance led to a still broader coalition with other criminalized communities like the unhoused residents of Skid Row to escalate the public confrontation with the city. On the other, feminist and queer activists arrested in the Tod@s actions felt that the legal battle left little room for them to continue the jail time conversations about the gender and sexual politics of incarceration and address the collective's reservations about undocumented youth supporting the DREAM Act. Brilliantly, they built a circle of care where they invented creative and joyous direct action to counter masculinist modes of protest. Their desire to address antideportation organizing in all its complexity took the shape of the *Octopus of Oppression and Transformation*—a massive installation of a papier-mâché octopus—accompanied by street theater staged in January 2011 in front of city hall.[57]

City Attorney Trutanich pressed criminal charges against the arrested Tod@s members for three misdemeanors. They were charged with obstructing traffic, refusing to follow police orders to disperse, and resisting arrest. The Tod@s members faced the prospect of up to one year in jail and $1,000 in fines each if convicted. While Tod@s members had gone into the civil disobedience prepared for felony charges, the city's prosecutors typically treated civil disobedience violations as infractions, Shiu-Ming, who was part of Tod@s's legal support team, explained. Protestors would appear for a city attorney hearing. Usually, they would be warned against reengaging in civil disobedience for a period and would be offered a diversion program or fined. Instead, the city took a punitive stance on the summer 2010 protests.[58]

Trutanich and his office repeatedly and publicly stated that they wanted to make an example of the thirty-three activists to deter future unpermitted civil disobedience. Trutanich, quoted in the *Los Angeles Times*, declared, "In order for us to have a civilized society, there has to be a predictable result when you break the law. I want to make sure that they don't do it again."[59] He cited the cost to that city caused by the traffic jam and the special equipment to cut the lockboxes. The irony of Trutanich words about a "civilized society" was not lost on Tod@s. They too decided to make an example of SB 1070 and bring it back to the LAPD's and immigration enforcement's inhumane policing and caging of brown and Black people. On September 22 and 23, 2010, when the Tod@ activists were arraigned, the collective launched its Days of Resistance with a rally and press conference with the clear message: "We will not let the threat of imprisonment silence our movement! End the criminalization of our communities and the criminalization of resistance!"[60] Another wave of public protest followed in November. Tod@s members visited public schools and college campuses and spoke with alternative media to continue their public education about SB 1070 and to raise awareness about why they engaged in civil disobedience that summer.

Assisted by their legal teams, a smaller group negotiated with the city attorney's office. Mariella Saba, one of the Wilshire 9, was nominated to be part of this group. In these meetings, Trutanich and his staff tried to browbeat the protestors into silence. Trutanich also played the tired card of pitting immigrants against African Americans in Los Angeles. Describing her first encounter with Trutanich in the early days, Mariella wryly recalled, "He entered like a sheriff, and very imposing with his big body and imposing with his language saying, 'I am not here to talk about content; I am here to talk about, about . . . ,' I don't know what the hell. . . ."[61] She grew serious as she remembered Trutanich's effort to shut down the activists in the room by lecturing them on the millions their protests cost the city. She describes her growing resolve to speak up and Trutanich's reaction: "He came at me. He talked about your 'Latino action.' He said that the money that was wasted could have gone to the African American people in Skid Row. You're a white man in a position of power and you're telling me this! You could do way more if you really wanted to, if [you] weren't racist, you could solve a lot of problems in the city. But he told me this. I was like, 'Whuh.' I am going to get back at this man but in a bigger way."[62] Trutanich's posturing and his cynical move to pit immigrants against African Americans strengthened the activists' collective determination to fight the city.

Mariella found out that Trutanich did monthly walks in Skid Row. The venerable Los Angeles Community Action Network (LACAN), which organized unhoused residents on Skid Row, had already been protesting these monthly "safety walks," part of the Safe City Initiative launched in the Business Improvement District with the Central City East Association. The association represented the interests of the district's property owners, businesses, employees, and the housed residents.[63] The unhoused Skid Row residents saw the walks as the city leaders' attempts at scapegoating them for the city's problems. Mariella contacted LACAN. For the next eleven months, she and Tod@s organizers like Hamid, who was involved with LACAN, followed Trutanich and his team on their walks, publicly calling them out for their sweeps on Skid Row residents. At every turn, they demanded the right to dissent and an end to the "criminalization of our communities," connecting the many faces of police power and enforcement.[64]

The city's decision to prosecute Tod@s members and the Wilshire 9 together exacerbated the already existing tensions over the place of feminist politics and the DREAM Act activism. Away from the public's eye, twenty-four Tod@s members worked with their legal team to prepare to fight their cases. In long meetings, they discussed the worst-case conviction scenarios and fears about infiltration. As Naazneen and Patricia perceptively noted, sometimes the infiltrator is patriarchy.[65] These legal defense discussions detracted from other urgent conversations about developing a feminist of color abolitionist stance within Tod@s and the broader movement. The feminist and queer Tod@s members, among the twenty-four charged by the city, wanted to draw attention to invisibilized forms of gender and sexual violence. They wanted the group to create and value a culture of care. Not finding a space for these conversations at these meetings, the queer and feminist activists turned to INCITE! In this alternative space where BIPOC feminists were at the center, they could talk about their bodies in relationship to state violence. They felt affirmed, cared for, and replenished, ready to engage with Tod@s critically. The Octopus Project blossomed from these incitements to imagine social change outside of masculinist modes of protest. It presented a worldmaking alternative to the intersecting systems of oppression experienced by BIPOC communities. It allowed members, exhausted by the legal defense, to care for each other.

Similarly, those Tod@s members who were escalating their tactics to press for the passage of the DREAM Act gravitated toward the Octopus Project, attracted to creating a visual and embodied representation of a capacious vision of liberation rooted in an intersectional analysis. They needed to be heard and seen by those in the coalition who opposed the military option in the DREAM Act and had reservations about undocumented youth in Tod@s backing the bill.[66] Reflecting on those tensions, Mariella noted, "So, it was not an easy space to navigate, as you saw. . . . It almost put the youth in a smaller place . . . *SINistas*, we pushed for the DREAM Act, but we were actively putting our bodies on the line against [military] recruitment. Not a lot of that was seen or visible. . . . We had to navigate it together but not . . . become obstacles to people's liberation. . . . That's where the Octopus of Oppression comes in to show the complexities of the system from different angles."[67] Even as coalitional politics were put to test, Tod@s became a brave space to experiment with and push for an intersectional analysis that could reflect queer, feminist, undocumented, and youth-led analyses of the carceral and militarized logics of policing and incarceration.

The octopus installation and play introduced "the creativity, the lightness, the joy" to public protest. Ten writers, actors, and artists came together to collaborate. It felt both exciting and unwieldy. New activists joined the effort. Some were involved in the student struggle within the California State University system against tuition hikes, the Bus Riders Union's protest against fare hikes, and LACAN's protest against the city's criminalization of unhoused Skid Row residents.[68] The group arrived at the idea of a street theater with multiple themes and overlapping scenes staged around the mobile installation—the octopus—with many artists constructing the parts at Chuco's Justice Center, home to the Youth Justice Coalition, which organizes against criminalization and incarceration.[69] Each octopus limb had one side that represented an axis of state oppression and another that offered a worldmaking alternative that presented "what was wholesome for our communities": bodily security and freedom from a scarcity economy created by intentionally siphoning resources away from already marginalized communities.[70] Tod@s decided to stage the play with the octopus on January 18, 2011, in front of city hall, where the city attorney's office was located, to show Trutanich that dissent is part of public life.

Explaining their decision to put their energies into a different type of protest and make particular interventions, Naazneen and Patricia said they wanted to connect the legal intent of SB 1070 and its punitive architecture to the enforcement of the gender binary imposed by US settler colonialism; Israel's settler colonialism in Palestine; and Islamophobia in US domestic and international national security policies. At stake, once again, was an expansive definition of the struggle for migration justice. The larger collective objected to a gender arm for the octopus up until the night before the action. But Naazneen and Patricia remained committed to directly

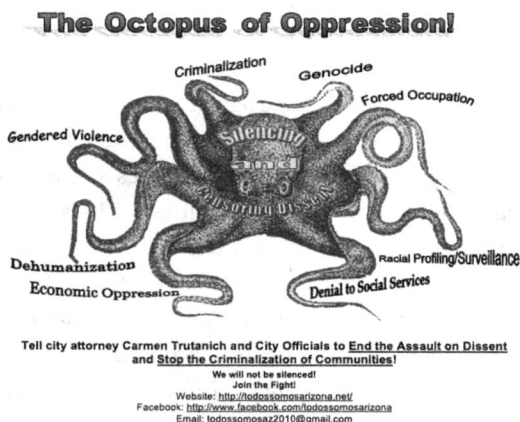

2.3. A Tod@s Som@s Arizona handout showing all the arms of the Octopus of Oppression. Tod@s members and allies performed a street theatre on January 18, 2011, in front of the LA city hall with a papier-mâché installation of the octopus.

addressing "the dominance of this sort of masculine mode of thinking." Patricia, who took the lead in writing the script for the gender arm, said, "The idea of these pieces was to give a little bit of life into what gender might look like, or what state oppression might look like."[71] Palestine produced another type of discomfort. Some members felt that addressing Israel's systematic removal, incarceration, and containment of Palestinians to control Palestinian land would draw the collective into unnecessary controversies. However, those, like Naazneen, who had come to Tod@s from the BDS movement continued to insert their intersectional politics into the collaborative creative process.

For the street theater, Patricia adopted poetry as her form. She and her companion actor, a cisgender Black man, created their scene as inmates in a jail cell. They juxtaposed Patricia's experiences in jail "around the violence of a gender binary and how state imposes it" with the criminalization of Black masculinity and the caging of Black men. Naazneen and her companion actor highlighted the effects of anti-Black and Islamophobic racial profiling by police. She cowrote her scene with a Cal State Northridge student who was being prosecuted because of protesting tuition hikes. Their scene recreated two settings, a mosque and a bus stop, to tie these spaces and struggles together. Naazneen's coactor, a Black youth, got picked up at a bus stop by a police officer after being profiled as a student skipping school. In a parallel scene, Naazneen was raising money for ground wells in Palestine at a mosque when she got arrested by an FBI agent for terrorist activities. They designed the scene to reveal the distinct modes of state surveillance, which put members of Muslim and Black communities in the clutches of the national security and prison industrial complex.

The actors performed each scene under an octopus arm during the street performance, which attracted a huge crowd. At the end of the scene, an actor flipped the arm to show the transformation of that oppression. The joy of the performance emanated from the uplifting message that people could transform the oppressive conditions in which they live. The action got people out on the streets and activated through theater and art in a way that bolstered the collective's and their allies' spirits, which were being crushed by the city's prosecution. Communicating the effects of the action, so different from the ones on May 6 and July 29, Patricia noted, "It was a piece of art activism, and really a healing way of confronting state power with creativity, and with alternative visions of a more just society." Their message in that action was one of hope: "We're showing that we can take these state arms of oppression and transform them, right. . . . This is the value of this type of grassroots work coalitional, antiracist work."[72] Did those committed to more traditional templates of direct action see any value in their labor or see street theater as organizing work? It is hard to tell, but it was certainly worth the effort of conceptualizing and performing the world Tod@s aspired to build.

By early March of 2011, the city attorney's office started to back down, first dropping the criminal charges against the Wilshire 9, and then those against Tod@s organizers.[73] The multipronged strategy of building a strong defense with a team of lawyers, public demonstrations, letter-writing campaigns, public education, and street theater swayed public opinion in favor of the actions. The city continued to defend its initial decision to press criminal charges by characterizing the activists as "professional" agitators. But the higher moral ground of disobeying unjust laws embraced by the Tod@s activists prevailed. They were able to expose and beat back the city's efforts to criminalize protest. This was no small victory, especially in light of the threat of a year of jail time. Tod@s continued to find ways to engage the city on policing and prisons while supporting undocumented youth activism. By 2012, Tod@s decided to disband because the collective had served its purpose. Subsequently, many Tod@s members continued to participate in militant civil disobedience launched by LA's Black Lives Matter and the "Undocumented, Unafraid" movement.[74]

Conclusion

I have presented a rare account of queer and feminist analyses of the prison-detention-deportation complex in the struggle against SB 1070. The visceral experiences of queer and feminist activists in Tod@s informed their position that gender-racial-sexual violence is fundamental to settler carceral structures. Their insights revealed that radical migrant politics aimed at dismantling all forms of carcerality needed to address racialized and settler-constructed gender and sexual hierarchies. The impacts of anti-Indigenous, anti-Black, and anti-immigrant laws like SB 1070 could not be understood apart from the policing and punishment of queer and gender nonconforming bodies. The attention to the different registers of violence activated a queer and feminist ethics of care. The Tod@s members who enfolded and enacted the care before, during, and after the direct actions demonstrated how necessary it is for activism.

Tod@s popularized the language of abolition and community self-defense as a collective, making it integral to antideportation activism. This political orientation articulated with later developments in the movement such as the emergence of the nationwide antideportation #Not1More campaign and organizing spaces like Mijente, which advocates the decriminalization of all immigration. Tod@s set its sights on transforming the systems that enable criminalization, captivity, and displacement. In doing that, its formulation of migration justice radically departed from the immigrant rights organizations' appeals to the state. Tod@s respectfully repurposed the philosophies of civil disobedience and elements of Black radical traditions to demand the elimination of all carceral institutions, establishing a meaningful coalitional space with Black and houseless communities fighting police brutality and mass incarceration. It forged a political course of action, which directly took on punitive legal regimes with their thriving marketplace of prisoners.

Tod@s members remain acutely aware that their experience as criminalized protestors was different from those who are routinely criminalized by police. Mariella reflected on the difference between her journey through the criminal legal system as part of the Wilshire 9 and that of her brother, a dark-skinned Latinx Palestinian. The Wilshire 9 appeared in court with a pro bono team of well-heeled Mexican American Bar Association lawyers. In those court appearances, Mariella bore witness to "all the people of color who were suffering through their cases. I know those faces. I recognize the situation without knowing each other's stories, and I know each story is heavy."[75] Like the people she encountered in the courtroom, Mariella's brother was navigating the system in a parallel universe without the moral weight of criminalized protestors.

The next chapter is devoted to understanding the treatment of "criminal aliens," who organize as Families for Freedom (FFF) in New York City to end deportation. Nevertheless, they are not legible to the public as principled political actors. Though they too are committed activists, their criminal convictions for a range of aggravated felonies lead them through a different legal maze. The FFF organizers, many of whom were immigrants of African descent living in hypersurveilled areas of New York City, have had to produce themselves as subjects of migration justice. The FFF members cut through the moral-legal barrier erected between innocent immigrants and those perceived as criminals to assert the value of their kinship ties. They reject permanent expulsion as an appropriate punishment for those with criminal charges and convictions.

3

"DON'T DEPORT OUR DADDIES"

"¡Alto a las redadas!" (Stop the raids), "End Deportation Now," "Keep Families Together." These signs and slogans convey the signature message of every immigrant rights march in the last decade. Public outrage has flared up from time to time since 2014 over the treatment at the US-Mexico border of Central American parents and children seeking asylum in the United States from drug, gang, sexual, and economic violence in their home countries.[1] In 2018, immigrants and US citizens vociferously decried the Donald Trump administration's separation of children from their asylum-seeking parents, who were put in criminal custody at the US-Mexico border.[2] These widespread protests mainstreamed the call "Abolish ICE." Numerous US citizen mothers accompanied by their young children joined "Abolish ICE" demonstrations. Ordinarily untouched by the fear of deportation that haunts migrant and mixed-status families daily, US citizens found themselves identifying strongly with the rage and grief of incarcerated parents forced by the state to abandon their terrified children at the border. The protests testified to the ideological power of families.[3]

In this chapter, I attend to the effects of deportation and separation of family members in the interior of the United States. The separation of asylum-seeking families at the border exists on a continuum with postentry enforcement. In the interior, immigration enforcement has been steadily tearing apart mixed-status and undocumented families since the draconian 1996 laws expanded the grounds for mandatory detention and deportation. As I explain in chapter 1, this pace has picked up because the Department of Homeland Security (DHS) is using old and new programs to facilitate the deportation of migrants who encounter local police or are under correctional control.

Migrants of color get entrapped in the unforgiving criminal legal system, which brutalizes US-born Black people, US citizens of color, and citizens of Indigenous Nations in distinct ways. When attached to a migrant, the label "criminal alien" has immigration consequences. It justifies the person's permanent deportation. Living in the interior, away from borders, does not translate to safety. Plenary power and citizenship—in short, US countersovereignty—regulates the bordered national space *and* intimate familial space. Neither the interior space of migrants' homes nor their authorized presence in the nation's domestic space affords Black and brown families privacy or protection from state violence under the current immigration enforcement apparatus.

I put the mainstream outrage we witnessed in 2018 into historical perspective by offering an account of a pioneering twenty-first-century antideportation organization, Families for Freedom (FFF), formed in 2002 in New York City (Lenape land). Uniquely, it is among a handful of groups that organize and defend migrants who are charged with or convicted of one or more of the fifty-plus aggravated felonies that make legal permanent residents (LPRs) and undocumented migrants deportable. Based on its members' experiences and research, FFF clearly understands that its members encountered law enforcement because they are Black or of color, first-generation working-class immigrant men living in overpoliced neighborhoods. The organization features deported daddies prominently.[4] It makes visible the care these criminalized men provide for their families because it is a material reality. The representation also humanizes these men considered too dangerous to live in the United States. The organization's focus on men and their care work illuminates the racial and gender politics of criminality and deportation.

Families or Freedom uses storytelling to mobilize deportees and their families to build a movement to dismantle the carceral system. To lay the groundwork for the rest of the book, I read settler power by comparing FFF's unusual approach to antideportation organizing with the settling stories within the immigrant rights movement about respectable immigrants who deserve to build a life in the United States. The new movement-building scripts generated by FFF members are transformative because their resistance to mass deportation is a rejection of mass incarceration. By examining these new scripts, I develop a methodology to detect settler power and resistance to it, *even in the absence of* FFF's direct engagement with Indigenous politics or a political framework that names the settler state.

Over the twenty years of its existence, FFF has sustained its commitment to end all forms of incarceration. It recognizes that the fundamentally anti-Black practices of policing and imprisonment structure immigrant detention and deportation. Racism, heteropatriarchy, impoverishment, and anti-immigrant backlash pave the way to prison and deportation. Its most recent campaign, "Free Them All / Defund Hate," conjoins the abolitionist call to end incarceration with the demand that the funding being poured into detention centers be shifted to serving the thousands of asylum seekers who have been bused to New York City by the anti-immigrant governors of Texas and Florida since the summer of 2022.[5] FFF has provided support services to these asylum seekers to contend with the city's inadequate response.

To call public attention to the "Free Them All" campaign, FFF has returned to in-person rallies, suspended at the height of the COVID-19 pandemic, such as the one it staged in March 2023 in front of 26 Federal Plaza, which houses the Department of Homeland Security.[6] A huge colorful sign with cutout letters strung across the base of a statue at the plaza read "FREE THEM ALL!" It amplified the message carved on a cardboard sign, "ABOLISH ICE." That day, FFF members and their supporters gathered to publicize the stories of three immigrant Jamaican Black men, Wayne Gardine, George Marks, and Garfield Green, each with over thirty years of residence in the United States and detained for deportation. All of them are fathers whose children have been profoundly affected. They all have old criminal convictions, one wrongful (in the case of Gardine), for which all three have served long prison terms.[7] All three men are organizing inside the detention centers and with those outside, including their family members, to be freed. Looking through the photos of the 2023 rally reminded me of a vigil I attended at the exact location in 2009 to stop the deportation of Roxroy Salmon and our chants about how he took care of his children and elderly mother.[8] I marveled at FFF's unwavering and open support for immigrants with criminal convictions, for their families, and for decarceration.

This transformative anticarceral work requires an internal process of raising consciousness and the outward-facing work of shifting dominant discourses in the immigrant rights movement as well as shoring up public support for people with criminal convictions. Internally, those directly impacted by deportation unlearn the dominant settler scripts that privilege innocent and, therefore, deserving immigrants. They build a culture in which people with criminal convictions are not shunned. As a result,

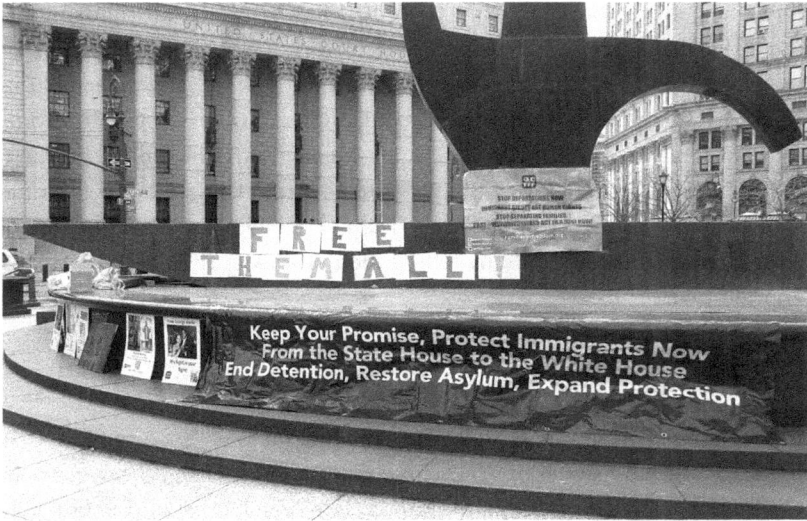

3.1. Banners and signs at the Families for Freedom "Defund Hate / Free Them All" rally at 26 Federal Plaza in March 2023. FFF organizers gathered to demand that Wayne Gardine, George Marks, and Garfield Green, each with over thirty years of residence in the United States and detained for deportation, be freed. Courtesy of Families for Freedom.

they start to imagine a future outside of carceral logics. Concomitantly, this unlearning of dominant scripts and bearing witness to each other's stories prepare the organizers to publicly take on the production of criminal aliens to demand their freedom from deportation and an end to carcerality. Their organizing shifts the discourse toward prison abolition in the broader immigrant rights movement.

Uniformly, deportable and deported men narrate their permanent separation from their children, elders, and other loved ones as a critical dimension of state-inflicted injustice. I characterize the stories FFF members tell as *testimonios* after the tradition of impactful protest politics in Latin America, where those directly affected by state violence frame and narrate their experience with it. The FFF *testimonios* subvert the conventional white heteronormative and settler scripts of domesticity and productivity by emphasizing men's care work in their families. The organization's attention to kinship, intimacy, and men's caregiving in their families initially puzzled me since antideportation organizing typically foregrounded familial care to stop the deportation of mothers. Like the valuation of care by Tod@s queer and feminist activists, FFF's attention to care work is radical;

it challenges the dominant expectation rife in the immigrant rights movement that female-bodied women do such work. Over time, I learned that FFF's focus on men provides an entry point into the racial-gender politics of settler carceral power. Criminal convictions devalue criminalized immigrant families of color and render their kinship ties illegible. This illegibility justifies settler power exercised to separate those labeled criminal aliens from their loved ones for life. The FFF members assert the value of their kinship and care work by telling their stories in their own voice and on their own terms.

Family Politics and Settler Carcerality

In its efforts to keep families together, the members of FFF learn to refuse the standard representations in mainstream immigrant rights advocacy of the innocent, hardworking, law-abiding, family-oriented, and assimilable immigrant, who struggles and is poised for success but for the limits of their immigration status under current law. While immigration scholars have amply critiqued these markers of the American Dream in the romanticized immigrant success story, I want to make a different point. These tropes mobilize a settler colonial imaginary that works through respectability politics. Deportability depends on migrants' transgression of heteronormative and capitalist expectations about conjugality, family, and work. As Evelyn Nakano Glenn reminds us, the political economy of the white settler state is organized around normative and nonnormative constructions of race and gender.[9] The rhetorical and political stances of FFF members depart from the settler colonial scripts in that they unapologetically assert the value of the kinship ties of "criminal aliens" and reject deportation as an appropriate punishment for those with prior or pending convictions.

The settling stories of the contemporary US immigrant rights movement emerge from a tendency Sunera Thobani explicates in her examination of North American settler governance. The nation-state offers correctives to immigrant grievances within logics that disappear Indigenous presence and sovereignty. Under those conditions, immigrants laying claims to the nation cannot question the foundational gendered and sexual violence that allows the nation-state to wield its sovereignty over its subjects.[10] By contrast, the centrality of the carceral state in FFF's organizing work enables it to offer alternatives to the dominant strand of immigrant politics that accepts and perpetuates settler carceral logics by remaining silent about "criminal aliens" and selecting to promote the stories of law-abiding families that conform to settler norms.

Activist valorization of families to contest deportation has led scholars to assume that the stories and images of family separation shore up heteronormativity to make calls for family unity palatable.[11] Instead of assuming that the deployment of families in the fight against deportation necessarily promotes conservative ideas about families, I follow the call of queer studies scholar Richard Rodríguez and Latino studies scholar Amalia Pallares to attend to the polyvalence of family politics.[12] I read the *testimonios* of FFF members for their disruptive use of families. This feminist line of inquiry has also led to an understanding of crimmigration as reproductive politics in the way Laura Briggs challenges us to name all regulation of families and households as reproductive politics, beyond childbirth, pregnancy, and reproductive health.[13] While immigration scholars recognize that public policy since the 1980s has cast immigrants as a demographic threat and have targeted their biological reproduction, I ask that we recognize the multiple ways in which deportation threatens the capacity of families to socially reproduce themselves through care work.[14] In the stories that FFF shares, men's participation in care work for kin is essential to the functioning of the family.

In the current enforcement environment, FFF's deployment of families helps us see that deportation policies unravel the links settler governance establishes among citizenship, citizenship-based rights, and normative heterosexuality enshrined in "the family." Criminality rationalizes, codifies, and normalizes the separation of loved ones. The FFF *testimonios* from mixed-status families amplify the diminished value of citizenship in this era of deportation. This diminishment of citizenship is similar to the Depression-era removal of US citizens of Mexican ancestry between 1929 and 1941.[15] When the citizenship of family members living in mixed-status families cannot protect their noncitizen kin from expulsion, then the US state sharpens its arbitrary right—plenary power—over the domestic space of the family as well as the bordered nationalized space that it illegitimately occupies.

Citizenship, the glue that holds together and legitimizes the nation-state, does not protect US citizen children, spouses, parents, and siblings from the dire effects of deportation. They lose their loved ones to prolonged detention. Their loved ones suffer from the lack of due process. Eventually, they are separated for life from their loved ones in the name of plenary power. Seemingly contradictory, the ineffectual citizenship of families affected by deportation in fact deepens settler (plenary) power through what

Aihwa Ong, in her discussion of the neoliberal state, calls graduated sovereignty.[16] Graduated sovereignty under the moral racial-gendered economy of neoliberalism fine-tunes differential rights and privileges. These are not clearly distributed along the citizen-alien divide. In this iteration, the status of the deportable "criminal alien" unmoors their citizen kin from civil and human rights.

About Families for Freedom

New Yorkers directly impacted by detention and deportation formed FFF in 2002 to organize against the post-9/11 domestic war on terror waged on the city's South Asian and Arab communities. Founders Aarti Shahani, Subhash Kateel, and Maria Muentes rallied around family members like Uncle Malik, a sixty-six-year-old ailing Bronx resident and Pakistani national who was placed into deportation proceedings when he complied with the George W. Bush administration's 2002–11 National Security Entry-Exit Registration System (NSEER).[17] Since then, FFF has grown into a dynamic multiethnic and multiracial organization.[18] The stepped-up enforcement of the 1996 laws, which expanded the grounds for deportation and eliminated judicial review (discussed in chapter 1), and the escalating political hyperbole around the threat of migrants with criminal convictions entrapped the city's Latinx, Caribbean, and other Black immigrants, who joined the organization. To contend with the crisis, FFF started to organize instead of relying on lawyers and advocates to represent their interests. Families for Freedom puts those directly impacted by the repressive immigration system at the center. It believes they are best positioned for collective action because they know that system from the inside.

Families for Freedom members live in working-class neighborhoods in Queens, Brooklyn, the Bronx, and northern Manhattan. While no recent data is available, a 2012 report cowritten by FFF and based on ICE data acquired through a Freedom of Information Act request established that ICE disproportionately targeted these neighborhoods, where immigrants of color encountered police because of NYPD's stop-and-frisk program. Between 2005 and 2010, most of those detained (91 percent) were deported. Of the legal permanent residents detained, 70 percent were deported. The Criminal Alien Program, which allows jails and prisons to transfer noncitizens to ICE, in conjunction with the stop-and-frisk program were the main driver of deportations. Even though only 9 percent of the cases during this period qualified for mandatory detention, by ICE's own admission, people were not released, leading to the overcrowding of local detention centers and resulting in 64 percent of detained New Yorkers being transferred out of state.[19] All of these patterns in enforcement and incarceration have endured.

The current executive director, Janay (Jani) Cauthen, directly impacted by the deportation of her ex-husband, Jean Montrevil, describes the organization's evolution over the last two decades this way: "The intersection between immigration enforcement and the criminal legal system is at the core of FFF's work. Most of our freedom campaigns consist of individuals who come in contact with ICE following a criminal conviction. FFF works to reform mechanisms of systemic oppression, most commonly mass incarceration, which has historically targeted Black men and resulted in broken families."[20] Its campaigns tackle the prison-to-deportation pipeline and confront the anti-Blackness that lubricates it. It is a leader in antideportation organizing with strong ties to local, state, and national organizations that recognize the criminal and corrections system as a driver of deportations.[21]

From the time it was founded, FFF has approached its work through the lens of racial justice. It has connected the deportation of migrants of color to the racially biased policing of Black and brown men and their overrepresentation in jails and prisons. It quickly recognized that many of its members were being targeted for mandatory detention and removal because of their criminal records. It folded the defense of "criminal aliens" into outreach, campaigns, and policy work. Former FFF executive director Abraham Paulos, a refugee from Sudan who moved to the United States when he was three, underlined the rarity of FFF among immigrant rights organizations in the city. It was the only organization that did not treat his criminal convictions as a problem when he called it after being released from Rikers Island.[22]

The organization understands that the prison industrial complex is designed to punish Black people and people of color. Historically, FFF worked with immigrants in prisons. Today, imprisoned citizens and noncitizens use its hotline. According to Jani, the calls have led the organization in a new direction. It has decided to support prisoners regardless of their citizenship status, such as Puerto Rican New York resident Michael Santiago, who is incarcerated in Pennsylvania, and it is building his case for clemency.[23] Its commitment to dismantling the racially unjust carceral system has drawn it to New York–based organizations like the Center for Community Alternatives, and the community-based Release Aging People in Prison

Campaign, seeking to reduce and eventually end imprisonment. Families for Freedom's "Free Them All" campaign, which gathered pace during the preventable deaths in prisons and detention centers during the COVID-19 pandemic, consolidates FFF's anticarceral abolitionist politics. It collaborates with the Queer Detainee Empowerment Project (QDEP), which supports LGBTQIA, Two-Spirited, and gender nonconforming migrants who have been released from detention, helping them access health care, education, and legal and emotional support and working to keep queer families together.

Based on their members' experiences, FFF campaigns to end the pipeline from street arrests, police stations, jails, and prisons to immigration detention centers. These grassroots efforts aim to build collective power to "lighten the burdensome load that families with members in the system are going through."[24] The organization teaches deportees and their loved ones how to navigate not only the maze of immigration courts and detention centers but also the criminal legal system. It conducts know-your-rights training and legal clinics for their members. Its handbook, *Deportation 101*, has become an invaluable resource for detainees and deportees, and serves as a model for deportee rights education. The right to equal protection under the law, the right to a detainee's day in court, and bond justice have been FFF's consistent demands despite the courts' and legal community's equivocation on the entitlement of noncitizens to these rights. To free a member from detention, FFF strategically floods ("zaps") detention centers, immigration courts, the New York City Council, and the district attorney's office with phone calls and emails to disrupt their routine work.

As FFF members campaign for their own release from detention and relief from deportation, they help countless others in detention centers or prisons access resources to build their own cases and speak up about the abuse incarcerated immigrants face. They have exposed the role of for-profit corporations like CoreCivic (formerly the Corrections Corporation of America) and the GEO Group. The organization has documented and protested the overcrowding of detention centers due to mandatory detention and the sudden removal of detainees from local detention centers in New York and New Jersey to those in faraway states, including Alabama's Etowah County Detention Center, which the Detention Watch Network listed among the top ten worst detention centers.[25] The dispersion means that FFF works with detainees spread out across the country so that they do not feel isolated and can continue to address the abuses they face. FFF's "ICE Out of NY / Release Not Transfer" campaign, in coalition with allied organizations like QDEP, continues to mount pressure on jails, prisons, and ICE to end the practice (see chapter 1). It organized to end the incarceration of families at Pennsylvania's Berks County Detention Center, which finally shut down in January 2023.

The organization educates the public about the scale and human cost of deportation through staging demonstrations and vigils at street corners in affected neighborhoods and at the ICE headquarters at 26 Federal Plaza in lower Manhattan. At the demonstrations, deportees and their loved ones read their *testimonios*. They publicize their stories through newspapers and radio shows. Many work with a network of progressive local churches. They were part of the now-dissolved local New Sanctuary Movement and sheltered those with deportation orders. Church leaders and congregants build a base of support to free people from detention and testify against deportation in immigration court. In some cases, FFF members' resistance has led to retaliatory deportation orders. Under the Trump administration, ICE targeted veteran FFF activists and the New Sanctuary Movement cofounders like Ravi Ragbir, a Trinidadian national, and Jean Montrevil, a Haitian national, in 2018. Both have publicly fought for their right to remain in the United States. I recount Jean's recent pathbreaking victory in immigration court below.[26]

To change city and state policies that facilitate the prison-detention nexus and to pressure local, state, and federal officials, the organization works in alliance with a wide range of groups that share its goals. One policy direction has been to end the cooperation of local police and corrections departments with ICE through information sharing and the use of detainers (see chapter 1). It continues to call for an end to ICE operations in the city and, more broadly, the state. Its current campaign, "Abolish ICE! NY-NJ," and "Defund Hate" evolved out of the older "ICE Out of Rikers" and "ICE-Free NYC" campaigns.[27]

Early on, FFF members realized that more was needed to protect noncitizens with priors. It identified postconviction relief as one area of policy change in the state's criminal legal system. FFF helps people with deportation orders file motions for postconviction relief (in cases of wrongful convictions in New York). It exposed the ICE practice of thwarting such motions by holding the deportees in custody and preventing their appearance in criminal court.[28] In 2020, FFF, acting in a broad coalition, changed New York state's misdemeanor law by reducing the one-year sentence for Class A misdemeanors by a day. This change protects those who would otherwise be at risk of deportation under federal immigration law because of a 365-day sentence.[29] It has introduced state-level legislation as part of a large coalition to increase the governor's utilization of clemency. An ally of FFF, the Clemency Coalition emphasizes an antiracist, pro-Black, queer-positive, and anticolonial framework to move from punishment toward restorative justice.[30] As I will explain, FFF is increasingly applying for clemency for deportees with priors.

The foundational work of FFF exposes the connection between deportation and criminality, and between criminality and migrants' race, gender, and nationality. It enables us to see how deportation cements settler carcerality. The organization's call to abolish ICE and reunite families puts forward a prison abolitionist vision that goes deeper than the critique of ICE for imprisoning unwitting victims of the deportation machine—asylum-seeking parents and children. Over the last two decades, FFF effectively used its literacy in the criminal-immigration pipeline to develop an expansive abolitionist agenda for change.

Testimonios and Affective Politics

Members of FFF use storytelling and bearing witness to each other's struggles as core tools of organizing, empowerment, and leadership. Many of these stories, from which I draw, were featured on FFF's older website.[31] The current campaigns tab on its revamped website and its social media posts circulate the stories of those detained and deported. The older website carried a mix of first-person testimonies from persons directly targeted for deportation and testimonies from impacted family members. The rest, including the recent ones, are third-person narratives by FFF organizers speaking or writing on behalf of an affected member. The majority of those who shared their stories faced detention and deportation for prior criminal convictions ranging from possession and sale of marijuana to attempted burglary, larceny, fraud, and violent crimes. Also, among those who turned to FFF for support were undocumented men or visa overstayers who were arrested, detained, and put into deportation proceedings during the NSEER program.

I characterize these accounts as *testimonios* because their telling incites social change.[32] They fit into the genre of life narratives that has popularized Latin American social movements and Indigenous voices. In Latin America, women, often asserting their identities as family members who have lost a loved one to state-sponsored violence or inaction, use *testimonios* to demand accountability from the state. Shannon Speed and Maylei

Blackwell have argued that *testimonios* are an important source of self- and political expression for Indigenous and Latinx women, despite social scientific suspicion about their reliability. At the same time, Blackwell warns against treating *testimonios* as unvarnished truth and a privileged vehicle for the oppressed. Instead, she asks that we learn to treat the life writing or oral histories of social movement actors as politically directed acts.[33]

Migrant *testimonios*, as sources for my work, help me read the organizers' analyses of power. Their thoroughly political and carefully crafted nature invites the listener to ask why the stories are narrated in a particular way and for whom. Although an individual tells the story, to function as a *testimonio* it must simultaneously represent a collective experience. By generating an affective space through which intensities circulate, FFF members build a common cause internally across difference; they then publicize the *testimonios* to confront the state with its violence, and they agitate the broader public to correct the injustices. Voicing the truth of one's experience carries the ethical force of *testimonios*. At the same time, the accounts are

3.2. Families for Freedom executive director Janay "Jani" Cauthen (*left*) speaks at the "Defund Hate / Free Them All" rally at 26 Federal Plaza in March 2023. FFF organizers Christiana Adebiyi (*middle*) and Sallimatou Diaby (*right*) hold the posters advocating to free George Marks and Wayne Gardine. Courtesy of Families for Freedom.

tightly scripted, rehearsed, and purposive tellings. They communicate an urgency that impels those who bear witness to act.

The stories of the FFF members and their loved ones are self-representations. They are not elicited by an interlocutor. They are not interviews or oral histories recorded by a researcher. They are told from detention centers, on release, and after deportation and gathered by the organization. Through these stories, we glimpse the havoc deportation causes in their intimate relations. Children, parents, spouses, and lovers speak of their suffering, confusion, and anger. Their ability to touch people's hearts depends on conventions of intimacy, a feminized realm. Dissolving the line between public and private, they create an "intimate public" in which it becomes possible for those who bear witness to validate "qualities, ways of being, and entire lives that have otherwise been deemed puny or discarded."[34] The tenderness of the *testimonios* analyzed here allows me to trace the gender and sexual politics of deportation.

Daddies and the Crisis in Caregiving

Families for Freedom pays conscious attention to men and their care work in their families. The organization publicizes the disruption to social reproduction of families when fathers face mandatory deportation. Making noncitizen fathers of color marked as felons publicly visible as caretakers rather than breadwinners rewrites the state's racial-gendered law-and-order project and redefines masculinity. Immigration and law enforcement tighten the connection between working-class men of color and criminality. Once deported, the men usually cannot reenter the US legally during their lifetimes. Their lifelong exile from their children, spouses, and elderly parents, often US citizens or legal permanent residents, must rely on the language of danger and lawlessness.

Deportation, increasingly defined as a national security issue, fortifies settler space by normalizing the violent separation of kin in the name of the rule of law. A strand of queer scholarship notes the institutional construction and disciplining of deviant family forms to produce a national culture, the ideal worker, and the ideal citizen.[35] The families are multiply marginalized and lie outside of state-approved conjugal arrangements, which are by default white, middle-class, and nuclear. The devaluation of migrant family ties and family separation shores up settler power. I argue that FFF's mobilization of affect in defense of criminalized men in their roles as caregivers turns our attention to the state's construction of aberrant families. Such constructions justify its encroachment into the private sphere and the separation of these men from their loved ones. The FFF narratives about family separation and reunification thus diverge from the heteronormative settler ones in the mainstream immigrant rights movement. As queer theorist Jasbir Puar observes, these state practices of family separation unmoor heterosexuality from nuclear, spatially intact heteronormative arrangements.[36]

The organization's campaigns foreground the intimate lives of migrants to usher in daddies, mommies, and kids as political actors. Documentation of FFF's countless rallies shows children holding photographs of deported fathers and magic marker signs with the appeal "Don't Deport Our Daddies." The *testimonios* circulated by FFF are overwhelmingly about or from men. The predominance of men among FFF's constituency mirrors the targeting of men by law enforcement and mimics the prison population, as Manisha explained it to me.[37] Nationally, according to the data available, men constitute the majority of those arrested (90 percent each year between 2013 and 2017), detained (79 percent in 2015), and deported (94 percent in 2012 and 93 percent in 2013) for immigration violations. It is important to note that the number of women detained and deported has risen.[38]

Before learning about FFF's work, I was very familiar with the iconography of mothers, signified as primary caregivers, in antideportation organizing. Media reports had made visible activist mothers like Elvira Arellano, who sought sanctuary in August 2006 in a Chicago church and was frequently photographed with her son Saul in front of posters that said, "Don't Deport My Mommy." Amalia Pallares credits Arellano with introducing family separation to the immigrant rights movement by politically harnessing her motherhood. Even though, as time went on, Arellano's activism challenged conventional notions of the family, making her a controversial figure even within the movement, activists continue to effectively link mothering and family integrity to attract public sympathy and highlight the inhumanity of deportation.[39] The recent public outrage over border enforcement shows that separation of parents, especially mothers from their children, was a public relations disaster even for the openly nativist Trump administration and its "zero tolerance" policy. Ideologies about motherhood and children continue to make their incarceration unpopular and provide a pressure point for antideportation activists. This chapter provides a counterpoint to the trope of motherhood by looking at the mobilization of "good fathering" in the migrant justice movement in context of deportation.[40]

Compared to women targeted for deportation, men with criminal convictions present organizations like FFF with a difficult public relations task. When deportees cannot profess their innocence and respectability, which are markers of "good" parenting, to gather support, how can they become politically effective? Prisoner advocates are all too familiar with the challenge of presenting felons as subjects of rights because of the widespread belief that those who break the law have no entitlements. Successful testimonies promoting prisoners' rights have to confound the clear-cut boundaries between perpetrator and victim, guilt and innocence.[41]

Reflecting the realities of FFF's membership, the organization adopts narrative strategies that place the men and their contributions in the private sphere. The stories become organizing tools that contest the stereotypical casting of men who have criminal convictions as uncaring and irresponsible. This political position makes it difficult to argue that FFF's focus on families provides recourse to respectability, a critique rightly leveled at those organizing efforts that valorize the normative family in the hopes of representing its members as responsible future citizens. In the United States, mothering or fathering does not rescue those with criminal records from their dominant representation as bad or failed parents. FFF cannot access the settler scripts about immigrant respectability. However, they can access their audience's feelings to stir a sense of injustice about the immigrants' treatment by police and immigration authorities. Those telling their stories create an "account of the social world as an affective space where people ought to be legitimated because they have feelings and because there is an intelligence in what they feel that knows something about the world, that if listened to could make things better."[42]

The FFF members' decision to share the intimate details of their lives points to their determination to expose the state's racialized and gendered violence and its invasion of the private, domestic sphere. This intrusiveness illustrates a basic insight of feminists of color—the private sphere cannot shield low-income people of color because their kinship systems and sexuality are suspect and open to intense public policing. In one of the paired *testimonios*, Kathy McArdle and her son Joshua tell how eight federal agents banged on their door early one morning in 2004 to arrest Joshua's father, Calvin James, for an old conviction. In a testimony to the UN Special Rapporteur on the Human Rights of Migrants in 2007, Joshua, who is now an adult and a father, paints a vivid picture of the violation of his home and the traumatic process of learning what happened to his father:

My name is Joshua. I am 9 years old. My Father was here since he was 12 years old. His mother and sisters and most of his family are still here. The INS took my dad away from me when I was in kindergarten. . . . They came to my house early in the morning and took him while I was sleeping. . . . For many nights after they took my dad, I asked my mom when he was coming back. Then I got it. He was deported to Jamaica almost 3 years ago. I miss my dad very much, but the people who took him just don't care. . . . They are leaving families heartbroken. I want them to stop the deportation laws. They should bring my daddy back. And I wish other kids could have their daddies back too. . . . That's why people everywhere should care about families like ours.[43]

FFF includes children directly in its organizing work, giving them a space to speak about the harm caused by deportation.[44] While the presence and voices of children emphasize their unjustified suffering, the children's political effectiveness also lies in acknowledging that they cannot lead innocent and protected lives because of state violence. They are encouraged by FFF to confront the public with their trauma and demand accountability. The moral reckoning staged by Joshua's story utilizes the conventions of sentimentality but by no means affirms conventional ideas about families or childhood.

In the adult narratives, one finds compelling accounts of how the deported men helped with the everyday tasks of caring for their children and how they desired to be good fathers. Writing in the first person, Barbara Georgiana, a US citizen, described the expedited removal of her husband, Howard, to Jamaica for an outstanding deportation order: "Life has turned upside down since our husbands were taken away. . . . They used to help with everything: pick up the kids from school; take them to the library, the park, McDonald's." In a transcribed telephone conversation with Howard from Jamaica, which was carried on the old webpage with Barbara Georgiana's story, Howard expressed the emotional turmoil of being separated from his wife and three small children: "Even though I'm not locked up, it feels like prison. . . . I don't want my kids to grow up without a father." Without any hope of reuniting with his children soon, Howard articulates how deportation has interfered with his ability to be a good father. Back in New York, Barbara Georgiana decided to send one of her children away to live with Howard to cope with the increased pressures she faced at work and home. The disruption in social reproduction led to what one study calls the "effective deportation" of left-behind family members, including those who are US citizens.[45]

The desire to be a good father imbued Joe's testimony. Addressing a congregation at St. Paul of the Apostle Church in 2007, Joe, an asylum seeker from China who had lived in Brooklyn for ten years, talked about his and his wife's fears of being separated from their young US-born children. Joe and Mei had been pulled over while driving to Vermont and had spent four months in detention. In this statement seeking sanctuary for his family, Joe said:

> I am here representing thousands of families with a similar situation. . . . As parents facing deportation, we feel helpless to protect our own children. . . . We love our children's smiles. We want to see them grow. We want to be in their daily life. . . . I have been working in a restaurant for 10 years. . . . Today I am 28. I am a young father. I want to be a good father. . . . My daughter here—she is the oldest child. She is 2 now. I take her to the playground, even if I am tired. . . . She deserves the best.[46]

Joe expresses his desire to be involved in his children's life despite his taxing work schedule. His reference to the ordinary pleasure he takes in his children's smiles opens a powerful affective space. Similarly, when testifying with her son Joshua to the UN Special Rapporteur, Kathy, who continues to sit on FFF's board, shared an ordinary but tender domestic moment while recounting the horrors of Calvin's arrest and its aftermath. She recalled, "Their greatest joy was probably the tickle fights they used to have, and just quiet moments together that can never be duplicated by phone calls." In a more elaborate feature in the magazine *Colorlines*, an older Joshua is quoted as remembering his father's cooking: "I miss his cooking. I really liked his rice that he used to make. It had coconut milk in it."[47] Memories of touch, smell, taste, and sight bring to life a daily presence that deportation ends. These details lend the narratives their emotional texture and give substance to the men's identities as good fathers and caregivers.

Enforcement, then, targets migrants' ability to care for their family members and households as well as their livelihoods, their biological reproduction, and their activism. Once the men are detained and deported, women become solely responsible for care work, and the crisis in social reproduction deepens as they juggle paid work with childcare and eldercare. The *testimonios* from the members of FFF challenge us to apply to their families the feminist insights about kinship arrangements in communities of color where men's place in their families cannot be read straightforwardly through the hegemonic scripts about masculinity contingent on breadwinning. As the FFF organizers repeatedly point out, the working-

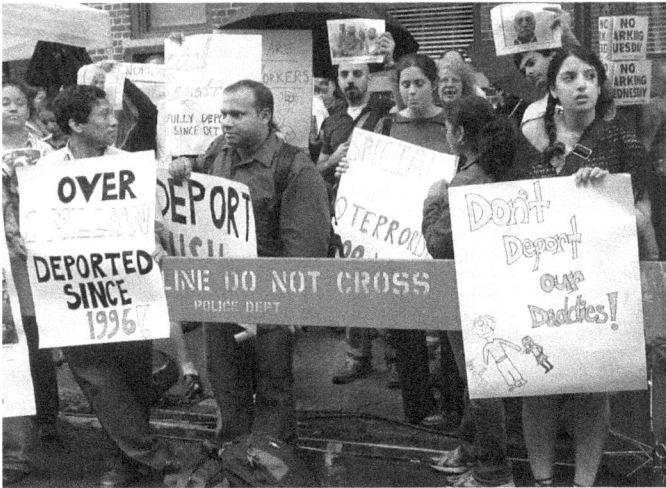

3.3. A Families for Freedom antideportation rally in downtown Manhattan in the early 2000s. Courtesy of Families for Freedom.

class realities of the members make men's caregiving and household tasks essential for their family's survival. In an interview, former FFF executive director Janis Rosheuvel reminded me that FFF members' daily struggles in the "private" sphere recounted in the *testimonios* arise from policing of their racially and class-segregated neighborhoods.[48] "Before the criminal justice system made their lives into a calamity," she pointed out, "they are, oftentimes, on the margins." The current executive director, Jani, makes the same point about the importance of fathering for otherwise socially marginalized men in relating the story of her ex-husband, Jean, and their nontraditional family.

The long-drawn-out and eventually successful struggle to reunite Jean Montrevil with his family underlines the power of movement building *and* the enormous emotional toll of state-sponsored violence. Throughout the campaign to reverse his deportation order, Jean insisted that reuniting families was at the heart of the movement and that he was fighting to be with his children.[49] I first came across Jean and Jani's story in 2009 on FFF's old website. I learned that Jean, who had moved with his family from Haiti as a teenager and was a permanent resident, had a deportation order for old criminal convictions. Jean had served eleven years of a thirty-three-year sentence for a non-violent drug offense. Testifying on his behalf at the same gathering for sanctuary at which Joe spoke, Jani, who identified herself as a Black woman born and raised in Brooklyn, talked passionately about Jean's fathering. He was "a good dad" to their young son, a loving stepdad to her daughter, and a supportive husband who cared for the children while she went to college. "My husband got a conviction when he was a teenager, back in 1989. He did his time. But here we are in 2007, trying to stay together. Deportation is hanging over us anyway" because immigration refused to look at Jean for who he was.[50] Jean and Jani have been committed antideportation organizers since. Even though their marriage did not survive the threat of deportation, Jani, Jean, FFF, and their allies organized tirelessly to keep Jean with his four children.

When I talked to Jani in 2023 after Jean's deportation order was permanently canceled, she reflected on the years of struggle, and the harm to their family. Jean was released under parole around 1996, just when mandatory deportation for those with criminal convictions became law. Postincarceration, he built a life with Jani, and he parented their children Jahsiah, Janiah, and Jamya. However, the fear of impending deportation strained their relationship. In 2005, Jean was identified by ICE for deportation during an immigration sweep when he went to report to his parole officer. Jani holds immigration policies responsible for destroying her marriage. Tying Jean's encounters with the criminal legal and immigration enforcement systems to his race and gender (a Black man and a Haitian immigrant who had felonies), she pointed out that these punitive measures repeatedly "rebrand" immigrants, driving home the message "You're no good; you're bad." She recalled the dehumanization they felt as a family when Jean, who was wearing an ICE-mandated ankle bracelet, was pulled aside at an airport security check on their way to a vacation at Disney World.

Despite these methods of surveillance and intimidation, Jean continued to speak out, becoming a veteran organizer in New York's New Sanctuary Coalition. He continued to be involved in the lives of his children. In 2018, during the Trump administration, Jean, already targeted for his activism, was arrested by ICE agents in his home and deported to Haiti. Jani said this came right when their son entered the best public high school in Brooklyn. She remembered the glow on Jean's face as he watched their son walk into his school on that first day. Jani directly experienced the havoc of deportation that she had witnessed as a FFF organizer. Growing up with a single mother in an immigrant family, she had not fully anticipated Jahsiah's distress. She talked frankly about the emotional difficulties Jahsiah faced and the impact of his father's forced removal on his academic performance. They constantly worried about Jean's safety in Haiti. At that point, Jani decided, "No one messes with my babies," referring to the enforcement apparatus responsible for separating her children from their dad. She used her skills as an organizer to bring Jean home to his family.[51]

The campaign to bring Jean home is a strategically brilliant and uplifting example of tackling the criminal legal and immigration system together. It successfully secured a pardon for Jean's three-decades-old convictions from Virginia's governor, Ralph Northam, in August 2021. To contest his deportation, Jean and his legal team filed a case against ICE for targeting him for his activism in the migrant justice movement. As a result, Jean was initially granted a ninety-day parole under which he returned to his family in New York. In the settlement with ICE, Jean was granted a three-year relief from deportation, and by January 2022, Jean's permanent residency was restored. With the pardon for the crimes and his status as a permanent resident, the next step was to reopen his immigration case; in April 2023, the judge ruled for permanent relief from deportation. The cancellation of Jean's deportation order resulted from the steadfast collective persistence on the part of FFF, Judson Memorial Church, New York University's immigrant rights clinic legal team, and numerous supporters who put pressure on ICE and elected officials.

Behind this legal story lay the power of *testimonio*. Jani shared with me the impact of her son's testimony in immigration court during the 2023 hearing. That day Jean's supporters packed two rooms. For the first time, Jani heard her son speak about the depth and extent of the effect of his father's deportation. Hearing her son express this pain broke Jani's heart. During his testimony, Jahsiah told the judge that his father did not have the freedom to go to high school because he was already behind bars at that age. Despite this history, he had raised a son and instilled important values in him. Jahsiah's testimony created an affective zone for all those present. Even the judge, Jani said, was moved to tears and declared Jean was a good man. Jani recalled exclaiming aloud in court, "Finally!" Though the immigration judge operated within a moral economy, which dictates that immigrants establish their "good character" in all considerations of relief, Jahsiah interrupted the narrative about irredeemable "criminal aliens," the moral basis for their mandatory and permanent banishment. His testimony allowed everyone present to absorb what is inhuman about our current immigration enforcement. It exposed the daily, insidious, and enduring ways in which state actions invade family life, long after the ICE agents have arrested and removed the parent. The power of such narratives to paint the emotional life of those affected by deportation carried the day leading to a historic victory in the migrant justice movement.

The expulsion of fathers like Calvin, Howard, and Jean, despite their publicly declared roles as caregivers, puts national belonging and non-belonging into play. Intertwined with fears attached to Black and brown immigrant masculinities, the questions of belonging revolve around who can settle and who cannot, whose family form is recognized and whose is not, who deserves a family and who does not. The US citizenship or legal permanent residency of a spouse or child affected by deportation fails to deliver its promise of belonging and should serve as a lesson for the main-stream immigrant rights movement, which vociferously advocates a path-way to citizenship. What does citizenship do for the US citizen children of Calvin, Howard, or Jean and the many others whose stories FFF has documented over the years?

Criminality rationalizes the forced separation of citizens and legal residents from family members. Given the introduction of the right to family unification (as narrowly as "family" was defined) into the 1965 Immigration and Nationality Act and the defense of this immigration preference since, the legal grounds to exile deportees from their nuclear family rely on the stringent sanctions against noncitizens with criminal records or immigration violations.[52] Though these family reunification preferences in immigration law helped many FFF members to sponsor their immediate family members for legal residency, once their noncitizen loved one became entangled in the criminal legal system, the sponsor's or the citizen child's status was not enough to keep their families together. This bears out the long history that shows that neither the state nor the economy valued or respected family integrity of racially and sexually minoritized, Indigenous, poor, and disabled people. By demanding accountability for how their lives have been ripped apart, FFF members enact the political and affective mandate of *testimonios* by mobilizing to end incarceration and deportation.

Movement-Building Stories

Testimonios serve as calls to conscience. They hail a public. They move people who are not directly affected to act in alliance.[53] Importantly, they create community among those who come forward to tell their stories. In the years that I have engaged with the political charge of *testimonios*, I have realized they have a crucial function of building community internally among those directly but differentially impacted. Members start to unlearn and address the internal relations of power—the separations among them created by the dominant white nationalist and gendered discourses of il-legality and criminality.

The FFF organizers produce a new political repertoire, offering alterna-tives to the settler scripts used widely in the mainstream immigrant rights movement. The process of sharing, listening, and rescripting personal stories in FFF's organizing space overcomes the toxic divide between de-serving and undeserving migrants. In a groundbreaking version of the call "All of Us or None," FFF creates a sense of common cause and courage. Janis crystallized this orientation when she said, "Our *family* is valuable; our family deserves justice . . . like any other family," asserting the worth of criminalized members.[54] In this section, I focus on the internal storytelling work of transformative movement building.

Settler carceral politics discipline migrants of color to invest in white su-premacist, settler, and heteropatriarchal ideologies about who deserves to reside in the United States. Such politics inflict incarceration and deporta-tion on those deemed undeserving on the grounds that they break laws and separate them from their community and loved ones. Social fragmentation and geographic separation facilitate the expropriation of land, labor, and life under racial capitalism and settler colonialism.[55] The mainstream im-migrant rights movement participates in these structures when advocates strategically select the stories of the ideal subjects of immigration reform. These stories promise compliance with settler arrangements. They remain silent about people with criminal records. Immigrant rights leaders, in their eagerness to end deportation through a legalization plan for undocu-mented people (who can pass criminal background checks), consent to US settler colonialism by supporting proposed legislation that strengthens the punitive links between crime and immigration, beef up interior and border militarization, and bring back guest worker programs for low-wage jobs.

Abolitionist antideportation politics cannot rely on the settler scripts. Criminal aliens are already considered to be "failed" fathers, mothers, chil-dren, siblings, lovers, and breadwinners. The FFF members learn to recognize that they have become targets of state violence *precisely because of* their race-based criminalization and their transgression of prescribed gender and sexual arrangements.

This critical understanding of families outside of the heteronormative imperative of respectability politics is not immediately apparent to those on the outside. The organization's name can give the impression of con-servatism, as it did for Abraham, who organized with FFF and served as its executive director. He recalled his reservations when a friend asked him to approach FFF. He confessed, "But this name, man. It seems like a very right-wing name." He eventually called FFF when no other organization was willing to help him because of his prior convictions. He says, "I still remember when I called Families for Freedom. It was a really therapeutic conversation. The person that picked up the phone told me 'Look, you know, I haven't exactly gone through, what you're going through, but my father went through that, and I think the system is unjust. . . . Here, at Families everyone is either at risk of deportation, or has a loved one in such a situation.'"[56] When I asked Janis, who preceded Abraham as executive director, about why the organization coalesces around families, she pointed out that "people directly affected by the issues fight at a whole other level— that's why it's crucial for families to be at the center of organizing."[57] In FFF, deportees and their loved ones become the base and start to control their own narratives. They radically depart from official state-controlled narratives as well as those told by immigrant rights advocates.

Yet, FFF's political analysis does not stop at the assumption that families' firsthand experiences with detention and deportation make them a "natural" and readymade constituency. The political work in FFF starts with inviting members to discuss their circumstances across divides of nationality, immigration status, convictions, and family arrangements. Since each member's experience with ICE agents, detention centers, criminal and immigration courts, and consulates is singular, it can be fragmenting rather than unifying. Before the testifiers can tell their stories publicly, they learn how to tell the stories to each other and listen to the consequential differences in the paths that led to their deportation order.

As organizing tools, *testimonios* construct a political collectivity, purpose, and vocabulary. The members learn to build a political platform that pulls together the skeins of their individual experiences to thematize criminalization and deportation as aspects of state violence. Writing about the Los Angeles organization Mothers Reclaiming Our Children (ROC), which challenged the escalating incarceration of Black working-class youth in the 1990s, geographer and American studies scholar Ruth Gilmore argues that the identity the Black working-class women shared as mothers who had lost their children to prisons was enormously powerful but not sufficient to define their political task.[58] To directly confront laws, police, the courts, and the carceral system, the mothers in ROC had to build a systemic critique that could articulate the coming together of race and criminality. Similarly, FFF could not stop at an appeal to the normativity and universality of families or rest its argument, as organizations like Chicago's La Familia Latina Unida did, on the state's violation of its professed commitment to family values.[59]

The organization's internal process has required developing a political vocabulary that rejects the settler carceral distinction between violent and nonviolent crimes and criminal and noncriminal deportees. The racialized and gendered distinctions among the levels of criminal acts and convictions have a long history. Immigration scholar Mae Ngai has shown how these moral determinations have informed deportation policies.[60] A colorblind conviction that those committing crimes must pay dearly for them is deeply rooted in US culture. Laying out the divisions within FFF and outside it in the movement, Manisha explained that many advocates buy into the reasoning that migrants with criminal convictions deserve to be deported. She said:

> I hear it all over—we want to keep the hardworking undocumented family-oriented immigrants in this country. But those criminals should be deported. *And there is no real analysis of what it means to be a criminal for immigration purposes.* . . . When people are so divided in terms of who is deserving and who is undeserving, it becomes really important that people are politicized.[61]

In this critique of the immigrant rights movement's acceptance of federal- and state-government-dictated terms of who is a felon, FFF rejects outright the appeal to family as an alibi for respectability. By extension, it rejects settler standards.

How does this process of politicization work? FFF engages its members in continual conversations about the tendency of, say, an asylum seeker with no criminal conviction to distance himself from a legal permanent resident with one and of both immigrants to deny any commonality with an undocumented migrant. In turn, FFF also hears undocumented migrants with no criminal convictions privileging their claims over criminally convicted legal permanent residents. Over time, undocumented migrants become aware of the struggles of LPRs with criminal records and of their US citizen family members whose legality cannot protect their loved one from deportation. All the groups start to see legalization for the mirage that it is and move away from that illusory settler promise.

Deportees and their families often feel condemned to shame, silence, and isolation in addition to wrestling with the moral discourse about the deserving subject of relief and immigration reform. It takes time for a deportee to piece together a story and prepare themself for the media spotlight and scrutiny that comes with going public. The process is painstaking and painful. The high visibility of Jean's story and others has resulted from years of media training and storytelling as leaders in the city's antideportation movement. The circulation of stories such as Jean's by corporate and alternative media shows that the public pressure built through collective power can stand up to what historian Rachel Buff terms "the deportation terror."[62]

The preparation, the rehearsals, the narrative choices, and the strategic use of print, broadcast, and digital media are part of the authenticity and power of *testimonios*. Though consciously crafted and selective, the FFF *testimonios* have space for the complexities of crimmigration as it plays out in the deportees' lives. The stories are at once raw and polished, politically geared and truthful. They are more capacious than the brief autobiographical testimonies used by DREAMers as messaging, which have become a widely used strategy in the immigrant rights movement to shift public opinion toward proimmigration legislation.[63]

When made public, the *testimonios*, a product of internal political education, function "to transform the immigrant rights movement and how it views the people who are most marginalized from it—people with criminal convictions—and then also the wider society," in Janis's words. Reflecting on a thread that runs through various FFF programs, she said:

> Part of what we do is unpacking the criminal justice system for people. Why is it unjust that 90 percent of stop-and-frisk in NYC are brown and Black men? We debunk a lot of myths about why people are locked up in the first place, why they have contact with the criminal justice system, which can lead to deportation proceedings. . . . We spread the word about the dangerous intersection of criminal justice and immigration.[64]

Discussions about the racialized and gendered processes through which migrants encounter local law enforcement help deportees find common ground across immigration status to make their case to the public. This helps shift the public's attention to the coordination among the carceral arms of the state.[65] In all its coalitional efforts to change public policy advocacy, it works to arrive at an anticarceral position, which refuses to create legal loopholes for the more "deserving" migrants, such as low-level offenders. In the last decade, FFF and its allies have shifted the national discourse on migration justice toward abolition. A far cry from the comprehensive immigration reform (CIR) platform, a 2023 bill reintroduced in Congress proposes an end to racial profiling, the retroactive punishment of migrants with criminal records, and the criminal prosecution of people who are crossing borders.[66]

The *testimonios* build a movement by drawing together people who bear the brunt of the prison-to-deportation pipeline as much as they appeal to those who do not share those experiences but can become staunch allies. The movement-building work of life writing and storytelling on the part of deportees and their loved ones can get lost if we start to wonder why these heartbreaking stories have not ended mass deportation. For whom are these stories told and how many more are necessary to turn the tide? I have learned that deportees and their loved ones tell their stories for each other. They comfort and console. They turn their frustration, rage, fear, confusion, and hopelessness into action. In putting the stories into public circulation, every FFF member hopes that someone going through some version of the deportation nightmare will find them helpful. This is the alchemic nature of *testimonios*. For those in detention, the information blackout locks up detainee voices. Releasing their stories becomes a political act.[67] Thus, Speed writes about visiting the Hutto and Karnes county immigration detention centers in Texas to smuggle the stories of Indigenous women out of these spaces of detention in order to release them into the world.[68] While FFF has had significant victories, it does not always succeed. Nevertheless, it frees deportees and their loved ones to directly tell their stories to fight for change.

Conclusion

In this chapter, I have used FFF's movement-building *testimonios* to qualitatively explain the Enforcement and Removal Operations (ERO) data ICE publishes about its steady success at expelling "criminal aliens." In its self-congratulatory report of its removal operations in fiscal year 2020, ICE noted, "The vast majority of ICE ERO's interior removals—92 percent—had criminal convictions or pending criminal charges."[69] This trend helps us understand the significance of FFF's work and the limits of CIR built on legalization without any curbs on crimmigration. The CIR advocates' continued reliance on a normative framework promotes the values of nuclear, law-abiding, self-sufficient immigrant families. Its disavowal of "criminal aliens" deepens the settler logics of immigration and deportation policies.

Deportation coproduces a settler space. Through mandatory detention and deportation, the United States asserts territorial control. Race, gender, class, sexuality, and nationality intertwine in the production of the criminal alien. Criminality lubricates the pipeline from the prisons to the planes, which carry shackled deportees out of the United States. The state manages immigration, national security, and cultural integrity through the punitive regulation of migrant families by mandating indefinite separation. Deportation continues to institutionalize US countersovereignty in the form of plenary power over territory and migrant and mixed-status households.

The FFF's defense of "criminal aliens," I argue, inoculates its political work against settler discourses that legitimize territorial and carceral power. This chapter aims to model an analysis that apprehends activist strategies and discourses resistant to settler colonialism, even when the organizing focuses solely on migrants. My approach is prompted by critical Indigenous studies, which spells out the obvious and insidious workings of settler colonialism and calls on all of us who live on Indigenous lands to challenge these mechanisms. As migration studies scholars and activists, we need to name and amplify all refusals on the part of migrants to participate in settler colonialism. Such critical consciousness has enormous potential to link migrant justice to Indigenous projects of decolonization and decolonize migration studies.

In the next chapter, I continue to develop this approach by examining the nested nature of imperialism, carcerality, settler colonialism in Long Beach, California. I turn to youth organizers of Khmer Girls in Action. Like other Southeast Asian refugee communities resettled in the 1980s across the United States in impoverished neighborhoods, Cambodians in Long Beach found their loved ones locked up and retroactively processed for deportation. Cambodian deportees' status as refugees with legal permanent residency introduces issues distinct from FFF members, who were also labeled criminal aliens. The KGA youth leaders learn to situate their analysis and activism in the legacies of the US war in southeast Asia, the lack of meaningful government support to their community's resettlement in the United States, and the relentless war on crime in their neighborhoods. These reckonings bring to the surface the distinct histories of genocidal violence directed at Cambodians and Gabrielino/Tongva people and land in Long Beach.

4

"DEPORTATION = GENOCIDE"

It was the holiday season in Southern California. I was headed toward a December 9, 2017, forum, "Not Home for the Holidays," at the Martin Luther King Jr. Park Community Center in Long Beach. The forum had been organized by Khmer Girls in Action (KGA) in partnership with other Cambodian-led organizations with deep roots in Long Beach.[1] Colorful signs painted by KGA teenagers decorated the auditorium walls. "'Tis the Season for Justice," reminded one poster; another unapologetically stated, "Daughter of Refugees / Not Your Model Minority / #freeourdreams." On the stage were large cutouts of two split halves of a heart with the message "Deportation Breaks Our Hearts / #KeepFamiliesTogether / Not Apart." The forum was precipitated by the impending removal of over ninety Cambodian refugees who were among the one hundred arrested and detained by ICE in October 2017. They were being held in ICE detention centers across the United States during the holiday season.[2] I joined more than 150 community members at the event.

KGA's young women leaders shared the stage with elders in the community to talk not only about the tearing apart of their families as a result of deportation but also about the poor socioeconomic indicators in Long Beach's Cambodian community documented by a new needs-assessment report, which was released at the forum.[3] All the speakers testified to their struggles with unrelenting poverty, unemployment, the lack of adequate housing, their own or their family member's poor physical and mental health, the lack of safety due to heavy policing, and the lack of educational support. The range of issues covered at the forum reflected KGA's approach to organizing, which recognizes deportation as one symptom of their community's experience of fifty years of political and structural violence and trauma. The organization partnered with others to produce the needs-assessment report and has developed its own research agenda to counteract the absence of Census Bureau data about the Cambodian community. The political voice KGA cultivates speaks in the same breath about refugee, gender, racial, and economic justice, breaking out of the discursive mold of immigration reform talk.

A high school student in KGA's three-year leadership program, Jocelyn Kong, whom I had met during my fieldwork with KGA the previous year, shared the story of her aunt, who was among the seventy in detention. Her aunt had moved to Long Beach in 1992 and settled in a poor neighborhood. All her life, she struggled with intense poverty. When she became a teenage mother, she coped with her deteriorating mental health by using drugs. She was incarcerated several times for her drug use. And now, she was being detained by ICE for removal as a "criminal alien."

Jocelyn, who had taken on the responsibility of financially supporting her family at a very young age, tried to imagine her life without her aunt. Her aunt had encouraged her to stay in school and bought her food, shoes, and school supplies. Reflecting on the fear of deportation that hung over her family, Jocelyn said, "All you have is family, and we support each other. Without family, there is no history; without history, we have no identity." This passionate declaration encapsulated a core lesson KGA youth learn during their leadership training.

Interrogating Resettlement

In antideportation organizing, stories of women detainees and deportees are rare. Rarer still is the presence of a multi-issue Asian American feminist organization rooted in a refugee community that puts young women's leadership at the center. Building the leadership capacities of high school age Khmer girls and women to become vocal, visible, and recognized in their community as agents of social justice constitutes the core of KGA's work.[4] Long Beach boasts the largest concentration of Cambodians outside of Cambodia. To know their histories and themselves, KGA encourages its youth members to interrogate the category "refugees" and the very concept of the United States as a "refuge." KGA executive director Lian Cheun calls this "coming to consciousness about *why* they [KGA members and their families] are Cambodians in the United States."[5] KGA's decolonizing curriculum resonates with the emergent field of critical refugee studies and insists that "the refugee" is more than a descriptor and a legal classifica-

4.1. KGA youth organizers at the December 9, 2017, "Not Home for the Holidays" townhall in Long Beach. Photo credit: Joy Yanga. Courtesy of Khmer Girls in Action.

tion. "The refugee" is an affective category that puts into circulation warm and fuzzy stories of rescue, rehabilitation, and refugee indebtedness to the United States to cover up the buildup of structural and political violence that produces the refugee.[6] The political education at KGA helps youth organizers piece together the circumstances that turned their families into refugees.

KGA adults guide youth to excavate the impacts of the United States' war in Cambodia between 1965 and 1973, the rise of Democratic Kampuchea under the Khmer Rouge (1975–79) as a result of that war, and the shoddy efforts of the United States in the 1980s at resettling those who fled Cambodia's political and social turmoil.[7] The curriculum helps KGA youth members connect their histories of displacement from Southeast Asia to the permanent ejection of Khmer refugees turned criminal aliens from the United States. They start to examine why their communities settled in a metropolitan area with one of the highest poverty rates in the country.[8] The political analysis developed by Southeast Asian refugee rights activists provokes all of us in the migrant rights movement to connect immigration and refugee policies, US foreign policy in Southeast Asia, and US domestic policies governing refugee resettlement, welfare, and crime.[9] Incorporating the shared experience of refugees with deportation expands the agenda for migration justice beyond immigration reform.

One aspect of the effects of refugee poverty is law enforcement's profiling of Cambodian youth as crime- and gang-involved. The ascription of gang violence on Southeast Asian youth arises from a pathologizing connection between race, gender, age, and space. The violence is attributed to their youth, pathological masculinity and femininity, innate cultural difference, the overseas environment in refugee camps, and their current residence in impoverished neighborhoods of color.[10] Consequently, citizen and legal permanent resident Khmer youth become ready targets of what Victor Rios calls the "youth control complex"—local police and punishment regimes in schools that feed them into the school-to-prison pipeline.[11] Legal permanent resident Khmer refugees were the first among those in Southeast Asian communities to be deported starting in 2002.[12] That year, the US State Department brokered a secret repatriation agreement with the Cambodian government under Prime Minister Hun Sen, which has a poor human rights record.[13] Between 2002 and 2022, the number of Cambodians deported from the United States had reached eight hundred, with the pace picking up in 2017. An estimated two thousand are under removal orders.[14]

Once more, Khmer refugees are uprooted, this time from their supposed refuge. They are forcibly separated from their loved ones, first through imprisonment and then through detention and deportation. The removal of family members puts the economic survival of refugee communities and their ability to care for each other, including their elders and ancestors, in jeopardy, exacerbating intergenerational trauma and refugee poverty. The youth who go through KGA's leadership trainings call into question the production of the failed refugee in the figure of the deportable "criminal alien."

The KGA's equation, that genocide equals deportation, powerfully intervenes in national amnesia, both American and Cambodian.[15] The equation performs memory work; it conjoins space and time. Its political intent is to serve as a wake-up call. As the following sections demonstrate, the KGA's transnational political education counters the United States' benevolent and heteropaternalistic narrative of rescue and refuge through resettlement. Its leadership development curriculum on Southeast Asian history directly implicates the United States in carpet-bombing Cambodia as part of its brutal war in Vietnam, creating the conditions for the rise of the Khmer Rouge, and causing the genocide that followed.[16] The KGA youth members are then encouraged to link these causes of devastation and displacement to their community's experiences in Long Beach. They learn how their community became casualties of neoliberal austerities, its accompanying discourses of self-help, and the rapid expansion of the law-and-order state and immigration enforcement targeting felons and gangs. By framing deportation as a genocidal practice, KGA unambiguously shows that forced family separations that result from deportation exist on a continuum with the death and destruction that caused their family members to flee Cambodia. The last section of the chapter shows how KGA also contests the Hun Sen regime's ideologically fostered forgetfulness about the genocide under Khmer Rouge and exposes the US government's refusal to hold Cambodia responsible for continued human rights violations. These excavations become particularly relevant at a time when migrant rights activists are unmasking United States' purported humanitarianism by demanding asylum or refugee status for those that the United States has displaced across the Americas and in Syria and Afghanistan.

The frame of genocide, used with care and historical specificity by KGA, brings to the surface the genocidal structures of settler colonialism. In this chapter, I explore two lines of analysis important for my larger argument about deportation as a form of settler carceral power. The United States wields this type of power by resettling people displaced by its imperial ventures on Indigenous land, casts the resettlement as humanitarian, and then polices and criminalizes the refugees to uproot them yet again. First, I underline the rich implications of KGA's interrogation of US resettlement as a practice and an ideology for illuminating the United States' authority as a settler state. The United States can project itself as a refuge for Cambodian survivors of genocide by papering over its own genocide of Native peoples and their persistent struggles against it. In turn, the induced forgetting of the US war in Cambodia perpetuates the memory lapses about US policies governing Indigenous lands, peoples, and cultures. Second, I juxtapose KGA's memory work with the struggles of Gabrielino/Tongva, the traditional caretakers of the Los Angeles basin and the southern Channel Islands, to reclaim land and culture as they battle for federal recognition.[17] KGA, of course, discusses US genocide against Native peoples during its trainings. However, at present, its political work is not directly connected to the Tongva struggles in Long Beach.[18] My desire to examine the KGA's rhetorical deployment of genocide is not intended to suggest an isomorphism between similar-sounding struggles. By adopting critical refugee studies pioneer Yên Lê Espiritu's methodology of critical juxtaposition, which requires thinking across "seemingly disconnected events, communities, histories, and spaces,"[19] I explore the questions about settler power that arise from placing two struggles—Khmer and Tongva—side by side.

In Long Beach, the story of refugee resettlement bumps up against Gabrielino/Tongva struggles to reclaim land and culture as they battle for federal recognition. In this space, we can trace two nested movements of resilience against genocide: Khmer and Tongva. About three miles west of Cambodia Town lies the historic site of the Tongva village of Povuu'ngna, which stretches downhill from Rancho Los Alamitos to the California State University at Long Beach.[20] At this site, Tongva activists resist the degradation of their lands and the desecration of sacred sites as a result of commercial development. To minister these sites, they revive their cultural practices and relation to the land.

In sifting through these layers of struggles in Long Beach, I aim to arrive at an understanding of how the imperial-settler carceral state operates through processes of displacement, dispossession, and resettlement. To do this, I keep in mind Karen Leong and Myla Vincenti Carpio's insight that the carceral state works by subjecting diverse communities to removal, displacement, dispossession, and economic precarity.[21] What does it mean for the United States to exercise its power to settle or remove migrants conditionally and to withhold or award the right of residence in a space where Indigenous sovereignty operates? How does one write about migration by always considering the present tense of Indigenous politics and peoples? I do not pretend to answer these questions in full. I approach them to expand what we can think about as migration studies scholars.

About KGA

Leadership building of high-school-age youth—with young Khmer women in the forefront and, since 2011, Khmer boys and young men as allies—forms the backbone of KGA's work. They represent the 1.5 and second generations. Born out of a commitment to attend to the reproductive health and empowerment of Khmer girls in 1997, the organization frames the right to maintain refugee family integrity as a gender and reproductive justice issue. It demonstrates what a migrant rights vision and agenda can look like if gender and sexuality are central. KGA has created a youth leadership development pipeline to combat the school-to-deportation pipeline. The leadership-building folds KGA's antideportation work into campaigns to end economic, educational, and health disparities; racial profiling by the police; and incarceration. Given the status-adjustment demands of the immigrant rights movement, this broad slate of issues, including KGA's campaigns to improve school climate and student wellness, are not easily recognizable as immigrant rights activism.

The members of KGA are students from two Long Beach high schools— Polytechnic and Wilson. Members are introduced to KGA by their peers, KGA alumni who are family members, and high school faculty with whom KGA has built a strong relationship over many years. KGA staff visit the campus and support the members' extracurricular activities related to KGA campaigns. In recent years, KGA has welcomed Southeast Asian youth throughout the Long Beach Unified School District. The leadership development spans three years, during which the students move through a three-tier afterschool program. These three tiers run concurrently every week during the academic year between August and June.[22]

KGA works intensively with Khmer youth in each tier. Students enter the leadership pipeline through the Young Women's Empowerment Program (YWEP) and the Young Men's Empowerment Program (YMEP). The YWEP and YMEP students train separately for most of the year to safely explore gender and sexual diversity and alternatives to toxic forms of masculinity. The first-year program is framed by the philosophy "KNOW HISTORY / KNOW SELF," which helps the students understand who they are politically and culturally.[23] In the second tier, Youth Organizing Long Beach (YOLB), students deepen their understanding of structural oppression and "start to build a lot of their skill sets around events planning, organizing, public speaking, outreaching, door knocking."[24] Through practice, they get initiated into the work that goes into organizing communities, readying themselves for the capstone Khmer Justice Program (KJP), which trains them to develop strategies and shape and lead campaigns. The KJP students are KGA's seasoned leaders.

The KGA members organize with their African American and Latinx peers to build campaigns to address their shared experiences with state, economic, and gender violence. In this coalitional space, KGA ensures that the experiences of Cambodian youth do not disappear in the larger Long Beach–wide discussions over discipline, health, and safety. Lian underlines the importance of inserting the Khmer youth's narratives into these issues. There is a lack of data about the Khmer community and, she says, "that is why establishing our own narrative is really, really important. It creates a resonance for our young people, but it could also echo out to other folks in our community."[25] By working in coalition, KGA and its youth members have effectively influenced policymaking and implementation by ensuring officials who can advocate for their communities get elected. In the Los Angeles area, KGA participates in various migrant rights coalitions, including Central American refugee-led organizations like Central American Resource Center (CARECEN). It has close ties with the Youth Justice Coalition, which organizes youth to fight their criminalization.[26] It was part of the LA area–based Allies, which proposed an alternative platform to comprehensive immigration reform in 2007 (see chapter 1). Nationally and transnationally, KGA partners with the Southeast Asian Freedom Network (SEAFN) and the Southeast Asia Resource Action Center (SEARC) in defining the agenda for refugee justice.

"Step into Long Beach": Struggles against Displacement and Dispossession

My steps turned toward Long Beach and Khmer Girls as a result of conversations during the very early stages of my research with veteran LA area activist Hamid Khan, fellow activist Richard Rath, former executive director of KGA Suely Ngouy, and New York City–based Cambodian American organizer Chhaya Chhoum.[27] Chhaya's clear and impassioned case for the transformations that a "refugee voice" could spark in the immigrant rights movement rang in my ears for many years until I had the opportunity to visit KGA for a month between March and April 2016.[28] I wanted to learn how KGA builds leadership among young people who do not see themselves and their history reflected in the pages of their public school textbooks. How did these high school students put into words and, beyond that, translate into action the multiple layers of state and structural violence?

To prepare for my visit, I spent several months developing my research plan and protocol with Ashley Uyeda, a longtime and key staff member who liaised between the rest of the organization and me. We decided I would observe but not participate in the weekly 3–6 p.m. trainings each Tuesday and Wednesday. The emotional safety of the space during trainings had been built as a result of the long-term trust between the staff and the students to allow the difficult journey involved in uncovering the layers of violence, neglect, and forgetting. The KGA lounge, where members gather after school and before the training session, envelopes them in love and care. From snacks to a speaker to play the members' favorite tunes, menstrual products stocked in the bathroom, evening rides home, and heart-to-hearts with KGA staff, the organization ensured that the members felt loved and accepted.

During the first week of my visit, I introduced myself and shared my project with the students. Over the month, the students and I built rapport with each other. Since my goal was to absorb KGA's political education curriculum, I concentrated on the content of the trainings, skills-building, and the learning objectives of each exercise. Reflected in this chapter is what I learned about the curriculum and the process of political education through my observation and my interviews with KGA adult staff members. I did not interview the teen members, nor are they directly quoted.

I was invited to prepare and participate in events related to the two cross-racial campaigns KGA was spearheading. These were the Every Student Matters (ESM) campaign to create a positive school climate and the outreach activities at the new wellness clinic housed in Roosevelt Elementary School. These campaigns opened my eyes to the connection between organizing for health and wellness, not always legible as immigrant rights issues, and organizing against deportation.

To understand KGA required understanding Long Beach. So, I lived there during my 2016 visit. I moved from the gentrifying shore area into the heart of Cambodia Town in east Long Beach. Cambodia Town is economically depressed and suffers from a lack of federal and city investment in it. Despite the neglect, it developed into the commercial, cultural, and residential hub of the city's twenty thousand Cambodian residents due to the efforts of Cambodian mutual assistance associations formed in the 1980s. Sustained community-based endeavors calling attention to the social-historical significance of this neighborhood eventually led the city in 2007 to designate the business corridor on Anaheim Street stretching between Atlantic Avenue and Junipero Avenue as culturally significant. Blue "Cambodia Town" street signs mark the strip. Though around 20 percent of Cambodia Town's residents are Asian, 70 percent of those categorized as Asian are Cambodian. By 2021, chains were replacing Cambodian-owned businesses, and citywide urban renewal plans were impacting the neighborhood.[29]

In the 1980s, the city was not equipped to address the needs of Cambodian refugees. As they started to step migrate to Long Beach, they found themselves inserted into urban decay. Even as the Ronald Reagan administration aggressively pushed to accept Cambodian refugees, valorized as "freedom fighters" in its ideological war against communism, its neoliberal low-cost approach to refugee resettlement was consistent with its hallmark economic austerity measures.[30] These neoliberal refugee policies emphasized self-sufficiency and contracted out support services to nonprofits, which were not up to the enormous task.[31] Lian pointed out that Long Beach did not provide the language assistance, cultural competency, and mental health support needed for a heavily traumatized group of people who found themselves in "already impoverished communities with overcrowded housing . . . and poor school districts. . . . For the most part, people were left to fend for themselves. . . . You had this *explosion* of racial tension in a lot of urban communities [like Long Beach], where there was already historical discrimination." Gang violence, which peaked between 1989 and 1995, and school dropout rates were only some of the consequences of a "very problematic resettlement process."[32] Reagan's dual wars on poor people and crime expanded the neoliberal carceral apparatus. These wars shifted resources to enforcement and the punishment of those in poverty by popularizing economic austerity and fomenting moral panics about drugs and crime.[33]

The part of Cambodia Town where I stayed in many ways instantiated the Long Beach of policy reports—economically depressed, polluted, and unsafe. At the same time, the neighborhood was culturally rich. The Mark Twain Neighborhood Library on Anaheim Street holds the largest collection of Khmer language books of any US public library. The two Buddhist temples within a block and a half of where I stayed on Orange Street signaled the vibrancy of Khmer culture transplanted from Cambodia and Vietnam. Social service offices with Khmer and English signs dotted the area. The Mekong Mart strip mall bustled with traffic into the Asian grocery stores and mom-and-pop eateries. All these institutions testified to painstaking community building since the 1980s.[34] Gorgeous murals brightened the walls on Warren Street and Mahanna Street, one depicting Long Beach's Cambodians alongside African Americans and the other fusing a bucolic scene evoking the countryside in Cambodia with the port city of Long Beach.

Invisible in these depictions are the long-term struggles of Tongva cultural leaders and educators to save and take care of the sacred site of Povuu'ngna at the nearby California State University, Long Beach (CSULB) campus. Since the Spanish incursion in 1790, Tongva residents have been scattered from their ancestral lands and urbanized due to dispossession.[35] Today, Tongva live dispersed in the area, dispossessed of a land base. Historian William McCawley, in his collaborative oral history cowritten with Tongva scholar Claudia Jurmain, astutely points out that "for California tribes such as the Tongva, the BAR's [Bureau of Acknowledgment and Recognition's] acknowledgment process constitutes a de facto denial, more than two centuries of governmental efforts to de-legitimize their authority and deprive them of their land."[36] Despite federal denial, Tongva have self-organized into three councils and engaged in the decolonial work of cultural revival and caring for ancestral sites, protecting them from the incessant threat of commercial development. While this part of my research is based on secondary, not primary, sources, I was fortunate to take part in the 2017 Indigenous Day Ancestor Walk between Costa Mesa and Povuu'ngna organized by LA and Orange County Tongva and Acjachemen community leaders who are part of the California Cultural Resources Preservation Alliance. The walk revivified Tongva presence on the land and marked the persistent efforts to protect the land from desecration and degradation from port activities and the suburban sprawl. Embedded in Long Beach are the cusped histories of US imperialism abroad, domestic occupation, dispossession, and displacement. Also lying side by side in this space are contemporary Tongva and Khmer works of cultural revival, resilience, and transgenerational care of ancestors.

How Cambodian Refugees Became Deportable

When I present on the deportation crisis in the Cambodian community, I am frequently asked how Cambodians become deportable when they usually have legal resident status as refugees. The KGA curriculum answers this question by contextualizing Khmer deportability in the convergence of US foreign policy in Southeast Asia, US immigration policy, and state and federal criminal laws. This evolving refugee justice approach departs from standard analyses of the deportation crisis, which focus solely on the inimical effects of two 1996 laws—the Illegal Immigration Reform and Immigrant Responsibility Act and the Antiterrorism and Effective Death Penalty Act.[37] KGA staff organizers have been developing this national and transnational analysis with SEAFN and the 1Love Movement. During my visit, they were introducing this approach to the local community.

KGA members recognize that deportation in their community is fundamentally linked to being criminalized as gang involved. Most refugees received their deportation orders while finishing their prison sentences. These refugees were the casualties of a battery of increasingly stringent federal and state laws starting in the 1980s (see chapter 1). These laws defined gangs, imposed gang injunctions, and enhanced sentencing for

ANCESTOR WALK

October 7th, 2017

20TH ANNUAL PILGRIMAGE OF THE TONGVA & ACJACHEMEN PEOPLE, CARRYING PRAYERS FOR OUR ANCESTORS AND FUTURE GENERATIONS

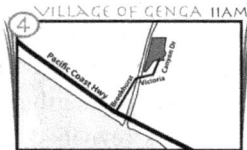

PANHE   7:30AM

1. Panhe is an ancient village nestled on the banks of San Mateo Creek. Throughout the years ceremony and reburials have taken place here. The site continues to be an important ceremonial site. We celebrate the efforts of all the community members who prevented the disruption of Panhe. This area is an irreplaceable spiritual and cultural site. We come together to pray for it's continued protection.

PUTUIDEM   8:30AM

2. Putuidem, located in San Juan Capistrano, is the mother village of the Acjachemen people. Our leaders Oyison and Corrone lived here. We remember and honor them. Meet at Northwest Open Space— 30291 Camino Capistrano, San Juan Capistrano, CA.

GENGA   10:00AM

3. This site is very ancient. The village and ancestors were over 9,500 years old, ancient when the Egyptian pyramids were built. Over 600 ancestors were moved to build the Harbor Cove housing tract at Newport Back Bay. We pray that this kind of disruption will never occur again.

VILLAGE OF GENGA 11AM

4. This is the main portion of the village of Genga, located above the Santa Ana River. This site was a trade route to the desert. Protected in the open space of Fairview Park for years, it is now threatened by plans to build sports fields on it.

BOLSA CHICA 12 & 1:30PM

5. We gather in the parking lot and walk across the Bolsa Chica Mesa to the memorial gardens. Bolsa Chica is the home of the cog stones, unique disk shaped stones used in ceremonial rituals.
6. For decades tribal members and preservationists have worked to preserve Bolsa Chica as sanctified burial grounds. The area is a sacred site, eligible for the National Register of Historic Places. 174 ancestors were disturbed to build homes.

MOTUUCHÉYNGNA 3:30PM

7. We visit the memorial gardens, walk and pray. Here, Native American monitors stood in a circle to protect Ancestors from further desecration while threatened by workers and heavy equipment building homes. The building was stopped, and the housing project was redesigned. Four less houses were built. We honor and remember all who worked to protect the Ancestors here.

PUVUNGNA   4:30PM

8. Join us at Puvungna, "The Gathering Place." This is all that remains of our creation site, located on the campus of CSU Long Beach. Attempts to build a strip mall and housing on the last open 22 acres of this sacred site were blocked by court order. Puvungna is listed on the National Register of Historic Places.

4.2. The handout, distributed to participants, names the places at which we stopped during the October 7, 2017, Ancestor Walk. At each site, a Tongva elder narrated its significance and the efforts to protect the land from development and said a prayer or performed ceremony. Courtesy of Tongva and Acjachemen leaders of California Cultural Resources Preservation Alliance.

activities marked by law enforcement as gang-related.[38] At the federal level, the criminalization of Southeast Asian refugee youth and efforts to block them from immigration benefits such as naturalization started in the Reagan era. With the 2002 US-Cambodia repatriation agreement, those who have not been able to naturalize because of a criminal record risk detention and deportation.

I witnessed the criminalization of Khmer youth within days of starting my fieldwork at KGA. I was invited to join a multiracial group of local high school students for a walk-through at the new wellness clinic in the same complex as the newly built Roosevelt Elementary School relocated on Linden Avenue. On my way to the clinic, I noticed Long Beach police cars with flashing lights on Atlantic Avenue. Two police officers loomed over two handcuffed teenagers of color sitting on the edge of the sidewalk, their heads lowered and baseball caps pulled over their eyes. This arrest, possibly a common occurrence in that neighborhood, stayed with me as I walked through the clinic's well-lighted, airy, welcoming space.

The contrast between the two projects of responding to Long Beach youth's challenges could not have been starker. As I listened to our guides introducing us to the reproductive health and mental health services at the clinic, which offered teen-only hours once a week, I started to understand the connection between KGA's wellness campaign and the commonplace brutalization of Long Beach's youth, among whom I stood. When I shared what I witnessed with a few KGA staff, they immediately told me that Atlantic Avenue is well known as an area where youth are surveilled, arrested, and entered into the state's gang database.

The Long Beach Unified School District (LBUSD) actively participates in the disciplining and criminalization of Black, Latinx, and Khmer and other Southeast Asian youth. KGA youth leaders' participation in the "Every Student Matters" campaign is a response to the elaborate architecture of punishment that creates the school-to-prison-to-deportation pipeline.[39] The campaign was part of a large coalition, Building Healthy Communities Long Beach, a California-wide initiative. The students' experiences bear out Victor Rios's observation that school teachers and administrators, probation officers, and social workers are all implicated in constructing this architecture that funnels youth into correctional control and triggers deportation for Khmer refugees.[40] The "Every Student Matters" campaign generated an infographic that states that one LBUSD student is suspended every nineteen minutes.[41] A 2012 school climate survey conducted as part of the campaign found that 9 percent of over 1,700 students who participated reported being arrested on or near school grounds.[42] These data, coupled with KGA's 2011 survey, conducted by and with Khmer youth, were published in its "Step into Long Beach" report. The researchers found that Khmer youth feel discriminated against in school, with 47 percent reporting that they felt wrongly disciplined. Of the youth surveyed by KGA members, 39 percent of young men reported being stopped by law enforcement, and 23 percent reported being arrested.[43]

As KGA, along with other Southeast Asian activists, argue, deportation triggers the unresolved political traumas of the war and the Khmer Rouge, exacerbating the mental health crisis in Long Beach's Khmer refugee community—62 percent of Long Beach's Cambodian residents suffer from post-traumatic stress disorders.[44] Khmer youth suffer from high rates of depression as a direct "result of consistently feeling unsafe and prone to criminalization."[45] KGA's formulation of refugee justice stitches together the era of US intervention in Southeast Asia and their community's experiences as refugees.

KGA's leadership pipeline provides its members with the tools to question and organize against this type of institutional violence. Like other immigrant communities, which bear the brunt of police and correctional control, Khmer refugees and their children find the calls for legalization ineffective without a direct contestation of the law-and-order platform encoded in the background checks built into every legislative proposal and of the commonsensical notion that criminal aliens deserve to be deported despite having served time for their criminal convictions.

In the case of deportable Cambodian refugees, the State Department becomes a key player, introducing the consideration of foreign policy into Southeast Asian antideportation organizing.[46] Until 2002, incarcerated Cambodians, often transferred directly to the custody of immigration authorities upon completing their criminal sentences, could not be deported, leading to a successful Supreme Court challenge to the indefinite detention of removable aliens (see my discussion of Kim Ho Ma's case in chapter 1). Recall here the State Department's advocacy role in pushing for Cambodian resettlement under the Jimmy Carter administration. Reagan actively promoted this policy position as well.[47] Two decades later, the children who had served as the posters for justifying the war against communism were turned into liabilities in the domestic war against crime and, yet again, became the targets of the State Department's intervention.

These developments have fueled the SEAFN and the 1Love Movement's evolving approach, which is to target the State Department and the United

Nations by demanding a revised and fair repatriation agreement. The 2015 Fair Repatriation Campaign demands that those who had entered the United States with refugee status in the period that preceded the 1993 normalization of US-Cambodia diplomatic relations be protected from deportation. Addressing the plight of those already deported, the networks have introduced language that would allow refugees expelled to Cambodia the right to return. The protection of refugees from deportation would apply to them retroactively in these proposals. The proposed revisions aim to align the US-Cambodia repatriation agreement with international standards and the 2008 US-Vietnam repatriation agreement. In October 2015, SEAFN launched its #right2return social media campaign to circulate the historical context within which deportation needs to be understood and escalate the struggle to restore the rights of those already deported and bring them back to the United States (see chapter 1).[48] In mid-December 2015, KGA organized a "Not Home for the Holidays" forum to spread these strategies to the Long Beach Khmer community and shore up support from Long Beach's city council members and the district's state assembly and congressional representatives.[49] The 2017 forum with the same theme amid escalating deportation is both sobering and inspiring, since it evidences the Khmer community's courage to speak up in repressive times.

KGA staff were critical of the stigmatization of noncitizens with criminal convictions well before the hashtag #FamiliesAreFelons started to circulate in late 2014 among migrant activists in response to President Barack Obama's assurance to the nation that immigration enforcement targeted "felons not families. . . . Gang members, not a mom who's working hard to provide for her kids." Obama was unveiling executive orders for the Deferred Action for Parents of Americans and Lawful Permanent Residents (DAPA) and an expansion of DACA eligibility.[50] For KGA, the distinction between families and felons did not hold for the Khmer community. At all levels of KGA's movement-building work, students learn to interrogate the characterization of their loved ones and community members as deportable "criminal aliens." They learn to reframe this story of refugee failure and deserved punishment by situating their crimogenic reality in history and structural discrimination. Ashley explained that KGA asks the students to think about how criminalized activities meet the needs of and for families: "This is one way in which they see that [crime and gang membership is] a way to make money, to have protection, and a way to have family. These are real basic needs but are not being provided." In a decriminalizing move, KGA asserts, "Our families *are* felons." This statement intervenes in the divisiveness rife in the immigrant rights movement about whether those with criminal records are defensible.

The affective power of KGA's call, "Keep Families Together," lies not in any innate goodness of the family form but in the welling up of grief, lying very near the surface, in those separated indefinitely from incarcerated or deported loved ones. These separations reopen the wartime wounds inflicted by the United States and, then, the Khmer Rouge.[51] Added to the state-designed deaths were the prolonged separation and disappearance of family members fleeing the Pol Pot regime and the chaos of refugee camps. These disappearances still haunt the parents and grandparents of many KGA students.[52] Reuniting with family members, rebuilding the ties, and constructing families of choice anchor resettlement, amplifying the value of families for this refugee community. KGA students learn to speak publicly about incarceration and deportation in terms of a fresh state-sponsored assault on their families and communities in the space of resettlement.

Deportation = Genocide

The April 5, 2016, Tuesday training was a time to prepare for the New Year, which, following the lunar calendar, the Khmer community celebrates in mid-April. That year, KGA youth members, like in other years, planned to join the April Cambodian New Year Parade on Anaheim Street, the main artery of Cambodia Town, culminating in the Cambodian Cultural Festival. That year, the KGA contingent's focus was the immigrant and refugee justice message of family unity. However, homeland politics, discussed below, led several Khmer organizations, including KGA, to withdraw from the parade in late March. This change, KGA staff knew, would disappoint their youth members, and they dedicated their training to the complexities of the New Year for the Cambodian community.

The training started with the students playing a boisterous icebreaker designed to move their bodies and interact with each other. Like every other training, KGA organizers Sophya Chhiv (now Chum) and Ashley unfurled a piece of butcher paper to display the theme that would structure the training for that day. I was not quite prepared for the bold letters on the butcher paper. They read, "Deportation = Genocide." I later discovered KGA had used this equation to frame its lessons and antideportation campaigns for many years. Sophya, a core staff member in charge of community organizing and currently KGA's associate director, led the facilitation that day. She asked the trainees to reflect on what the New Year meant for

4.3. Khmer Girls in Action's YWEP, YMEP, and YOLB organizers gather for a group photo after their training on the topic of deportation on April 12, 2016. That day we marked Khmer New Year with flowers and incense. Photo credit: Joy Yanga. Courtesy of Khmer Girls in Action.

their families, communities, and KGA. She then asked us to dwell on the two words on the butcher paper. One was about a whole group of people targeted for mass murder, and the other was about the banishment of migrants from their families and from the communities in which they grew up to another country. Could these two distinct types of violence be equated? she asked. And why were we talking about issues like genocide and deportation in the celebratory context of the New Year? Below, I show the historical specificity the trainers brought to the equation. They also used the equation to stitch together historical and life events to correct national amnesia and erasure.

The New Year, KGA youth said, was family time and an occasion to express pride in Khmer culture and identity. It was a time to honor ancestors. Adding to this understanding, Sophya reminded us that it was also a time to mark all that the refugee community in Long Beach had gone through to escape war and genocide; it was a time to celebrate all they had achieved. Furthermore, the celebration of the Khmer New Year has been fused with the fateful day, April 17, 1975, when the Khmer Rouge soldiers drove everyone out of Phnom Penh, inaugurating four years of torture, starvation, and death. Since then, the celebratory tone of the New Year has mingled with grief and loss. In fact, this emotional landscape was spatially expressed on Anaheim Avenue, a couple of blocks past MacArthur Park, where the New Year Parade ends and the Cultural Festival takes place. A black banner on the street marked the forty-first memorial of the killing fields, reading "Remembering three million victims of the Cambodian genocide" in Khmer and English.

Asking the students to connect the 2015 KGA public forum "Not Home for the Holidays" to the Khmer New Year, Sophya reminded them that many of their loved ones could not gather because they had been torn away by different forms of state-sponsored violence—whether by the genocide under the Khmer Rouge, the carceral system in the United States, or the permanent removal of refugees from the United States. Without diffusing the tension between the two types of violence—genocide and deportation— from which the Khmer community in Long Beach suffers, she steered us to think about the *impact* of genocide and deportation on the families of the participants in the room. Genocide lethally targets the intimate sphere to break down social norms.[53] Deportation, too, breaks apart families, inflicting more loss, more grief, more emptiness in a community that already suffers from extraordinarily high levels of post-traumatic stress disorder.

These assaults on families were inseparable from the loss of sons, daughters, husbands, lovers, and siblings to prisons and detention centers in the United States and then, post-2002, to their expulsion with no legal avenue for the deportees to return. Refugee parents are once again separated from their children, whom they had snatched from death in the midst of war and the Khmer Rouge's genocide. Many of the children who made the perilous passage to the United States are now themselves parents faced with indefinite separation from their loved ones. Lest we relapse into what Asian American studies scholar Cathy Schlund-Vials calls the "Cambodia Syndrome," it is important to remember, as KGA does, that the United States' fixation on the Cambodian genocide depends on its deliberate "nonadmission of U.S. culpability before, during, and after the Democratic Kampuchean era."[54] "Deportation = Genocide" redirects our attention to the United States and its perpetuation of traumatic practices, which directly target families in the form of deportation.

We ended the two-and-a-half-hour lesson with the screening of Cambodian American filmmaker Socheata Poeuv's *New Year Baby*, a documentary about Poeuv's efforts to recover her history through that of her parents.[55]

Our laughter, elicited by the lighter moments in the film, gave way to intense grief as we watched her parents' fragmented, and many times unwilling recollection of labor camp life under the Khmer Rouge as they visited these sites of violence in Cambodia. Watching the animated representations of the disembodied yet all-permeating control of the Angkar (the organization) over camp dwellers, I was reminded of the complete control that US prisons and detention centers exert over every aspect of the lives of those incarcerated, including their emotions and the contact they have with loved ones.[56] The previous weeks' trainings had laid the groundwork for us to remember that the violence inflicted by the Khmer Rouge on Cambodians lay on a continuum with the preceding political trauma of war and US carpet-bombing and postsettlement racialization, refugee poverty, and distress driven by US public policies.

These powerful entry points into the creation of refugeehood and Khmer Rouge's legacy in the diaspora prepared the participants for the announcement of KGA's decision not to participate in the 2016 Khmer New Year Parade. To explain KGA's decision, Sophya and Ashley pointed to how a high-ranking Cambodian military official, Hun Manet, the son of the Cambodian People's Party's then prime minister Hun Sen, was to visit Long Beach and attend the parade. Prime Minister Hun Sen had served as a commander in the Khmer Rouge and, among his many atrocities, spearheaded the massacre against the Muslim Cham community in Democratic Kampuchea. He defected to Vietnam in 1977, and in 1985, the occupying Vietnamese government appointed him prime minister of the People's Republic of Kampuchea. He installed himself in that office in the postoccupation state of Cambodia and was in power for nearly forty years.[57] He operated like a dictator, violently suppressing public protests for labor and land rights and political freedom. Hun Manet, who is now prime minister, trained at the US Military Academy at West Point, and was a lieutenant general in the Royal Cambodian Armed Forces. Cambodians in the diaspora see him as having perpetrated human rights violations under the Hun Sen regime.[58]

To contextualize KGA's decision to withdraw from the parade, Sophya and Ashley shared with the students a March 23 protest by more than 250 Khmer elders, the majority from Long Beach. They had gathered at the Long Beach city hall to testify to city council members in an hour-long period dedicated to public comment on how the city officials should respond to Hun Manet's invitation to the parade. The elders spoke of the deep scars left by the Khmer Rouge and the continued human rights abuses under Hun Sen's authoritarian rule.[59] Testimonies read in Khmer and English moved several council members to tears. Two council members and Long Beach mayor Robert Garcia said they would not appear at the parade if Manet was present. On March 28, Manet announced he was not going to attend, attesting to the political effectiveness of the Long Beach Cambodian community. The parade took place, but KGA and other social justice groups stayed away. Protestors lined both sidewalks during the parade, which was smaller than usual, holding the signs they had made for the city hall rally. They announced, in no uncertain terms, "We are Khmer community in Long Beach and don't want to see dictatorship government join our parade." Their presence and voice marked a win. Though the young men and women at KGA had been excited for weeks about taking part in the parade, they were able to understand KGA's withdrawal in the context of what they were learning and express their admiration for the courage of their elders, whom they otherwise had seen as being wary about delving too deeply into their past.

These transnational intergenerational connections and memory work become critical in mobilizing students, who were not themselves at risk of deportation because they are US-born. They are encouraged to ask what laws and policies expose community members to deportation and force them back to "that place where they are still having to survive and still having to struggle."[60] Toward the end of my visit, Sophya shared with me the story of her older sister who was criminalized and put into deportation proceedings in 2003. The story shows how American-born Cambodians continue to feel intimately the impacts of harmful US policies and the ways in which KGA provides support and purpose to similarly affected youth leaders, who, through their social justice work in the organization, raise their voices passionately to demand change.

A second-generation Cambodian American, Sophya had just graduated high school and completed KGA's leadership training. She was working with the organization as staff when her older sister was put into deportation proceedings. KGA had just turned a year old as an autonomous organization when the 2002 repatriation agreement made the threat of deportation real for the Khmer communities. Former KGA executive director Suely Ngouy described how challenging it was for the fledgling organization to create a rapid response network to respond to the deportation crisis.[61] But it quickly put resources in place in alliance with two well-established local organizations, the United Cambodian Community and the Cambodian Association of America. Sophya's sister was among those whom KGA assisted.

Sophya is one of six children. Her mother and her older siblings migrated to Long Beach as refugees. As a single parent, her mother supported her children by working long hours in a restaurant. Sophya remembered moving a lot as she was growing up and wryly remarked that her family lived everywhere in Long Beach except for the affluent parts. Her oldest sister, who was three or four years old when they moved to Long Beach, had a difficult transition. Reflecting on the challenges her sister must have faced, Sophya said, "I know that in the '90s it was hard growing up, especially having to resettle and assimilate here in Long Beach during the '90s when gang violence in the community was really high and not knowing or having a sense of who you are and your culture and identity." Sophya's sister got gang-involved in this social ecology of imperial-settler neglect. Since she was the oldest, she was expected to take care of her younger siblings. She took them everywhere, including gang meetings. The gang members also visited their home. Sophya grew up among them. "You know, those people were family. They were family to my sister; family to us," she pointed out. Eventually, her sister was arrested; she cycled in and out of prison. During these periods of incarceration, Sophya's family cared for her children.

The news that her sister had been transferred from prison to an immigration detention center was sudden and unanticipated. To communicate the speed with which the deportation regime kicked in after the repatriation agreement, Sophya snapped her fingers. How would her sister be treated in the detention center? How was she going to be treated by the Cambodian government, if she were to be deported? Through KGA, Sophya accessed legal assistance, financial support to pay for a lawyer, advocates who wrote letters of support for her sister, and experts who could testify in her case. Her family dropped everything to make day trips to another part of the state to attend the hearings in immigration court as her sister filed for asylum.

Sophya's father, who was struggling with terminal cancer at the time, testified in court. Sophya did not know him well since he had been long divorced from her mother. She recalled the intensity of that moment. She prefaced it by saying that at the time, the deportation of criminal aliens was a wedge issue in Cambodian communities. Gang members did not cut sympathetic figures. But, she observed, "There is so much more behind that if you connect it to history!" Her father provided that living history in front of the immigration judge. Sophya recounted that day in court:

> I remember that was the last thing my dad did before he passed away. Because . . . yeah, it was really hard to see him in a wheelchair and having to talk about what happened to him. . . . We filed for asylum, that's

why [my father had to tell his story]. So, my sister had to file, saying that, you know, if she were to go back, it would be an endangerment to her because my dad fought against Khmer Rouge. . . . My dad had to tell the story. I had *never* heard that story until that day in court. Till this very day . . . I couldn't even . . . I . . . I stepped out of the room because I couldn't, I couldn't handle it. . . . I never really knew my dad because my parents were divorced. But the moment that my sister got detained, he was like, "What do I need to do?" You know. Because that's his daughter. And then, when he told the story, I was like, I can't be in this room. This is the first time ever hearing him talk about it. I can't imagine what he was going through.[62]

As the asylum case dragged on, the Department of Homeland Security impounded Sophya's sister's documents. Without her green card, she was not authorized to work and was unable to support her family. For Sophya, her sister's case revealed "the part of the system that is corrupted and [is] pushing her back into prison, pretty much, and waiting for her to make another mistake."[63] These barriers to employment and survival that people face upon being released from prison have been framed by Michelle Alexander in the case of African Americans as profound civil rights violations.[64] When these barriers posed by criminal histories combine with immigration controls, the lens of civil rights and enforced second-class citizenship requires widening to grasp the transnational politics of deportation of US residents who are not citizens. The use of crime to deport refugees throws into relief settler carcerality.

This story exposes multiple layers of colonial and settler carceral violence. Criminality sets the groundwork for expelling refugees, sharpening US territorial control or countersovereignty, and consolidating its neoimperial interests in Hun Sen and his son Hun Manet's Cambodia. Sophya connects the violence of her family's dislocation from Cambodia with the combined violence of institutional neglect and active criminalization of refugee youth on resettlement in the United States. She draws out the gendered effects of these structures on women. To grasp the horror of these enactments, one does not need the details—unbearable to Sophya—that her father presented to the judge, breaking intergenerational silence. As Latinx studies scholar Leisy Abrego reminds us in the context of weaving her family's story of escaping El Salvador with the larger political context, the silence that stretched between Sophya's father and his daughters stemmed from unspeakable and many-layered state terror the family had experienced in Cambodia.[65] A deadly silence also enveloped the immigration courtroom: the silence around US war that entangled the country Sophya's father fled, the silence about the bombs that rained on Cambodia day and night between 1965 and 1973, forcing people to take sides in a war that was not theirs. Decades later in the California courtroom, the US state, in an exercise of its plenary power, appointed itself as the adjudicator of whether Sophya's father's story was credible and whether Sophya's sister deserved relief from deportation based on credible fear.

Sophya knew this violence in her bones. As a KGA youth leader turned organizer, she learned about this history as part of getting to know herself in community and taught it to activate other youth. It felt unbearable when she heard this history from her father's mouth. In stepping out of the courtroom, she refused to accept the United States' repudiation of its violence and its role in creating the monstrous conditions the Khmer Rouge unleashed. Her witnessing of intergenerational pain and scarring exceeds an encapsulation in words, inviting those who hear her account to recognize that her stepping away creates an epistemic space. Through Sophya's story, I discern a sadistic will-to-know characteristic of voyeuristic hearings in immigration courts and a refusal on the part of Sophya and her family to submit to the power-knowledge constitution of a failed refugee subject who has to justify seeking asylum in the United States yet again. This space that eludes enunciation has been identified by sociologist Grace Cho, in the case of the Korean diaspora, as a "haunting" and by ethnic studies scholar Khatharya Um, in her textured analysis of the making of the Cambodian diaspora, as "refugee refusal." Sophya's recoiling from the layered violence is another manifestation of this noncompliance.[66]

In discussing the impacts of deportation on women with KGA staff, I learned that they contextualize these lived experiences in the organization's foundational commitment to gender and reproductive justice. When KGA members learn about deportation, they think about the impact of taking away women from their families as a result of incarceration and deportation. Khmer culture is hardly exceptional, Sophya observed, in expecting women and girls to be the primary caregivers in the community. But this culturally expected carework stabilizes the refugee community. In an underresourced, impoverished community, girls and women like Jocelyn and her aunt provide income through their livelihoods; they feed their families; they are responsible for their families' health; they take care of small children who are their own and those in their extended and adopted family; they translate for their families and friends; and they organize for justice. The experiences of Sophya's sister instruct us to understand the intersections of gender with the structures of the death-dealing imperial-settler state, which continues to generate its disavowals to perpetuate its exceptionalism.

Coexisting with KGA's efforts to name the multiple forms of genocide across space and time are Tongva struggles in Long Beach against the ongoing genocidal actions of the United States directed against them. KGA's analysis effectively intervenes in the controlling image of the "killing fields" as the only site of genocide by implicating US imperialism in the creation and treatment of Khmer refugees. By naming this imperial violence, KGA intervenes in how the United States projects itself as a refuge. But, going a step further, we need to see that settler colonial forms of genocide underpin US imperialism abroad, as does racial capitalism that has produced refugee poverty in the spaces of resettlement. The naming of deportation as a form of genocide cannot but call attention to Tongva battles in the present to secure Tongva sacred and burial sites, places shared with Acjachemen tribes, in the face of ongoing US settler logics.[67] To write against these logics would require bringing to the foreground the practices of cultural revival, particularly the introduction of Tongva culture to youth; acts of remembrance through art, navigation, ceremony, and storytelling; and the protracted battles to protect burial sites from real estate development. At the same time, we must remember that Tongva struggles are rooted in dispossession through colonial settlement, while Khmer struggles are rooted in forced displacement and failed resettlement on lands occupied serially by the Spanish, the Mexican government, and the United States.

Just a few miles away from Cambodia Town, where the CSULB campus is located, Tongva activists—scholars and cultural practitioners—continue to fight land dispossession and the related assaults on their culture by warding off commercial development of a sacred site and burial ground on the western corner. The ancestral village of Povuu'ngna became the property of Long Beach State College (later CSULB) when 283.5 acres were taken from Rancho Los Alamitos in 1944 to build the campus.[68] Rancho Los Alamitos, created in 1833 under independent Mexico, was a small fraction of the 300,000 acres of land which was appropriated from Tongva in 1790 by the Spanish. In 1974, the site of the village was listed under the National Register of Historic Places as a result of the efforts of Tongva organizers and their allies, who succeeded in getting CSULB to designate the site as Povuu'ngna, a "sacred place then and now, where Ouiot, the omnipotent first chief was born, and where Chinigchinich appeared to give the people their ways."[69]

In the early 1990s, CSULB proposed to commercially develop the twenty-three acres of land designated as sacred to build a strip mall. The plan threatened to desecrate the sacred site and burial grounds. Members of the Tongva community and their allies again organized protests. Cindi Alvitre (Tongva), American Indian studies professor at CSULB, and poet and writer Gloria Arellanes (Tongva) recounted the struggle mounted by tribal members, community activists, students, and faculty.[70] Many Tongva activists refused to leave the site. Alvitre recalled her brother camping on the land for eighteen months between 1993 and 1994 as a form of protest. Plaintiffs within the Tongva community, including Arellanes, and the California Native American Heritage Commission, sued the university. The plans for developing the site were suspended in 1995 but CSULB has not returned the land to its caretakers. In fact, in 2019, CSULB, in a classic settler colonial move, dumped soil excavated from construction at the sacred site of Povuu'ngna, underlining for Tongva the urgency of their struggle to protect it from such desecration.[71] Through the community's struggles over Povuu'ngna, and the recovery and practice of its ties to this sacred site, Tongva exercise some measure of sovereignty.

The movement for Tongva self-determination has led the state of California to recognize Gabrielino/Tongva as a tribe. But the federal government's policies governing recognition testify to the settler colonial, blood-quantum-dictated terms to which it subjects Indigenous nationhood.[72] I call attention to this local struggle because it reveals the ties of Tongva people to the land and the continuing assertion of Tongva sovereignty in the face of settler colonial practices of dispossession through which the university reserves the right to use the land by reinforcing private property laws. This form of colonial control undercuts the relational ethics between land and people. Khmer refugees find themselves settled in this political economy of dispossession and experience the settler colonial and racist violence already stamped on the land.[73] In this environment, KGA and Tongva leaders undertake decolonizing projects that spring up to counter the violence but have yet to coalesce. KGA staff and youth are well aware of Indigenous struggles and other communities with histories of genocide. For Khmer youth to connect to Tongva resurgence, Kanaka 'Ōiwi scholar Hōkūlani Aikau's call for insurgent critical learning anchored in responsibility for and obligation to place and stories (as told during the Ancestor Walk) offers a way to move toward "the *how* of decolonization."[74]

Conclusion

The memory work required to excavate US imperial ventures abroad and settler colonial violence at home must be multidirectional. The mode of inquiry stimulated by KGA's leadership programs calls into question US benevolence by exposing the structural violence that creates the "failed" refugee turned deportable "criminal alien." Contending with Tongva presence and struggles in Long Beach brings to the surface the violence of settler colonialism on which the materiality of refugee resettlement depends. Indigenous studies scholar Jodi Byrd (Chickasaw) reminds us, "In geographical localities of the Americas, where histories of settlers and arrivants map themselves into and on top of Indigenous peoples, understanding colonialism as a cacophony of contradictorily hegemonic and horizontal struggles offer an alternative way of formulating and addressing the dynamics that continue to affect people as they move and are made to move within empire."[75] In seeking those horizontal points of contact as a migration scholar, I do not want to create an isomorphism between struggles of Khmer refugees and those of Tongva. Nor am I suggesting natural grounds for solidarity between the two groups of survivors. KGA curriculum and organizing and the SEAFN–1Love Movement platform underscore the hollowness and impossibility of the "gift" of US permanent residency. Tongva resistance against land development and desecration has mounted for decades regardless of federal recognition. Drawing on Kahnawà:ke Mohawk anthropologist Audra Simpson's work, I see Tongva intergenerational will to protect land and culture as one expression of a refusal.[76] It is a refusal to be short-circuited by US settler colonial power to decree which Indigenous Nations can be recognized.

The struggles are distinct because the political projects are distinct. For the Tongva people, the struggle against US colonialism centers on restoring cultural and political sovereignty. For Khmer refugees, the struggles focus on the restitution for the conditions fomented by the United States. My effort in the chapter is focused on writing about Khmer resettlement and the creation of the refugee-turned-deportee by remembering US genocidal acts. In writing about the multiple registers of political violence wrought on Khmer people, I try to keep in mind the Tongva exercises of sovereignty in the present—the cultural resurgence, the protection of sacred sites, the struggle over federal recognition, the reeducation of Tongva youth to revalue their culture through everyday practice, and the grieving for the long history of forced separation of young children from their families, the scars of which continue to open up in the present through the intergenerational transmission of trauma. While common ground for activism may or may not emerge between the two groups, juxtaposing the two movements helps us unmask the imperial-settler carceral nature of the US state.

As I show in the next chapter, also about migrant youth organizing, solidarities with Indigenous people *are* emergent. In Hawaiʻi, a training facilitated by undocumented members of the Immigrant Youth Coalition (IYC) and the National Youth Immigrant Alliance sparked allyship between non-Indigenous and Pacific Islander immigrant youth to support each other's struggles. I explain how the IYC's queer politics, attuned to all the ways in which BIPOC youth get criminalized, allowed the two immigrant groups— one Indigenous and the other not—to discuss their unjust treatment in schools and by the various arms of enforcement. Just like the discussions of an exclusionary and punitive school climate in Long Beach drew Khmer youth to their Black and Latinx peers, Micronesian youth felt supported to share their experiences of criminalization and discrimination with non-Indigenous immigrant youth who lived in fear of deportation. Taken together, this chapter and the next chart the power of youth who learn from and teach each other to connect the violence they face upon migration to US military and imperial control.

5

NOT DREAMING

After an exhilarating weeklong Youth Empowerment Summit (YES) in February 2012, I drove Johnathan, an undocumented queer youth organizer and cofounder of the San Gabriel Valley Immigrant Youth Coalition (IYC), to the Honolulu airport.[1] Over the course of that week, they and four other IYC–National Immigrant Youth Alliance (IYC-NIYA) leaders trained high school students and college age youth from Oʻahu, Maui, and Hawaiʻi Island. The youth participants represented the diverse migration streams forged by US imperial labor and military circuits. Some had migrated with their families to Hawaiʻi from Tonga, Fiji, and the Federated States of Micronesia. Other participants identified as Mexican, Peruvian, Filipinx, Black, East Asian, and South Asian. The training seeded a new organization, Hawaiʻi Alliance for Local Immigrant Voices and Empowerment (HĀ)LIVE, aimed at making discrimination against non-Hawaiian Pacific Islander and non-Indigenous immigrant youth visible. The summit also fueled a non-Indigenous and non-Hawaiian Pacific Islander student alliance, which campaigned successfully for in-state (resident) tuition for undocumented applicants to the University of Hawaiʻi.[2]

The day Johnathan was leaving Honolulu, they wore one of their "Undocumented, Unafraid" T-shirts. As I took this in, fear coursed through my body. These feelings clamored against all I had learned during the week of training. The five trainers, four of them undocumented, had repeatedly emphasized at every event that the more public one was about one's undocumented status, the harder it became for police and Immigration and Customs Enforcement (ICE) agents to target that person. A basic message of the summit was the importance of undocumented youth organizing and building collective power to declare their status in spaces of surveillance.

Yet, in that moment, faced with the reality of immigration enforcement and how it might impact my friend, my courage failed. I confessed to Johnathan that I did not want them to get arrested and hauled off to the nearby federal detention center. After all, this was the Honolulu Transportation Security Administration (TSA) known for profiling and detaining Latinx travelers. Johnathan laughed. If they were arrested, IYC-NIYA would immediately launch a campaign to free them from ICE custody through their impressive social media network, reinforcing the power of being out about one's status and exposing the state's punishing hand.

I accompanied Johnathan to the security checkpoint. I hugged them close, said goodbye, and anxiously watched as they snaked through the long line to where the TSA officer screened them. Johnathan presented their document. The officer waved them on. Johnathan walked through the checkpoint and the body scanner—their shirt announcing their status— calm, collected, and unhurried. As this happened, I registered it as an act of civil disobedience. I had met Johnathan in 2010 during the Tod@s Som@s Arizona civil disobedience against SB 1070 I detail in chapter 2. Johnathan was among some of the youngest participants. Their political acumen about the place of undocumented youth in the migration justice movement and their passion led us to plan the training in Honolulu to intentionally build momentum for local undocumented youth-led activism.

In many later reflections on this moment, I asked myself what such an act means in US-occupied Hawai'i. I am situated in Oceania, a space Pacific Island studies scholar Epeli Hau'ofa (Tongan and Fijian) has characterized as a sea of islands—a boundless and interconnected world over which the United States has violently extended its political, military, and commercial power.[3] I am particularly aware of how Johnathan's act presents us with an opportunity as scholars and activists to interrogate the legitimacy of US control over this space in the form of immigration enforcement. The United States illegally overthrew the Hawaiian Kingdom in 1893. Its authority over the islands and Kanaka Maoli (Native Hawaiians) continues in the form of statehood—countersovereignty writ large. To naturalize the presence of the arms of US immigration enforcement constitutes what Kanaka 'Ōiwi scholar and nationalist Haunani-Kay Trask calls "peaceful violence."[4] An indicator of the normalization of settler law, habits, and language, this term stands for the unquestioned everyday erasure of Kanaka

Maoli sovereignty (ea, which also constellates life and breath) over their lands and the ocean.[5]

Similarly, the treatment of Pacific Islander residents, Micronesians in particular, as undesirable migrants normalizes US tropes of anti-immigrant racism, the sway of US immigration laws over Hawai'i, and the primacy of US strategic interest in the Pacific. Micronesians from three freely associated nation-states migrate to Hawai'i under a unique arrangement with the United States. Harsh immigration laws have introduced new conditionalities inimical to Micronesians, despite their unique status, even as the United States continues to exercise absolute military control over these nations' land and ocean. As with Southeast Asian refugees, US foreign policy, immigration policies, and criminal law configure the realities of Micronesians in Hawai'i.

The YES training set into motion local youth-led reckoning with the complexity of migration to Hawai'i as a settler colonial space where the state and federal governments disproportionately incarcerate Native Hawaiians and Pacific Islanders and target Latinx residents for immigration violations.[6] Questions about Indigenous migration, in this case of non-Hawaiian Pacific Islanders to Hawai'i, and their treatment under federal immigration law and by local law enforcement surfaced powerfully during the training. At the university, students asking for resident status and in-state tuition eligibility for undocumented students had to reflexively seek ways to express allyship with Native Hawaiian and Pacific Islander students, who faced multiple barriers to education equity.

As I elaborate below, these Indigenous and Oceanic considerations of place and politics, in conjunction with the abolitionist ideologies advanced by queer undocumented youth of color, reveal the settler colonial, imperial, and carceral nature of US power. These considerations exceed the discursive limits of the assimilative and exceptional scripts of the DREAMer narrative, the symbolic terrain created by a branch of undocumented youth activism associated with efforts to pass the federal Development, Relief, and Education for Alien Minors (DREAM) Act. The chapter title, "Not DREAMing," alludes to the IYC's intersectional and queer politics, which scrambles the normative desires to become part of the American Dream embedded in DREAMer storytelling.[7] The IYC marked such assimilative discourses to be anti-Black, anti-Indigenous, and anti-queer because they disavowed death-dealing state violence visited on these communities in the form of criminalization. In that sense, the IYC's work is akin to what queer migration scholar Karma Chávez calls counter-DREAM activism, which refuses exceptionalism, rejects reducing "queer" and "migrant" to identity categories, and contends with the vulnerabilities of criminalized people. This chapter, thus, adds to a small body of scholarship critical of the assimilative DREAM narrative ensconced in neoliberal respectability politics.[8]

The task of this chapter is two-fold. First, I explain the kinds of analyses and actions IYC members developed between 2010 and 2017 to put into practice a queer and abolitionist imagination. How did its public "Undocumented, Unafraid" stance articulate with abolitionist principles leading to the solidarity declaration "All of us or none"? Answering that question brings us full circle to my preface, which opens with the antideportation and abolitionist message that the IYC sent out on October 5, 2017, in Westwood when they used ten prison beds to shut down traffic as part of the protest against the cutoff date for Deferred Action for Childhood Arrivals (DACA) recipients to file for a renewal of their status. I lay out the evolution of the IYC's political principles and its development of undocumented, queer, and transgender youth leadership. I weave the story of the IYC with Johnathan's story of their life and activism as a queer and undocumented youth. The organization's antideportation activism, which started with joining the wave of "Undocumented, Unafraid" actions and training, propelled it toward abolitionist alternatives. These politics committed the IYC to work for the collective liberation of multiple and overlapping vulnerable and criminalized communities.

Second, I lay out the implications of the discussions initiated by Indigenous Pacific Island migrant youth at the Honolulu YES for migration justice. Indigenous Pacific Island youth, whose families migrated to Hawaiʻi from the Federated States of Micronesia (FSM), Republic of Marshall Islands (RMI), and the Republic of Palau (ROP), together commonly referred to as Micronesians, voiced their experience of the intense discrimination they face in Hawaiʻi, often in the form of criminalization.[9] Currents from decolonial and migration justice movements crossed in our Oceanic space. Pacific Islander and non-Indigenous migrant youth started to build power and presence in conversation with their Native Hawaiian peers. This type of multiethnic solidarity-building across socioeconomically divided groups offers an example of what Kanaka ʻŌiwi scholar Ty Kāwika Tengan conceptualizes as the intentional enactment of hoa or binding relations. Tengan deploys hoa, which takes the material form of braided cordage used to tie and secure, to capture Oceanic decolonial projects dependent on connections.[10]

The operation of settler laws and ideologies in the state of Hawaii, along with US imperialism in the Pacific, fuels the anti-immigrant, anti-Black, and anti-Indigenous backlash against the Micronesian community.[11] The backlash, which draws on racist discourses about immigrants and African Americans in the United States, erases the periodically renewable Compacts of Free Association (COFA) between FSM, RMI, and ROP and the United States. In exchange for the United States' exclusive territorial control for defense purposes over these nations, including over a million square miles of waters in the Pacific, nationals of these freely associated states are allowed to migrate visa-free for education, employment, and health care, the provision of which on their islands are grossly inadequate because of US policy failures. COFA citizens migrate to cope with the fallout of nuclear weapons testing (1946–58); ongoing military buildup in the form of US naval bases, ballistic missile defense structures, and test ranges; and the failure of the US to deliver on moving the countries toward self-sufficiency when it held these Pacific islands in trust after World War II.[12] The position of COFA citizens as Indigenous Pacific Island migrants to Hawai'i thus illuminates the relationship between Indigenous migration and land dispossession. While youth organizing by Khmer Girls in Action detailed in the previous chapter peeled away the benevolence of US refugee resettlement, Pacific Islander Indigenous migrant youth exposed the convergence of settler colonial rule in Hawai'i, the stranglehold of US military power across the Pacific, and the state-sponsored discrimination they faced on migration.

The YES trainers encouraged local youth to identify and address geographically specific concerns. The Native Hawaiian sovereignty movement exposes the public to the US occupation of Hawai'i. Social justice actors across multiple movements contest Hawai'i's image as a racial paradise. This awareness about settler colonialism in Hawai'i meant that local youth navigated a political terrain different from California's, leading to distinct reckonings. Place molds what immigrant youth learn to fight for and how they fight.[13] The generative nature of the IYC-NIYA training connects the two tasks of this chapter. I draw on my ethnography in Los Angeles, formal interviews with IYC youth leaders, and my immersion in struggles led by immigrants, Native Hawaiians, and Pacific Islanders as a settler ally living and working in Hawai'i. In Honolulu, I was a coorganizer of the YES and a supporter of the push for in-state tuition for undocumented students as a university faculty member and an active member of the Hawaii Coalition for Immigration Reform. As an adult, I was often not part of youth-led spaces in Honolulu, and I write as a person who observed the results of the extraordinary dedication of our youth leaders. I close the book with this chapter on Hawai'i and Los Angeles to underscore the expansive possibilities for freedom generated at the meeting point of youth-led radical migrant and decolonial Indigenous politics.

"Undocumented, Unafraid": The Formation of the Immigrant Youth Coalition

I begin with Johnathan and the formation of IYC in San Gabriel Valley (SGV), a majority Latinx and Asian suburb of LA County. Johnathan's story is, of course, uniquely theirs. At the same time, it illustrates the larger story of radical undocumented and queer youth organizing.[14] Johnathan and a handful of undocumented youth cofounded IYC in 2010. The organization began modestly with small meetings in coffee shops in Pasadena. During its first statewide retreat, the organization articulated an abolitionist vision, which it folds into its workshops on power analysis, racial-economic justice, direct action, and the prison industrial complex. The IYC allowed its members and summit participants to explore abolition beyond asking for decarceration. By 2011, IYC networked with NIYA to create an autonomous space where queer undocumented youth could define their own struggles. Johnathan became an organizer for NIYA. With NIYA, the IYC escalated their demands to stop deportations. They staged their first independent civil disobedience against deportation in 2011 at the Metropolitan Detention Center in downtown LA. Undocumented organizers blocked buses carrying people to be deported. Inside, their undocumented peers occupied the offices, demanding an end to programs allowing police and ICE collaborations.

Johnathan risked arrest countless times in direct actions, including declaring themselves undocumented in 2011 at a Border Patrol office in Mobile, Alabama, for which they and a fellow activist were detained at a Louisiana correctional center. In 2017, Johnathan was arrested during the "All of Us or None" Westwood blockade.

Collaboratively, the two organizations formalized a curriculum for peer-to-peer training by convening Youth Empower Summits across states to undertake militant actions to stop the criminalization and deportation of undocumented migrants on the one hand and, on the other, push for immigrant-friendly state legislation. Though IYC's relationship with NIYA dissolved by 2013, the IYC continued to organize in the Inland Empire, SGV, San Fernando Valley, Los Angeles, and the East Bay to "build capacity across California to address the issues that affect undocumented youth and

5.1. *Left*, the Immigrant Youth Coalition, along with Los Angeles's immigrant-led organizations, block Westwood with a sit-in and a massive rally during President Barack Obama's visit to the city on June 7, 2013, demanding that his administration stop deportations. *Right*, ɪʏᴄ cofounder Johnathan Perez is at the mic at the blockade. Photos courtesy of Sergio Jimenez.

focusing in areas where immigrants traditionally haven't been organized."[15] Over the years, ɪʏᴄ clarified its identity as "an undocumented and Trans* & Queer youth led organization" with the purpose of organizing "youth, families, and incarcerated people to end the criminalization of immigrants and people of color." It fought to stop jail, prison, and detention center expansion. It intentionally developed undocuqueer and undocuBlack leadership.[16] It mobilized hundreds of young persons in California and across the United States with its summits, inspiring at least a hundred to risk arrest during ɪʏᴄ-led direct actions.

Johnathan self-identifies as Latinx (Colombian) of African descent and queer every time they tell their story. They model movement-building storytelling, a skill the ɪʏᴄ fosters in undocumented youth. The way Johnathan tells their story puts a face and feelings to the analytical points they make during presentations. Their self-identification as queer announces their refusal to be disciplined into neoliberal citizenship's productive and reproductive demands to qualify for legal status someday. In short, they refuse to straighten up, to use Chávez's words.

When Johnathan was three, they and their family fled corrupt and dangerous conditions in Colombia. "I still remember crossing the border," they said. It was dark, and everyone was ducking and running. At some point, they got separated from their mother and siblings but were picked up and carried by someone rounding up the group. Johnathan fell asleep in the person's arms. When they woke up, they remembered "seeing the strangest thing! A basketball. Someone was bouncing a basketball." Their family made East LA their home, and Johnathan attended public schools that were predominantly Latinx. Once Johnathan started to work with the dissident Dream Team in Pasadena, they trained to organize with youth across Southern California as part of a non-profit-funded initiative. They enrolled at the East Los Angeles College in Monterey Park in SGV, where they started to form friendships with Asian immigrants, including newcomers who were struggling with documentation. The decision to organize in SGV came out of the realization that Latinx and Asian undocumented youth there had no resources or support. These interactions with Asian Americans shaped Johnathan's commitment to crossracial undocumented organizing when they cofounded IYC. The IYC's birth in SGV and the founding members' sensitization to the race-, ethnicity-, and class-based rifts and commonalities between Asian and Latinx youth reflects ethnic studies scholar Wendy Cheng's insights into SGV, where regional racial formations decenter hegemonic, white-centered racial alignments.[17]

Johnathan's growing determination to test the immigration enforcement system is rooted in their family history and the courage it took to be an openly queer teenager. In 1986, their family received their deportation order, which began the long legal battle for asylum. Johnathan links the tenuousness of their family's status to their attraction to the "Undocumented, Unafraid" movement because they learned that they were safer as an organizer who came out of the "shadows."[18] At the Honolulu YES, Johnathan described their dual process of "coming out" this way: "What really gave me the strength to come out of the shadows was coming out of a closet first. Because, you know . . . , it's hard, and you're afraid of losing friends. And similarly, with coming out of the shadows, it's like—you're afraid that people are going to tell the authorities and you're going to get deported." For Johnathan, joining the "Undocumented, Unafraid" movement helped them combine queer and undocumented politics.

Politicized in public schools through organizing against military recruitment, Johnathan quickly developed a critique of the immigrant rights movement's and the DREAM movement's priorities because of the challenges posed by poverty, lack of documentation, and coming out to their family as a queer person. As a freshman in high school, they were interested in attending college. However, their older brother warned them that a college education was out of their reach as an undocumented student. By the time Johnathan applied for college, California's 2001 AB 540 allowed undocumented students who had attended high school in the state to pay in-state tuition, but there was no financial aid. They had to drop out for several reasons. They came out as queer to their family. They had to move out and rent their own place. They could no longer afford to pay tuition. Johnathan also wryly described themselves as not succeeding in school, directly intervening in the achievement-oriented DREAMer narrative. All these developments impacted their mental health, a subject not discussed outside of politicized undocumented youth circles. They started questioning the single-issue agenda for college access when another youth organizer asked them why they were fighting so hard to access higher education when students like them could not afford it. From that point onward, Johnathan started to frame the equity issues confronting undocumented youth broadly, beyond access to a college education. They embraced the intersecting issues arising from poverty, homophobia, transphobia, and the marginalization of youth of color within K-12 and higher education.

The series of civil disobedience actions led by queer youth in the summer of 2010 marked a significant political moment for Johnathan. Seeing unapologetic queer youth like Mohammad Abdollahi, Tania Unzueta, and Yahaira Carrillo in the forefront of the sit-in at Senator John McCain's office in Tucson, Arizona, in May 2010 gave them the courage to take public action as a queer undocumented youth. This sit-in followed on the heels of Chicago's Immigrant Youth Justice League's (IYJL's) first "Coming Out of the Shadows" event in March with the rallying cry of "Undocumented, Unafraid." Chávez notes the significance of these moments in articulating a new subjectivity and politics: "undocuqueer."[19]

Johnathan's resolve that queer, trans, Black, Indigenous, people of color (QTBIPOC) and gender nonconforming youth lead their own movement was further strengthened from feeling dismissed by the straight older leadership of cisgender men and women when they traveled to Arizona to protest SB 1070. Heterosexism and cisgender privilege are rampant in the immigrant rights movement. On returning to LA, Johnathan and other queer undocumented youth, contributed to queer and feminist interventions in Tod@s's organizing and civil disobedience against SB1070 (see chapter 2). Simultaneously, they supported the hunger strikers pushing for the DREAM Act at Senator Dianne Feinstein's office. They and other undocumented youth like Neidi Dominguez Zamorano exhorted documented Tod@s members to support the hunger strike and respect the young people's organizing against the military instead of distancing Tod@s from the DREAM Act because of its military service provision. For Johnathan, inhabiting their identity as a queer and undocumented youth activist to articulate a migration justice agenda from that experience "felt like home."[20] Claiming radical politics arising from the coalitional space of queer migration, Johnathan coauthored a widely circulated September 21, 2010, *Truthout* article with Neidi Dominguez Zamorano (who would go on to play a vital role in the campaign for DACA), Nancy Meza, and Jorge Guitierrez.[21] In that manifesto, as I like to characterize it, they declared that undocumented youth needed to lead their own movement and give voice to their own experiences without being told how to get their message across by nonprofits aligned with Washington, DC, and led by older, straight, cisgender, US citizen advocates.[22] In his study of the emergence of DREAMers as powerful political actors, public policy scholar Walter Nicholls lays out the challenge undocumented youth mounted to the control exerted by large foundation-funded coalitions like Reform Immigration for America and United We Dream on the priorities of the immigrant rights movement.[23]

Furthermore, the authors of the *Truthout* article asserted the leadership of radical, mainly queer migrant youth, veering away from normative demands associated with DREAMers. To understand the course that the youth movement was taking, the writers pointed out, "We must look to the women and men in the DREAM movement, undocumented queer and transgender young activists with emerging ideologies that challenge the capitalist, heterosexual and misogynistic systems here in the United States."[24] These activists risked deportation because they were no longer willing to put up with the fear and exploitation they faced due to their age, gender, and sexuality. They invoked Ella Baker and her foresight in encouraging young people to organize autonomously outside of the control of what Baker's biographer, Barbara Ransby, calls the "old guard" leadership of the Southern Christian Leadership Conference.[25] The authors declared that "the DREAM movement is a genuine large-scale movement; we have taken from what happened in the '60s, learned from it, fine-tuned it to our current context and relentlessly moved forward."[26] They ended the op-ed with Gloria Anzaldúa's exhortation in her foreword to the second edition of *This Bridge Called My Back* to travelers, inspiring them to build their own bridges because there are none. The authors, thus, constructed a radical lesbian, Black, Chicana, Native American, and Third World feminist genealogy of struggle. In the vein of radical traditions of the Black freedom movement and multiracial intersectional feminism, they connected their struggles as undocumented youth to those against US imperialism in Europe, Oceania, Asia, and Africa.

Undocuqueer Leadership and Abolitionist Migration Justice

While initially connected with the DREAM Act activism, the IYC forged its own path, following the principles laid out in the 2010 manifesto. From that point onward, undocuqueer youth have dynamically shaped the IYC's ideology, analysis, empowerment, leadership pedagogy, actions, and campaigns to define an inclusive migration justice agenda. By 2014, the IYC consciously grounded its work in queer, transgender, and undocuBlack politics. Its all-out efforts to address the realities of low-income communities under assault from racist policing, immigration enforcement, and gentrification led it to cast migration justice within an abolitionist frame.

The IYC built its political framework around four key elements. The organization made room for capacious storytelling that allowed undocumented youth to narrate their lives through the prism of queerness, gender nonconformity, impoverishment, and criminalization. Second, the IYC members taught each other to connect their local conditions to those that drove their migration. Third, the seeds of abolitionist politics lay in the IYC's refusal to abandon criminalized people. Along with deportation defense, they educated themselves about the various arms of enforcement, their expansion, and their collaborations with corporations to target them for civil disobedience. The IYC's trainings uniformly built participants' capacity to work through their fears and take direct action. Lastly, the IYC engaged with California's legislative process to successfully push for policies that create some level of security for undocumented people. This savvy engagement pressed state legislators to shift public funds away from punishment toward health care, housing, food security, and quality education. As demonstrated by the IYC's people's budget exercise I describe in chapter 1, redirecting public spending priorities is a goal of abolition.

The IYC was one of the few organizations in LA that consciously defined itself as immigrant and queer.[27] There, youth felt supported to name and connect the violence of poverty, police brutality, heterosexism, and transphobia they faced every day to envision change. This approach was urgent because, as Nicholls shows, complex storytelling as part of movement building started to pose a problem for DREAMers who felt that intersectionality did not lend itself to a clear message palatable to the general public.[28] Explaining how the sole focus on legalization ignored the lived experiences of undocumented youth and their families, former IYC organizer Marcela, who was radicalized in Chicago's IYJL and took part in the Westwood direct action in 2017, said: "[We know] the fact that in a lot of low-income communities, the police was an issue. Mental health clinics were being closed. Schools have been defunded. So, we are getting attacked . . . because of being low-income and people of color. But, within the immigration movement our intersectionalities were not being brought up. . . . Actually, we are facing so much abuse by the state, by institutions *outside of and within our status.* So, that's when we started having those conversations that there was so much more need than papers."[29] The IYC's leadership training linked the deprivations they experienced to neoliberal cutbacks in public education, health, and social service and the concurrent shift to policing and punishment. Through activities like "Care Not Cages" (chapter 1), the organizers started to articulate what their world would look like with a robust investment of tax dollars in education, health, and housing. The peer-to-peer storytelling then got polished into compact and powerful public narratives.

This type of storytelling propelled youth to explore the root causes of migration. What brought their families to the United States beyond the oft-repeated myth of the hope for a better life? Analyzing the root causes throws into relief the injustice of the punishing domestic policies, which, along with restrictive immigration laws and militarized border enforcement, aim to deter migration. The IYC's political education, similar to Families for Freedom and Khmer Girls in Action, pinpointed US economic policies and overt and covert military actions that displaced people like themselves. They recognized that these policies have been particularly devastating for Indigenous people, who have been uprooted from their ancestral lands in Latin America and the Pacific.[30] Claudia, an organizer who was building the IYC's new LA chapter when I met her in 2016, recounted her dawning awareness as an IYC teenager of the role of capitalism and imperialism. Expressing her understanding of the drivers of migration, she said:

> I think something that woke me up is when we think about the way that forced migration was created because of the United States. Born into our countries and being displaced whether it was economically, politically, and very violently from parts of Central America, and other countries. Well, what I know, is more about Latin America, to be honest, and just seeing the history of imperialism in our countries and the reasons why we leave. *Nobody wants to leave their home* and their culture and their families and be broken apart. But it's a decision that is forced on us because we can no longer live there; because our resources and money are taken away by the United States. And it creates that migration.[31]

Given her own political growth, she was generating young-adult-friendly materials on the roots of displacement to contextualize deportation in US domestic and foreign policies. Acutely aware that this type of analysis had no place in the immigrant rights policy discussions, including the DREAM Act, the IYC fostered internationalism, following the radical liberation traditions their members admired.

Education about crimmigration—the collaboration between the US criminal legal system and the civil immigration administrative system—was intrinsic to the IYC's antideportation work. This education tapped into their members' familiarity with the pervasive punitive policies and their carceral impacts on youth and adults, especially those who are Black, of color, gender nonconforming, transgender, and queer. Its position, "All of Us or None," evolved from its commitment to the freedom of all those criminalized and caged. Members recognized the dearth of resources for migrants with criminal records. Marcela recalled her own family's struggles to find someone to defend her uncle, who was put into deportation proceedings for having been criminalized as a young adult. This experience sensitized her to the acute need for community-based responses to the intersection between immigration and criminal law. As an organizer who was building the Free the People Network, a deportation defense project across six California IYC chapters, Marcela noted the particular vulnerabilities of low-income, unhoused, queer, and Black youth and youth of color who frequently come in contact with police. Many are thrown in jail for survival activities. With undocuqueer and Black voices in the foreground, the IYC was able to break the silence around these stigmatized experiences. Using their social media savvy, they stepped into the advocacy gap left by organizations that consider it "too hard" to fight for detainees with criminal records.[32] The IYC's deportation defense project evolved into immigration court accompaniment during the hardline Donald Trump administration, which made it nearly impossible to release people from ICE custody by exerting public pressure. Johnathan recalled the presence of IYC members and their allies in LA County–based Familia Trans Queer Liberation Movement during the hearings with detained migrants—many of them LGBTQ+ asylum seekers. Such actions led to the release of around forty persons in deportation proceedings. One of them was asylum seeker Valeria De La Luz Ramos, a transgender woman who was charged with involuntary manslaughter in 2015 and put into deportation proceedings in 2017 after serving two years in the Orange County men's jail.[33]

Direct action that confronts local police and ICE agents through non-violent protest was a signature IYC movement tactic, which built on the lessons the founders learned when they came out as "Undocumented, Unafraid." While civil disobedience made DREAMers nationally visible as undocumented youth taking big risks, IYC's direct actions were not tied to a piece of federal legislation. Instead, their actions exposed the connective tissues of the various organs of enforcement. This focus allowed the IYC to remain relevant once the DREAM Act failed and to escalate their demands to end deportation and dismantle the entire punishment industry.

In escalating their protest in the post–DREAM Act environment, IYC built California-wide capacity to sustain civil disobedience with trainings and militant public actions. Explaining the "why" of civil disobedience once the DREAM Act failed, Johnathan, who has risked arrest at many direct actions, clarified that it activated a movement to politicize and empower youth who did not have stellar academic records or dreams for college. They stressed how "ordinary" young people engaging in civil disobedience discovered "that they're worth it, you know, worth it, that they can do acts of courage. Because we weren't valedictorians. We weren't anything."[34] The political grit of such undocumented young people established their credibility. Slowly, well-resourced immigrant rights groups started to acknowledge the IYC's work.

Risking arrest by taking over an intersection or blockading an ICE detention center amid heavy police presence required IYC trainers to teach and enact something counterintuitive—to collectively confront the outsized presence of police and ICE in their lives to gain safety. The more visible they were to police and ICE as a community of activists, the safer they felt because "ICE is a greater threat when you accidentally come into contact with them."[35] Their militancy took shape in the affective field of fear, support, mutual care, and love.

In training undocumented participants to undertake nonviolent direct action, the most difficult level of coming out of the shadows, IYC leaders talked openly about their lifelong fears of ICE and police. Every action brought up enforcement-related fears, even for seasoned activists. The queer leadership in IYC permitted discussions of the fears and the trauma these confrontations can trigger in queer, gender nonconforming, and transgender Black and migrant youth of color. Within IYC, a culture of care validated these feelings and enabled activists to speak about their fears instead of hiding or dismissing them. The peer support, care, and love from

5.2. Immigrant Youth Coalition members gather for a Coming Out of the Shadows event at Mariachi Plaza in Boyle Heights on March 25, 2016. The event emphasized the voices of those directly impacted and the stories told by undocutrans, undocuqueer, and undocumented Black, Asian, and Pacific Islander migrants. Courtesy of Immigrant Youth Coalition.

adults in their community also empowered the activists to risk public action for change. Claudia described the battle between fear and collective love when risking arrest: "I have always been in that space of growing up in fear, you know, so I was really scared [when I decided to participate in direct action]. But at the same time, I wanted to get rid of that fear that we, that I, carried growing up. And it was very powerful for me and very eye-opening. Because when I was doing the action, a lot of community members were hugging me and saying 'thank you.'"[36]

The outpouring of community support, being seen and heard, and building the collective will to stop the persecution of immigrants and youth sustained such difficult activism. It also attuned the activists to the broader issues of mass incarceration impacting Black and other minoritized communities of color, steering them toward the utopian abolitionist cry: All of us or none.

Lastly, the IYC had a very pragmatic bent. They worked in creative coalition with progressive and liberal advocates for state-level legislative change across the United States. To stop copycat SB 1070 bills proliferating in anti-immigrant states, which were also restricting access to housing, employment, and education for undocumented migrants, IYC-NIYA visited states like Arizona, Georgia, and Alabama to train and cobuild with youth to protest these bills. At the same time, the organizers emphasized that there was little cause for complacency in immigrant-friendly states like California.

The IYC worked intentionally to pressure California legislators to undo the damage of the state's prison industrial complex. It also pushed for access to health care for low-income communities, regardless of their immigration status. The 2013 California TRUST Act (AB 4) to get ICE out of jails was one of IYC's major victories. To press for the bill's passage, the IYC and its allies organized caravans of people in deportation proceedings to travel to Sacramento to tell their stories. Under the act, county jails could no longer hold immigrants with low-level misdemeanors and nonviolent offenses. However, those with felony charges and convictions and high-level misdemeanors committed in the last five years could still be turned over to ICE, confirming the power of crimmigration.[37] At the 2017 IYC YES I attended, the organization distributed literature on the avenues for immigrants to avail of postconviction relief provided under California law and to petition for resentencing if those in prison or on parole had marijuana convictions (see chapter 1). Another area of legislative action for IYC was access to physical and mental health care for undocumented queer and transgender youth, transgender detainees, and asylum seekers. These ambitious demands, Johnathan noted, were initially dismissed by many immigrant advocates as asking for "too much."[38] Despite this pessimism, the IYC has been vindicated with California steadily passing laws starting in 2016 to extend state-funded health care to undocumented children, youth, and the elderly living in poverty.[39]

Undocuqueer leadership from the founding moments of the IYC gave members and YES participants the foresight to channel their power to rein in carcerality and push for broader issues to ease the crisis which undocumented youth, their families, and communities face every day. Its abolitionist turn strategically combined unapologetic direct action with more conventional political action, resulting in concrete measures to divert taxpayer money from punishment toward life-affirming social goods. The key elements I detail above were already in place by 2012, when IYC, in collaboration with NIYA, brought the two-pronged strategy of militancy and state legislative change to Honolulu.

Oceanic Currents: Criminalization and US Insular Control

Five IYC-NIYA trainers, Johnathan, Isabel, Maria, Andrea, and Eric, flew to Honolulu in February 2012 for a week-long series of trainings, public presentations, and meetings with the Hawaii Coalition for Immigration Reform, local immigration lawyers, and state legislators. The IYC's expansive migration justice framework, developed through a queer lens, informed the training and public engagements. Localized definitions of struggles and empowerment started to take shape as ideologies and strategies circulated across the 2,500 miles of ocean that separated the continental United States from Hawai'i. Indeed, the YES trainers consciously designed the summit to inspire youth participants to identify place-specific values and issues and then leverage the power of their voices to address them.

In my analysis of these Oceanic currents, I underline the force of settler laws that govern crime and immigration to subjugate and criminalize dispossessed Micronesian migrants living in Hawai'i, an occupied space. They, with their Indigenous hosts, Native Hawaiians, are disproportionately incarcerated. Criminalization and incarceration attempt to destroy Indigenous Pacific Islanders' relations to land, ocean, and communities.[40] Hawai'i's undocumented non–Pacific Islander youth and their families are subjected to the same US and state laws and threatened with deportation. The summit provided a space to discuss the impacts of these legal regimes on non–Pacific Islander youth who feared deportation and Micronesian youth who suffered multiple forms of discrimination, including anti-immigrant cultural racism in schools. The racism feeds the widespread perception that Micronesian youth and their communities are crime-prone. Under the 1996 federal immigration laws, COFA citizens, too, risked deportation as "criminal aliens" (see chapter 1).

The summit gave rise to two organizing directions, one that spun off in an independent community-based intergenerational decolonial project of cultural revitalization for Micronesian youth, who, in turn, supported undocumented youth. The other effort centered at the university, focused on winning in-state tuition for undocumented college-bound students within the broader framework of education equity. This campaign stemmed directly from the YES participants' increasing awareness of the barriers Micronesian and other Pacific Islander students faced within the education system in Hawai'i.

While Hawai'i has the image of a state shaped by immigration and is held up as a model for harmony among ethnic groups, the settler colonial state disproportionately imprisons Native Hawaiian and Pacific Islander youth in the juvenile detention system.[41] Native Hawaiians have the highest rates of incarceration. Micronesian, Latinx, and Filipinx youth face harsh disciplinary measures in school, consequent suspension, and incarceration at high rates. The day-long youth empowerment training for high school and college students from Oʻahu, Maui, and Hawaiʻi Island encouraged the participants to tackle the public aversion to confronting anti-immigrant racism in Hawaiʻi and its role in criminalizing immigration across the islands. In 2012, crimmigration was still a new concept. Youth-led conversations about carcerality were also rare before the 2014 police killing of Michael Brown in Ferguson, Missouri. The YES discussions cut through what ethnic studies scholar Roderick Labrador calls "racial vog," a metaphor that references volcanic smog, which "blankets Hawaiʻi society, sometimes suffocating its residents, but it is mostly tolerated as a naturalized part of the ecological and sociopolitical order."[42] Harmful perceptions of newcomer immigrants, including Micronesians, have permeated Native Hawaiian communities.

Starting in 2009, the state of Hawaiʻi targeted the Micronesian community as invasive and too dependent on public assistance, and these discourses became popular. To intervene in settler state and media-circulated oppressions directed toward Micronesians, Native Hawaiian and Micronesian leaders and scholars have undertaken multiple projects to connect and explore their heritage and issues together in the spirit of hoa (binding relations). They include Ka Holo Waʻa, which introduces students to Native Hawaiian and Micronesian canoe building and voyaging traditions, annual Oceanic Connections conferences at the university, and multiple programs run by community-based organizations such as Kōkua Kalihi Valley and We Are Oceania.[43]

The involvement of non-Hawaiian Pacific Islander high school and college youth in several YES events introduced the intersection of racist and anti-immigrant policies with the United States' colonial and military subjugation of large swaths of the Pacific. Pacific Islander youth testified to the injustice they faced at school, in the criminal legal system, and in other institutions on migrating to Hawaiʻi, where their dispossessed families had relocated. These discussions were attentive to the devastating effects of US occupation on Native Hawaiians and the resilience of the Hawaiian Nation. Though Native Hawaiian students did not attend the one-day YES training, they were part of the large public events, classroom visits, and debates that followed over an in-state tuition policy for undocumented students.

The YES session on crimmigration revealed enforcement policies and practices that knit together local law enforcement, correctional control, and immigration enforcement. It also explained why the IYC targeted detention centers, ICE offices, prison corporations, and the border patrol for their civil disobedience in a radical departure from the cap-and-gown DREAMer direct action aimed at legislators. The trainers broke down why encounters with the police had become so risky for migrants by contextualizing them in racial profiling, and programs like 287(g) and Secure Communities (S-Comm) in authorizing local police to enforce federal immigration law (see chapter 1).

By 2012, the Obama administration favored S-Comm, a county-by-county agreement with the Department of Homeland Security, as an efficient way to deport non-US citizens who came in contact with police officers. Unlike the 287(g) program that entailed expensive officer training, S-Comm depended on a cheaper way. The program allowed biometric data sharing across government agencies, including ICE, at police precincts to identify if the arrested person had immigration violations. Even if the person was not charged with a crime, they could be held for forty-eight hours for an ICE pickup. Where Johnathan grew up, petty theft or driving without a license was a survival activity. Those who engaged in them could be easily arrested because of racially biased policing in poor communities. To connect these policing practices to the monetization of detention by private prison corporations, which aggressively lobbied anti-immigrant politicians, the trainers screened a short video, "Immigrants for Sale." It presented these otherwise obscured corporate interests through infographics to unearth the generation of private profit through policies like S-Comm, which guaranteed a steady flow of criminalized immigrants into the deportation factory. While Hawaiʻi did not have private detention centers, the profit model of private corporations like Corrections Corporation of America (CCA) was familiar to those YES youth participants who were involved in local activism exposing the shipment and abuse of Native Hawaiian prisoners to CCA-run prisons in the continental United States because of oversentencing and overcrowding of local prisons.[44] Native Hawaiian activist Healani Sonoda calls this practice deportation, evidencing US colonial legal control over Native lands and people at the expense of Native Hawaiian sovereignty.[45]

S-Comm was activated in Oʻahu, Maui, and Hawaiʻi Island in 2010, resulting in a jump in deportations.[46] Those of us working locally on immigration issues were not able to immediately identify the cause of the uptick and local police involvement because there was no public debate about the program's activation by the state attorney general's office. We initially (and mistakenly) wondered whether the insular nature of Hawai'i meant that the deportations were part of the hundred-mile enforcement range of the Customs and Border Protection. On the ground, several YES participants were only too aware of the effects of S-Comm—arrests of loved ones, their disappearances into local jails, their unexplained detentions even when no charges were pressed, and, then, their removal to the federal detention center on O'ahu. In fact, we were connected to the neighbor island youth participants because we had been documenting with community assistance the encounters with police that led to detainers and detention.[47] The YES session helped participating youth make sense of the driving-under-the-influence checkpoints set up by police, immigration detentions after knock-and-talks, and ICE workplace raids with police cooperation. The workings of crimmigration resonated deeply with youth who lived in heavily policed neighborhoods like Kalihi (O'ahu), Kailua-Kona (Hawai'i Island), and Honokowai (Maui). As they listened to the youth, the trainers emphasized the importance of publicly holding police and immigration enforcement accountable for targeting immigrants and, in the process, dispel the notion that Hawai'i was immigrant-friendly.

COFA citizens—who have a unique immigration status under Compacts of Free Association and can travel to the United States visa-free and reside there indefinitely—face a heightened risk of deportation under the 1996 Illegal Immigration Reform and Immigrant Responsibility Act (IIRAIRA) and Antiterrorism and Effective Death Penalty Act. These two laws reclassified a slew of offenses as aggravated felonies to remove those who are charged or convicted of such crimes. Peculiarly, COFA citizens do not have the status of legal permanent residents (LPRS) or any of the immigration benefits of permanent residency. Yet, they are impacted by the same deportation regime as LPRS with criminal charges or convictions. This aspect of the legislative change in their treatment as immigrants has not received much attention as compared to the loss of Medicaid. Hawai'i's Micronesian community struggled for years to restore COFA citizens' access to Medicaid eliminated by the 1996 federal welfare law and IIRAIRA. To add to this, in 2009, the Republican governor moved them from the state-funded Medicaid program to one with minimal access to health care. As migrants who relocate to Hawai'i to access medical care for the life-threatening and chronic diseases resulting from nuclear testing and drastic changes in nutrition caused by colonialism, this fight was crucial.[48] Micronesian youth uniquely contributed to the battle to reinstate Medicaid. They played in volleyball and basketball tournaments to raise money for litigation, as longtime community organizer and youth mentor Innocenta Sound-Kikku (Chuukese) remembers in reflecting on the many facets of youth empowerment, in step with IYC's fierce advocacy for health care.[49]

At the same time, the risks of deportation to the very places COFA citizens were forced to leave are consequential for this heavily criminalized community.[50] In 2012 (when YES came to Hawai'i), ICE deported seventy-one citizens of FSM, nineteen citizens of RMI, and seventeen citizens of the ROP.[51] Micronesians living in Hawai'i had a lower age of arrest compared to other groups in 2010.[52] Research shows that these early contacts set up such individuals for repeated encounters with the criminal legal system.[53] More recent criminal legal data, which do not disaggregate Native Hawaiians and Pacific Islanders, confirm the trend of racially biased overpolicing and use of force. Settler laws are writ large on the criminalization of poverty and the lack of resources for meaningful diversion programs for Native Hawaiians and Pacific Islanders, whose presence in prisons has swelled since the late 1990s. This aggregated group, which represents 25 percent of Hawai'i's population, experienced arrests at a rate of 38.1 percent. Recent data analysis has shown that 59 percent of Asian/Pacific Islanders bear the brunt of the Honolulu Police Department's use of deadly force, and, not surprisingly, police argued that the (dis)proportion reflects arrests of Native Hawaiians and Pacific Islanders.[54] While YES attendees did not have much empirical data on disproportionate policing of non-Hawaiian Pacific Islanders, our Micronesian youth participants had experienced or witnessed such criminalization.

Readers may wonder how the awareness of these policies and their dreadful consequences could be empowering, especially for youth. To counteract the fear that haunted many of our participants, the trainers gave examples at every step of how they worked through their fears of police and ICE by engaging in civil disobedience in various contexts to confront the legislated injustices that they, their families, and communities faced. Isabel, who was undocumented, talked about walking into Senator Harry Reid's office in Washington, DC, with four others in 2010 to demand the passage of the DREAM Act. When they refused to leave after three warnings, the DC police arrested and booked them. However, they were not turned over to ICE. Maria, who grew up in San Bernardino, where a 287(g) agreement between local police and ICE was in force, said she was moved to participate in a civil disobedience action led by undocumented youth at the spur of the moment. She was fearful; the very recent deportation of her uncle after an encounter with local police was on her mind. With a catch in her voice, Maria said, "I feel that the more you are open about it [immigration status], it becomes harder for you to become targeted for ICE. So that's why I decided to take action [a few weeks before she traveled to Honolulu]. . . . It was really a life changing experience."[55] When explaining S-Comm, Johnathan revealed that ICE placed a hold on them in November 2011 because of the biometric data sharing authorized by the program. The detainer was triggered after they and another undocumented activist walked into a Border Patrol office in Mobile, Alabama, in an act of civil disobedience. They were detained at the South Louisiana Correctional Center and were released within a few days as the DreamACTivist.org campaign to free them and their comrade gathered steam. All five trainers reminded us they were in Honolulu to empower youth to take that first and most difficult step of coming out as undocumented.[56]

The trainers provided peer-to-peer support at the media training workshop to create a safe space for undocumented youth to come out and rehearse their stories with youth allies. Adults were not invited to the session; we saw a short practice video based on the workshop. The training emphasized that in creating a public narrative, the narrator needed to communicate the "why" of an action to their peers. Only then could they use it to build political will among advocates and policymakers. One person, who told his story on camera, was a junior at a Maui high school. Like numerous young people, some of whose stories I have shared in the book, he was growing up without a parent and feared losing the other parent to deportation. His father was deported in 2009 when his employer reported his undocumented status to ICE. The agents had come to their home looking for his father and placed the rest of the family in removal proceedings, which his mother was fighting with the help of a lawyer. The family, headed by his mother, was struggling to survive. His eighteen-year-old older sibling was working full-time to support the family. They lived with the constant dread of deportation: Would he see his mother when he returned home from school? What if he or his siblings were stopped by police and deported? These anxieties were always present as this young person tried to keep up with schoolwork and graduate. On graduation, he wanted to attend a technical school to become an automotive mechanic. But when the school's counselor visited his school to recruit, he noticed a question about status at the bottom of the form. This stopped him in his tracks. A young man from Tonga, who moved with his family to Hawai'i in the early 1990s, talked about aging out before his family's petition for this permanent residency was processed. The youth participants featured in the video filmed at the summit practiced these narratives to build power and learn to use storytelling in antideportation campaigns.

The video broke out of the "Undocumented, Unafraid" messaging mold by featuring two legally present Micronesian youth, Gina Ifenuk, who proudly identified as being from the island of Chuuk, and Max, who asserted the power of youth organizing while noting with a trace of irony that he was from a "micro island of the Pacific." The decision to feature Gina and Max reflected the trainers' sensitivity to place and the wide-ranging experiences of migration. One-third of the YES participants identified as non-Hawaiian Pacific Islanders, the majority listing FSM. The NIYA training manual emphasized collective values over issues because "values are experienced emotionally, people can access the moral resources—the courage, hope, and solidarity that it takes to risk learning new things and explore new ways of doing things."[57] This NIYA philosophy, put into practice by the trainers, allowed diverse groups of political actors, such as undocumented youth and youth with undocumented family members to work with Micronesian youth, who were not undocumented, but also experienced "othering," silencing, and criminalization. Paralleling sociologist Katherine Irwin and Asian American studies scholar Karen Umemoto's observation in their ethnography of Native Hawaiian, Samoan, and other Pacific Islander teenagers in Oʻahu's public schools, the YES youth participants understood that damaging anti-immigrant US continental discourses crossed over to Hawaiʻi, tainting Indigenous and immigrant groups who were perceived as abusing public assistance and as threats to public order.[58]

The last event of the week-long summit was dedicated to bringing local youth together to seed an organization that reflected their values and needs. During this time, Micronesian youth testified to the disempowerment they faced at school and in their neighborhoods. They felt the constant suspicion of schoolmates, teachers, and neighbors. Decrying the treatment of the youth she mentors, Innocenta said, "Everywhere they go, they're being targeted. Everything they do is being scrutinized by those that are supposedly their mentors or their protectors," impacting their mental health.[59] They were seen as troublemakers and written off by their teachers as underachievers.[60] Their culture was regularly demeaned in the media and through racist jokes, some calling for extermination.[61] State-produced discourses of COFA citizens' dependency on public assistance and cultural deficit fomented the anti-immigrant narratives, which gained credence under a Republican governor and continued unchecked under Democratic leadership. Editorials, reports, and COFA citizens' own narratives about the imperial drivers of their dislocation and health needs arising from nuclear testing did little to shift public perception.

At the meeting, Micronesian youth participants expressed their outrage at a recent statement made by the deputy city prosecutor in the trial of a twenty-seven-year-old Chuukese man. The prosecutor asked the judge to impose the maximum sentence for manslaughter to *"send a message to the Micronesian community, mainly males who take it upon themselves the idea that they can just drink all they want and not be responsible for what happens after that."*[62] As critical race theorist Charles Lawrence III observes in his analysis of the message, the public intelligibility of the prosecutor's exhortation testifies to collective and institutionalized bias.[63] Remarkably, the youth did not distance themselves from the Chuukese man on trial. Instead, they said they found the discrimination operating in the courtroom intolerable. They experienced a version of such criminalization in school. Recent data and research bear out the alienation that Micronesian public school students reported in 2012: Native Hawaiian and Pacific Islander students are suspended at a rate of 47 percent in school and 51.3 percent out of school, and a staggering 56.2 percent were referred to law enforcement.[64] These punishments have resulted in 43 percent of Micronesian high school students dropping out before graduation, leading to adverse economic outcomes.[65] The stories and data lay bare the dominance of settler laws with their settler modalities of punishing, removing, and caging Native peoples.

The organization seeded from these discussions articulated an Oceanic notion of migration justice rising from a space where Native Hawaiian, other Indigenous Pacific Islander, and immigrant issues converged. The stories shared by Micronesian youth led to a thoughtful discussion among the participants about the organization's name. During the brainstorming, the trainers supported them to be authentic. They landed on a long name, Hawaiʻi Alliance of Local Immigrant Voices and Empowerment (HĀ)LIVE. With the use of hā (breath, exhalation), the youth want to recognize their host, ʻāina (land and bodies of water) and Kanaka Maoli. They honored the collectivity signified by the shared space created by the life-giving force of breath. "Voices" in the plural and "empowerment" emerged as touchstones that bound together youth with different histories of migration.

Local organizing postsummit took two directions. Each direction required visioning a migration justice agenda that meaningfully incorporated the issues raised by Micronesian youth. One direction steered the community-based (HĀ)LIVE members to link the issues Micronesian youth faced to local immigrant rights activism and develop a supportive space for those who were undocumented. The other coalesced at the University of Hawai'i at Mānoa (UHM) to push for in-state tuition for undocumented students, first aimed at the state legislature and then, when the bills failed, at the University of Hawai'i (UH) Board of Regents (BOR). Both efforts required intentional alliance-building with Micronesian youth because their needs for cultural revitalization and their unique legal status was not easily translatable into straight forward "Undocumented, Unafraid" narratives and actions.

Within two weeks of the summit, (HĀ)LIVE youth came out in full support of a young Tongan telling his story of falling out of status as part of the national Coming Out of the Shadows week to a large accountability assembly in Honolulu organized by the local chapter of Faith Action for Community Equity. The following week, (HĀ)LIVE members gathered at the state Capitol rotunda to build momentum around two in-state tuition bills that had been introduced in the wake of the IYC-NIYA leaders meeting and sharing their stories with key state legislators. One of my favorite posters at that action announced, "Immigrant Youth Voices Matter." In the summer of 2012, with the announcement of DACA, several (HĀ)LIVE members joined outreach efforts to spread the word about DACA and connect youth (among them the YES participant from Maui) to resources to request deferred removal action and work authorization.

In a related development, YES youth and adult participants from community-based Micronesian organizations started to plan a Micronesian Youth Leadership Conference (MYLC) to answer their own prompt: share a dream. With Innocenta at the helm, the planners defined youth leadership as grounded in cultural revitalization and the intergenerational transmission of knowledge and traditions of leadership through the lens of the rich diversity of islands and nations, reduced to the colonial shorthand, "Micronesia." To prepare for the conference, Innocenta guided the youth to practice a Chuukese Um protocol to honor and invite the support of community elders. The protocol framed intergenerational cultural revitalization as an antidote to settler carceral logics, which alienate youth from their roots, relational practices, ancestors, and elders.[66] She also reminded me that unlike US definitions, in Micronesia, "youth" included people in their forties. In keeping with Micronesian traditions, youth organizing, broadly defined, necessarily involves elders because, as Innocenta put it, elders help the younger generation stay on course. Elaborating on this, she said, "Our spirituality is connected to the land, to the ocean, and to each other. And if

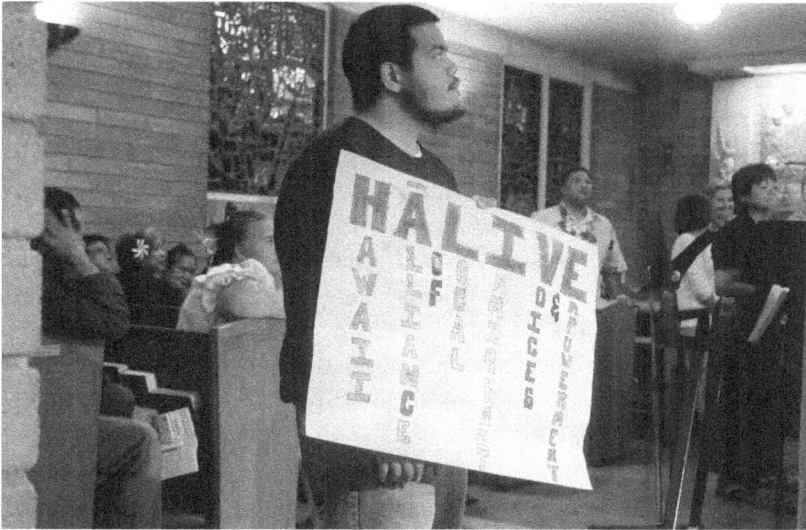

5.3. A Micronesian youth and cofounder of (HĀ)LIVE shows support as a Tongan youth, also a cofounder, tells his immigration story for the first time at a Faith Action for Community Equity Accountability Assembly in Honolulu on March 12, 2012, following the IYC-NIYA Youth Empowerment Summit. Photo credit: Angela Haeusler.

the youth lose that wisdom of connection, then they lose the core identity of who they are and their purpose—why do they even have to mobilize for themselves?"[67] As an outsider who attended the initial planning meetings for the MYLC at Stevenson Intermediate School, I had to make a real effort to broaden my notion of what counted as migration justice.

Since 2015, Innocenta has acted as a "cultural navigator," recruiting young adult Micronesians and involving the youth of Pacific Voices in the working-class neighborhood of Kalihi for *Masters of the Currents*, the first play with young Micronesian actors taking center stage to tell their own stories across Hawai'i and on the US continent.[68] The play emerged from workshops with Kalihi's Micronesian youth and story circles with Micronesian elders. The title of the play is based on an observation of an elder, Tamana (Papa) Poli (Paul) Otoko, quoted often by Innocenta: "We used to be masters of the currents but today we are slaves to the currencies of the United States." The play reclaims the celestial wayfinding traditions, which were revived by Papa Mau Piailug of Satawal (FSM), to give voice to the ways in which young Micronesians navigate the stormy conditions they face in Hawai'i. The youth's rendition of their migration to Hawai'i, the daily toll of harassment, which made them ashamed of their culture and language, and the elder-supported awareness of their navigational prowess as well as pride in the immense diversity of their cultures have nurtured an empowering Oceanic conceptualization of their identity. They enacted Hau'ofa's reconceptualization of Oceania as a vast and connected space where myriad everyday social practices of interdependence, not dependence, thrive.[69] Claiming public space through performance is one way to counteract the Micronesian youth's hopelessness with their futurity.[70] In one scene in the play, the young actors and elders point to the sky in wonder against a projection of a shimmering ocean and a canoe traversing it. Innocenta, who acted in that scene, mused that along with referencing the celestial wayfinding, the actors could be interpreted as pointing to a promising future guided by the power of ancestral knowledge.[71] Popularizing Papa Mau's role in introducing Native Hawaiians to celestial navigation in voyaging has encouraged other Pacific Islander and Native Hawaiian youth to honor their kinship with Micronesians and, in the words of Innocenta, "stand up for their cousins."[72]

The second direction, more recognizable as migration justice, took the form of student activism to institute an in-state tuition policy for those who were undocumented. The University of Hawai'i BOR approved of in-state tuition eligibility for undocumented students in 2013.[73] It was a direct outcome of the IYC-NIYA training. While this was a middle-of-the-road win, a far cry from undertaking civil disobedience or militantly taking on the arms of crimmigration, student leaders took to heart the consistent message of IYC-NIYA trainers that in-state tuition needed to be framed within the broader issue of education equity. This understanding came directly from the IYC's queer and radical framework. At every opportunity, including at meetings with state legislators, the trainers taught the participants to intervene in the exceptionalism of the DREAM narrative, which presented college-bound students as innocent and deserving, and, in the early years, their parents as culpable for crossing the border. The trainers reinforced the need to highlight the multiple challenges of poverty, lack of resources, criminalization, and the corrosive fear of deportation that stood in the way of multiply marginalized undocumented students. Agitating for access to higher education came with the responsibility of working to dismantle all the socioeconomic barriers that reproduced inequities.[74]

This political consciousness about education equity and its localization mobilized the student leaders to build a broad multiethnic coalition on the

UHM campus. Named Hawai'i Alliance of Immigrants for Action (HAIA), it included members from another student group Micronesian Connection. In preparation for the summit, many UHM YES participants were already researching how the system's tuition policy impacted Pacific Islander students. Under a BOR policy implemented in fall 2007, nonresident students from Pacific Islands, including FSM, RMI, and ROP, were being charged 150 percent of in-state tuition until they could establish residency by paying taxes and living on the island for twelve consecutive months. The BOR policy also set a six-year schedule over which tuition for all students would increase by 140 percent.[75] The adverse effects of these increases for Native Hawaiian students, already underrepresented in the UH system and at the flagship, which professed to be a Native Hawaiian place of learning, were not lost on the student activists. Student leaders at UHM, among them Carolina Torres Valle, Doorae Shin, Ryan Mandado, Gina Ifenuk, Leonard Leon, Genesis Shin, and Paul Martin, consulted with Native Hawaiian students. The HAIA representatives had to address concerns raised by the student government about whether the expansion of in-state tuition to new groups would affect Native Hawaiian students' access to financial assistance, including their eligibility for in-state tuition regardless of their domicile, under UH's Native Hawaiian tuition exemption policy. During the student government debates over a proposed resolution for in-state tuition for undocumented students, HAIA navigated these tough questions in a politically conscious way without falling prey to zero-sum arguments. They clearly and passionately expressed their understanding that Native Hawaiians are the Indigenous people of Hawai'i, and UH needed to live up to its mission of a Native Hawaiian–serving institution. They presented their research to show that extending in-state tuition to undocumented students would not come at the expense of UH financial support for their Native Hawaiian peers.[76] With Micronesian Connections, the HAIA members resolved to move forward with demands to reduce the tuition charged of Pacific Islanders if they won the campaign for undocumented students. The students made sure to create a broad understanding that affording in-state tuition to undocumented students was not coming at the expense of other marginalized students as they made their case in front of classrooms, faculty meetings, the student government, and, after they secured the support, to the UH regents. In an impressive feat, the students and off-campus supporters organized across neighbor islands so that youth testified at the Hawai'i Island and Maui BOR meetings.

Empowered by winning the in-state tuition policy for undocumented applicants, the student leaders dedicated 2013–14 to working with Micronesian Connection, Pacific Islander faculty in the Office of Multicultural Student Services, and academic departments across UHM in planning a campaign directed at the BOR to correct the inequity caused by the tuition increase for Pacific Islanders. Unfortunately, the efforts to reduce tuition for Pacific Island students have yet to succeed, even as the COVID-19 pandemic, which disproportionately affected Pacific Islanders, has sharpened the inequities in college access.[77] The university administration's refusal to respond to the disparate outcome of tuition hikes for its Pacific Islander students entrenches settler colonial logics. A recent report on educational inequity among Micronesians in Hawaiʻi, coauthored by UHM ethnic studies scholar Jonathan Okamura, bears out his prediction that the tuition hikes would lead to severe disparities for Native Hawaiians, other Pacific Islanders, and Hawaiʻi's ethnic minorities. These disparities were rooted in the state's chronic underfunding of public higher education and its refusal to move away from tourism, a tool of settler colonialism, to solve its fiscal problems. At UHM, only twenty-seven undergraduates were listed as Micronesians in 2020.[78] Retrospectively, the alliance in (HĀ)LIVE and at UHM among Micronesians, other Indigenous Pacific Islanders, Asian Americans, and Latinx students emerged because the YES training departed from the standard DREAM script. This departure, specific to Hawaiʻi, expanded the purpose of undocumented youth activism by legitimating struggles that addressed the intersections of racism, heteropatriarchy, colonialism, and capitalism.

Conclusion

The course I have charted in this chapter demonstrates that IYC's training, scaffolded by a radical and queer migration framework, guided Hawaiʻi's youth activists toward contextualizing Oceanic decolonial projects in the critiques of crimmigration. When introducing me to Los Angeles's complex immigrant rights landscape in 2009, veteran rebel lawyer Susan Alva told me to pay close attention to the undocumented youth who were at the forefront of making brave demands by refusing their erasure and criminalization. Indeed, radical and queer undocumented youth, such as those in IYC, enacted liberatory politics unapologetically and refused to distance themselves from "criminals" to confront intersecting power structures. Its activism demonstrates the opposite of the fears in the movement that radicalized undocumented youth and their intersectional organizing would dilute the clear and disciplined message of the DREAMers. Value-based cross-issue organizing produces strength and solidarity.

I would argue that IYC-NIYA's training in Hawaiʻi put into practice the solidarity ethos of "All of Us or None," binding youth across islands and ethnicities to draw on Tengan's attention to the verb form of hoa taken from voyaging traditions. Expanding on this polysemous word, Tengan points out that the canoe, secured and rigged together, also requires that crew members learn to be reliable.[79] The journeys I describe were turbulent for youth as they struggled to overcome cultural alienation, as in the case of Micronesian youth, or grapple with the distinction between sovereignty projects and those against the oppression of racialized minorities, as in the case of the fight for educational equity.

Both Indigenous and non-Indigenous migrant youth identified the common theme of criminalization in their lives. Ethnographically, the example of Hawaiʻi provides the starkest example of settler carcerality in the book, only because it is the most familiar to me. It gives clear examples of solidarity efforts across Indigenous and non-Indigenous groups. The intersections of US settler colonial power in Hawaiʻi and US imperialism, which have dispossessed and displaced the COFA citizens, require a reformulation of migration justice. Relatedly, IYC's abolitionist politics sought to shift public spending away from the architecture of punishment toward social goods. This approach resonated with Hawaiʻi's youth organizers, who were guided by the goal of achieving equity in public higher education. They embraced this mission within a broader decolonial framework.

Just as IYC's radical stance on policing and prisons has led to its solidarity with the Black Lives Matter movement in Los Angeles, in Hawaiʻi, two momentous events have reinvigorated connections among movements for Kanaka Maoli sovereignty, abolition, and demilitarization. In 2019, the state of Hawaiʻi deployed police and the National Guard to clear out the thousands of Kanaka Maoli and their allies who gathered on Hawaiʻi Island at the puʻuhonua (sanctuary from unjust laws) established at the base of Maunakea, sacred to Kanaka ʻŌiwi. The protectors had gathered to block the addition of a thirty-meter telescope at the summit, already degraded by a complex of thirteen observatories. They modeled a self-determining community that flourished with mutual care and provided food, shelter, health care, childcare, and classes offered by farmers, fisherfolk, Kanaka ʻŌiwi scientists, hula practitioners, frontline activists, and university instructors for all those gathered. The arrest of thirty-three kūpuna (elders), who nonviolently put their bodies on the frontline to stop the state's attempt to resume the telescope's construction, exposed the state's repeated willingness to criminalize Indigenous people and counter the assertion of Hawaiian sovereignty with sheer police force.[80]

In 2021, Honolulu police shot and killed sixteen-year-old Iremambar Sykap, a Chuukese youth and Kalihi resident, during a chase over a car theft.[81] The chorus of anti-immigrant and criminalizing discourse against the Micronesian community was vindicated in the judge's dismissal of the case against the police officers who killed him.[82] The judge justified the police use of force by likening the threat to one posed by "a caged animal," while denying that police action had anything to do with their victim's race or age.[83] The judge's dismissal disavowed, yet again, the imperial violence that pushes out COFA citizens and Hawai'i state's willful discrimination against this group. Following Lawrence, the harmful characterizations of Iremambar, his family, his community, and the residents of Kalihi remind us of the need to question their widespread intelligibility because they distort the lifestories of those so condemned.

Iremambar's killing was met with immediate community-led resistance against these state actions. A youth actor in *Masters of the Currents* and community organizer, Jayceleen Ifenuk, who was born in Chuuk, grew up in Kalihi and is YES participant Gina's sister, spoke in the memory of Iremambar the day after he was shot dead. She stressed the unity, carefully built over time, among Kalihi's Micronesian youth and with their Native Hawaiian and Pacific Islander peers to counter the deadly actions and discourses directed at Micronesians.[84] Iremambar's death in the hands of police is an immigrant issue, a racial justice issue, an anti-imperial and demilitarization issue, and a decolonial issue. Calls ranging from police accountability to abolition rang across the islands with community activists memorializing the many Honolulu Police Department killings. As Native Hawaiians and Pacific Islanders grieved Iremamber by expressing their Oceanic kinship and shared rage over US occupation, two daring projects of our times, abolition and Indigenous sovereignty, steered themselves toward each other.

CONCLUSION

JAILBREAK

The message "No Ban on Stolen Land" popped up on signs at airports across the United States to protest the Donald Trump administration's 2017 travel ban on refugees from seven predominantly Muslim countries. It circulated widely on social media. The message, coined by scholars and organizers Melanie Yazzie (Diné) and Nick Estes (Kul Wicasa), interrupted and intercepted the authority of the United States to dictate who is welcome and who is not on Indigenous lands. It also short-circuited the usual incantations by immigrant rights advocates who, faced with restrictive immigration policies, reinscribe American exceptionalism—the belief that the United States is a nation of immigrants and, thus, fundamentally committed to welcoming them. Yazzie, who participated in a welcoming ceremony led by Native people to receive refugees at the Los Angeles airport, posted the reception on social media. She noted that the land as well as Indigenous people recognized the humanity of the refugees and their need for safety. "No Ban on Stolen Land" asserts the agentive power of land tied to self-determining Indigenous polities. It lays bare the violent and exploitative control the United States exerts over that land, instrumentalized for profit. It is a call to conscience—the collective responsibility of those of us hosted on the land to do everything we can to join the struggles to restore Indigenous people's rights to protect it and care for it. The message carries the urgent charge of building solidarities across Indigenous and migrant rights movements.[1]

In Hawaiʻi, where I am located, I feel the daily throb of Kanaka Maoli decolonial movements. Indigenous politics operates in the here and now at the university, in organizing spaces, in the streets, and over the vast expanse of salt water and the valleys and mountains with their fresh water sources. This book about antideportation activists who defend migrants with criminal charges or convictions has been written in the presence of Indigenous politics and Kanaka Maoli and Micronesian organizers. The approach I develop here reveals that deportation is a carceral technology through which the United States stabilizes its settler-imperial power in the face of Indigenous sovereignties, which operate across the same territory. Migrant-led and Indigenous politics have a common object of analysis, US countersovereignty. My analytical focus treats Indigenous politics as a force even in instances when migrant politics do not clearly engage with Indigenous struggles. The crimmigration-sensitive antideportation activism I document does, however, directly challenge settler logics and discourses circulated by the immigrant rights movement. I find much hope in that.

The activism provides points of entry into the gender and sexual politics of settler carcerality, deportability, and the movement for migration justice. Throughout the book, I use "feminist" and "queer" as analytics, rather than descriptors, to place the constitution of normative and nonnormative sexualities and genders at the center of punitive mechanisms as well as ideologies of liberation. These analytics illuminate the intimate toll of settler respectability within the immigrant rights movement and the obstacles to intersectional organizing within radical spaces. Feminist and queer worldmaking within the organizations and collectives to address these dynamics makes it possible to imagine and practice what care not cages can feel like.

My work joins scholarly and activist efforts to bring resistance to migration control into conversation with Indigenous decolonial projects, which foreground the materiality of land and its connections to Indigenous identity and culture. Indigenous sovereignty executes care, responsibility, and consent in relation to land and elemental forms so as to be recognized by them, not by the state.[2] This conception of sovereignty requires a profound shift in human-centered and nation-state-bound notions of politics. To make this shift, I have been guided by insights basic to critical Indigenous studies. First, Indigenous people's particular relations to land and land rights mean that they are not racial minorities. Second, while Indigenous land-based struggles for sovereignty are distinct from those of racialized minorities, anti-Indigenous, capitalist, extractive, racist, and heterosexist power structures are chain-linked. The interdependency among these violent structures creates grounds for coalition politics based on difference, not sameness, as theorized and practiced by Black, Indigenous, and women of color feminists. Third, those of us who are migrants have a responsibility to stand up against land-appropriative settler politics.

The types of migration justice organizing I detail in the book reject settler politics encoded in the clarion calls of the immigrant rights movement. The activists eschew proimmigration characterization of the United States as a "nation of immigrants," a benevolent host to refugees, and the appropriate homeland for undocumented deportable youth, who are represented as culturally American and as untapped labor. These proimmigrant representations circulate and reinforce settler tropes at the expense of Indigenous presence and self-governance. They demand compliance with heterosexual norms.

In their defense of the most expendable of migrants—those branded with the felon label—the antideportation activists offer sophisticated understandings of the convergence of the regimes of mass incarceration with immigration enforcement. This convergence has the dual effect of controlling migration and undercutting Indigenous self-determination. These controls, which police the bordered interior, target the intimate. They punitively regulate gender, sexuality, kinship, and community. Through direct action, storytelling, political education, and youth leadership, the organizations and collectives have reformulated immigrant rights. They expand the vision of justice, encompassing those who are erased, dismissed, or disavowed. The antideportation activists generate new stories about their realities and visions, which do not rely on the settler scripts about deserving, innocent, productive immigrants ensconced in normative family arrangements. The US refugee resettlement and asylum-granting projects on stolen land are myths that the activists inventively debunk. The attention to the layered experiences of dispossession and displacement induced by US occupation and imperial actions informs the intentional rearticulation of the demands for migration justice. The antideportation activists incite us to move toward abolitionist visions, away from state-reliant, reform-oriented immigration policy proposals that prop up settler colonialism. In that sense, they perform what Mariame Kaba calls a "jailbreak of the imagination," daring collective action, radical care, and transformation to encourage their communities and allies to flourish.[3]

The organizers have taught me much about the power of storytelling in bringing about such transformation. The heartbreaks caused by deportation have sometimes made me question the value of storytelling. But in the process, I have realized that these stories bind people with very different experiences with migration and state apparatuses. Internally, the exchange of stories and the acts of bearing witness build a movement and open coalitional possibilities. The organizers make space to imagine what antioppression politics aligned with Indigenous struggles for decolonization can look like.

While I do not have any prescriptions, I do have a story about ʻaha, a word in ʻŌlelo Hawaiʻi used for gathering, coming together in conference, or performing ceremony. It also refers to a braided cord. In 2015, my colleague in ethnic studies and Kanaka ʻŌiwi scholar Ty Kāwika Tengan, opened our department's conference, Our Future, Our Way: Directions in Oceanic Ethnic Studies, with an activity.[4] He asked the participants to stand in a circle (it was big!) and passed out a long segment of sennit cordage for each of us to hold. The cordage was made either by master navigator Mau Piailug of Satawal atoll (Yap, Micronesia) before he passed away in 2010 or his students. It had been woven and distributed as part of a fundraiser for Papa Mau to travel from Satawal to Guam or further away to Hawaiʻi to get treatment for a chronic health condition. As we stood in the circle holding a part of the cordage, which connected us to each other, Kumu Kāwika called on Native Hawaiians to reaffirm their kinship with Micronesians, who were (and continue to be) the target of virulent discrimination. The cordage we gripped in our hands was meant to remind all of us of Papa Mau's centrality in reviving voyaging traditions among Native Hawaiians by sharing the art and science of navigation and wayfinding, instrumental in the first Hōkūleʻa voyage to Tahiti. The rope also connected Native Hawaiians, Micronesians, and all other ethnicities represented in the circle. Our commitment to each other's liberation, as distinct as they were, bound us to each other. Through this tactile, place-based, Oceanic activity, we sensed the political-intellectual commitments required of coalition building. The rope materialized the organizing power of ʻaha (gathering) and hoa (binding), encouraging us to be reliable voyagers during good as well as dangerous times.

NOTES

PREFACE

1   Burns, "Leaked Palantir Doc Reveals Uses." Palantir is a billion-dollar data-mining, tracking, and analytics company that contracts with law enforcement and ICE. The federal government contracts the GEO Group to run detention centers for ICE. The GEO Group received $184 million in federal contracts to incarcerate immigrants in FY 2017 and, together with CoreCivic, is responsible for detaining fifteen thousand people daily. See Freedom for Immigrants, "Detention by the Numbers"; Detention Watch, *Influence of the Private Prison Industry*; Human Rights Watch, "US: Poor Medical Care, Deaths, in Immigrant Detention."

2   On March 5, 2018, the Trump administration rescinded the Deferred Action for Childhood Arrival program, established as an executive order by President Barack Obama, making the renewal urgent. President Obama's executive order allowed undocumented youth with no criminal records to receive temporary Social Security numbers and work authorizations. An estimated 690,000 DACA holders were projected to be affected by the rescission. See Zong et al., "Profile of Current DACA Recipients."

3   Agarwal, "Black Lives Matter."

4   NBC Los Angeles, "9 Arrested at DACA Protest in Westwood"; CNN Wire et al., "LAPD Declares Unlawful Assembly."

5   CBS Los Angeles, "ICE Arrests 101 People in LA Immigration Sweep."

6   I am indebted to Karen Leong for crystallizing this formulation of settler colonialism in her reading of my work. I am inspired by Karen Leong and Myla Vincenti Carpio's theorization of the carceral state. See Leong and Carpio, "Carceral States."

7   Das Gupta, "Of Hardship and Hostility."

8   Batalova, Das Gupta, and Haglund, *Newcomers to the Aloha State*; Das Gupta and Haglund, "Mexican Migration to Hawai'i and US Settler Colonialism"; Das Gupta, "Shadowed Lives."

9   Buff reminds us of the rich history of organizing against deportation and for immigrant rights in the twentieth century, starting in the early 1930s. Buff, *Against the Deportation Terror*.

10 I have not ascribed abolition politics to the organizations or coalitions unless they explicitly embrace them. The IYC and FFF are explicitly abolitionist. Individual activists in Tod@s aligned themselves with such politics. Youth leaders in KGA demand a reinvestment in their futures instead of the school-to-prison pipeline. My thinking on abolition has been influenced by Davis, *Are Prisons Obsolete?*; Davis, *Freedom Is a Constant Struggle*; Thuma, *All Our Trials*; Kaba, *We Do This 'Til We Free Us*; Khan-Cullors, *Abolitionist's Handbook.*; and Spade, *Normal Life*. Spade explicitly links immigration detention to the neoliberal punishment regimes. See also, for example, Spade, "Impossibility Now." I continue to learn about abolition from organizing spaces like Critical Resistance, Survived and Punished, Creative Interventions, and Transform Harm.

INTRODUCTION DEPORTATION AS SETTLER CARCERALITY

1 Critical migration studies situates the development of borders in colonial cartographic practices and the evolution of state controls over where and under what conditions people can move. Scholars connect migration to colonial and neocolonial circuits. For exemplary works, see Buff, *Against the Deportation Terror*; Buff, *Immigrant Rights in the Shadows of Citizenship*; Buff, *Immigration and the Political Economy of Home*; Camacho, *Migrant Imaginaries*; Coleman, "Immigrant Il-Legality"; De Genova, *Working the Boundaries*; Das Gupta, *Unruly Immigrants*; Espiritu, *Home Bound*; Espiritu, *Body Counts*; Gutiérrez and Hondagneu-Sotelo, *Nation and Migration*; Hondagneu-Sotelo, *God's Heart Has No Borders*; Luibhéid, *Pregnant on Arrival*; Menjívar, "Central American Immigrant Workers"; Menjívar, *Fragmented Ties*; Nevins, *Dying to Live*; Nevins, *Operation Gatekeeper and Beyond*; Ngai, *Impossible Subjects*; Park, *Illegal Migrations and the Huckleberry Finn Problem*; Sharma, *Home Economics*; Zilberg, *Space of Detention*. Some exemplary early works that opened up the conversation between migration and Indigeneity are Buff, *Immigration and the Political Economy of Home*; Menjívar, *Fragmented Ties*; R. Ramirez, *Native Hubs*; Stephen, *Transborder Lives*.

2 J. Barker, *Native Acts*; Byrd, *Transit of Empire*; Moreton-Robinson, "Writing Off Treaties"; Morgensen, *Spaces between Us*; Kauanui, *Hawaiian Blood*; Wolfe, "Settler Colonialism and the Elimination of the Native."

3 US exceptionalism turns on professing its respect for the rule of law. Feminist and Indigenous studies scholar Shannon Speed (Chickasaw) cuts through these professions by implicating the US state in "neoliberal multicriminalism," which is a transnational web of violent, illegal practices that fall on the bodies of Indigenous women migrating north from Mexico, Honduras, and Guatemala. Speed, *Incarcerated Stories*.

4 Vimalassery, "Prose of Counter-sovereignty," 88. Manu Vimalassery now publishes as Manu Karuka.

5   J. Barker, "Introduction: Critically Sovereign," 10.

6   J. Barker, "Introduction: Critically Sovereign," 7–14. See also Tuck and Yang, "Decolonization Is Not a Metaphor."

7   Leong and Carpio, "Carceral States."

8   See Das Gupta and Haglund, "Mexican Migration to Hawai'i and US Settler Colonialism." The article presents one articulation of the argument I make in this chapter.

9   Metzl, "Structural Competency."

10 Kanstroom, *Deportation Nation*.

11 Amy Kaplan's theorization of the centrality of domestication in US expansion in the nineteenth century, including the reduction of Native American polities to the status of domestic nations, is instructive. Kaplan, "Manifest Domesticity."

12 Macías-Rojas, *From Deportation to Prison*.

13 Walia, *Undoing Border Imperialism*, loc. 153 of 4008.

14 Simpson, *Mohawk Interruptus*, 11.

15 On the colonial imposition of sex and gender binaries, see Driskill et al., *Queer Indigenous Studies*; Lee-Oliver et al., "Imperialism, Settler Colonialism, and Indigeneity," 234–36; Kauanui, "Indigenous Hawaiian Sexuality."

16 Hong and Ferguson, *Strange Affinities*. In the same volume, see Chandan Reddy's warning to movements against drawing analogies between racial and sexual liberation, 148–74. See also Karma Chávez's nuanced discussion of the coalitional possibilities of the appropriation of the LGBTQ strategy of coming out by undocumented youth activists as well as the risks of containing the activism to a desire for national belonging through citizenship. Chávez, *Queer Migration Politics*, loc. 1833–2514 of 5401.

17 Teves, *Defiant Indigeneity*.

18 Castellanos, Gutiérrez Nájera, and Aldama, *Comparative Indigeneities of the Américas*.

19 Blackwell, Boj Lopez, and Urrieta, "Introduction: Critical Latinx Indigeneities"; Blackwell, "Geographies of Indigeneity"; Blackwell, "Líderes Campesinas."

20 Lyons, "Dole, Hawai'i, and the Question of Land under Globalization."

21 Sharma and Wright, "Decolonizing Resistance," 121. My emphasis.

22 Volpp, "Indigenous as Alien," 324.

23 See J. Barker, *Sovereignty Matters*; Goeman, *Mark My Words*; Goodyear-Ka'ōpua, *Seeds We Planted*; Million, *Therapeutic Nations*; Simpson, *Mohawk Interruptus*.

24 Exemplary works by Indigenous feminists are J. Barker, *Native Acts*; J. Barker, "Introduction: Critically Sovereign"; Byrd, *Transit of Empire*; Goeman, *Mark My Words*; Million, *Therapeutic Nations*; Goodyear-Ka'ōpua, "Kuleana Lāhui"; Simpson, *Mohawk Interruptus*; Trask, *From a Native Daughter*. For influential theorizations of settler colonialism, see Fujikane, "Introduction: Asian Settler Colonialism"; Fujikane, "Foregrounding Native Nationalisms"; Saranillio, "Why Asian Settler Colonialism Matters"; Saranillio, "Colliding

Histories"; Trask, "Settlers of Color and 'Immigrant' Hegemony of 'Locals' in Hawai'i"; Wolfe, "Settler Colonialism and the Elimination of the Native"; Wolfe, *Traces of History*; Veracini, *Settler Colonialism*; Franklin, Njoroge, and Reiss, "Tracing the Settler's Tools."

25   J. Barker, "Indigenous Feminisms." Barker argues that "Indigenous feminism has asserted the polity of the Indigenous: the unique governance, territory, and culture of an Indigenous people in a system of (non)human relationships and responsibilities to one another."

26   I began developing this framework in Das Gupta, "Rights in a Transnational Era."

27   For a powerful theorization of this dynamic, see Speed, *Incarcerated Stories*.

28   See Hong, *Death beyond Disavowal*; Reddy, *Freedom with Violence*. The Landback movement names the border patrol, ICE, and police as mechanisms of white supremacy which separate Indigenous people from land, thus connecting demands of the Black Lives Matter movement and the migrant justice movement to the struggles of Indigenous people to get "Indigenous lands back into Indigenous hands." NDN Collective, "Landback Now: Land Back and Hawaiian Kingdom (US Occupation of Kingdom of Hawai'i)," November 28, 2020, YouTube video, 2:28:32, https://youtu.be/ezMA9DcJZk8. See the segment 16:40–25:16, in which Krystal Two Bulls (Oglala Lakota and Northern Cheyenne), director of the Landback campaign, explains the demands and political framework of the collective.

29   Macías-Rojas, *From Deportation to Prison*.

30   Omi and Winant, *Racial Formation in the United States*.

31   Byrd, *Transit of Empire*, xxvi–xxxv; Kauanui, *Hawaiian Blood*, 194.

32   Rifkin, "Around 1978."

33   Byrd, *Transit of Empire*, 129–37.

34   Byrd, *Transit of Empire*, xxvi–xxxv, 133–34; Arvin, Tuck and Morrill, "Decolonizing Feminism."

35   Trask, *From a Native Daughter*, 25–40.

36   Das Gupta and Haglund, "Mexican Migration to Hawai'i and US Settler Colonialism"; Fujikane and Okamura, *Asian Settler Colonialism*; Goodyear-Ka'ōpua, *Seeds We Planted*; Saranillio, "Colliding Histories"; Saranillio, "Why Asian Settler Colonialism Matters."

37   Simpson, *Mohawk Interruptus*.

38   Kanstroom, *Deportation Nation*, 63–74. The substantial body of literature on the Supreme Court rulings on the Cherokee Nation and precedents they set for Indian policy are beyond the scope of this chapter.

39   Volpp, "Indigenous as Alien."

40   In chapter 5, I show what happens when Indigenous Pacific Islander migrants are treated as racial minorities in US-occupied Hawai'i governed by US immigration laws.

41   Wilkins and Lomawaima, *Uneven Ground*, 98–116.

42 Tamez, "Indigenous Women's Rivered Refusals in El Calaboz," 241; Tamez, "Soveryempty."

43 Volpp, "Indigenous as Alien."

44 Kanstroom, *Deportation Nation*, 64. My emphasis.

45 Vimalassery, "Antecedents of Imperial Incarceration," 142.

46 Simpson, *Mohawk Interruptus*.

47 For a model, see Park, *Illegal Migrations and the Huckleberry Finn Problem*.

48 Tamez, "Soveryempty," 210.

49 Estes et al., *Red Nation Rising*, 6, 7, 83, 113–16.

50 Alexander, *New Jim Crow*; Browne, *Dark Matters*; Davis, *Are Prisons Obsolete?*; Davis, "Racialized Punishment and Prison Abolition"; Haley, *No Mercy Here*.

51 Cacho, *Social Death*; Fernandes, *Targeted*; Macías-Rojas, *From Deportation to Prison*; Zilberg, *Space of Detention*.

52 For exceptions, see the magisterial work of Hernández, *City of Inmates*; Leong and Carpio, "Carceral States"; Walia, *Undoing Border Imperialism*; Vimalassery, "Antecedents of Imperial Incarceration"; Sonoda, "Nation Incarcerated"; Estes et al., *Red Nation Rising*.

53 Leong and Carpio, "Carceral States," ix.

54 Wilkins and Lomawaima, *Uneven Ground*, 106–9.

55 Wilkins and Lomawaima, 102–6.

56 Wilkins and Lomawaima, 110–11.

57 Rifkin, "Around 1978," 174–82.

58 Deer, *Beginning and End of Rape*.

59 Alexander, *New Jim Crow*.

60 The IYC trainers, who visited Honolulu, facilitated a public discussion titled "New Jim Crow: Crimmigration, Youth, and Dissent" on February 28, 2012.

61 Deer, *Beginning and End of Rape*, 39–40.

62 Sudbury, *Global Lockdown*. Julia Sudbury now publishes as Julia Chinyere Oparah.

63 Stanley, Spade, and Queer (In)justice, "Queering Prison Abolition, Now?," 127.

64 Prashad, *Karma of Brown Folk*.

65 Freedom for Immigrants, "Detention by the Numbers."

66 Davis, "Masked Racism."

67 Fink, "Labor Joins La Marcha"; Robbins and Correal, "On a 'Day without Immigrants.'"

68 Smith, A., "Heteropatriarchy and the Three Pillars of White Supremacy."

69 Miranda, "Extermination of the *Joyas*," 259. For the multiplicity of gender and sexuality articulated in Indigenous practices, knowledges, and languages that talk back to the colonial imposition of heteronormativity and heteropatriarchy, see Driskill et al., *Queer Indigenous Studies*.

70 Stanley, Spade, and Queer (In)justice, "Queering Prison Abolition, Now?"

71 Blackwell, *¡Chicana Power!*, 8, 23, 44.

72   See Mingus, "Transformative Justice."

73   Drawing attention to care as essential yet often invisible labor in social movements, Hiʻilei Hobart and Tamara Kneese state that radical care is "a set of vital but underappreciated strategies for enduring precarious worlds." Hobart and Kneese, "Radical Care," 2.

74   Cvetkovich, "Public Feelings."

75   State of Arizona Senate, Senate Bill 1070; Detention Watch Network, "Detention and Deportation Consequences."

76   Berlant, *Female Complaint*, 22.

77   Speed, *Incarcerated Stories*; Blackwell, *¡Chicana Power!*; Fujiwara, *Mothers without Citizenship*. See also Archuleta, "I Give You Back"; Million, "Felt Theory"; Franklin, *Narrating Humanity*.

78   Literary critics John Beverley and Lauren Berlant emphasize the orientation of these stories toward those who are removed from the effects of subordination but implicated in its reproduction. I am more interested in the ways the stories bind together people in the movement. Beverley, *Testimonio*; Berlant, *Female Complaint*.

79   Examples of scholarship that bring feminist and queer analyses to bear on US deportation policies as they have been shaped since the nineteenth century include Canaday, *Straight State*; Chávez, *Queer Migration Politics*; Das Gupta, "'Don't Deport Our Daddies'"; Gehi, "Gendered (In)Security"; Lee, "Exclusion Acts"; Luibhéid, "Heteronormativity and Immigration Scholarship"; Luibhéid and Cantú, *Queer Migrations*; Luibhéid, *Pregnant on Arrival*; Chávez and Luibhéid, *Queer and Trans Migrations*; Ngai, *Impossible Subjects*; Pallares, *Family Activism*; Shah, *Stranger Intimacy*. It is worth noting that studies of contemporary deportation have been slow to integrate the scholarship on queer migration, which urges us to understand the regulation of immigration as the regulation of sexuality, gender identity, and family arrangements.

80   See also Audre Lorde Project (ALP), *Community at a Crossroads*, 43–48. The hard copy of the report is in the author's possession.

81   J. Barker, "Indigenous Feminisms." My emphasis.

CHAPTER 1 "ALL OF US OR NONE"

1   Legislative Analyst's Office, "2017–18 Budget." See also *Correctional News*, "California Corrections Budget Continues to Increase."

2   Spade, *Normal Life*.

3   The South Asian Network, which was instrumental in radicalizing the immigrant rights discourse in Los Angeles between 2001 and 2010, explains its attraction to a transformative justice approach to imagine social justice responses that are not reliant on punishment. South Asian Network, *From Displacement to Internment*, 32. On the link between transformative justice and abolition, see Mingus, "Transformative Justice."

4   Alianza Indígena Sin Fronteras and Christina Leza, *Handbook on Indigenous Peoples' Border Crossing Rights*. This handbook names the crossborder nations, reservations, and pueblos of Yaqui/Yoeme, O'odham, Cocopah/Cucapá, Kumeyaay/Kumiai, Pai, Apache, and Kickapoo/Kikapú. The continued militarization, walling, and enforcement of the border disrupt these Indigenous communities' autonomy and self-determination over their social, cultural, and spiritual lives and their mobility in their homelands. Tamez, "Indigenous Women's Rivered Refusals in El Calaboz," 8. Tamez names Ndé homelands and the relationship between Ndé and Nahua, Tlaxcalteca, Comanche, Kiowa, Kickapoo, and Jumano peoples and their homelands along the Mexico-Texas border. For the destructive effects of the Department of Homeland Security's (DHS) surveillance and militarization across O'odham lands, see Schaeffer, *Unsettled Borders*, 64–75.

5   See Camp, *Incarcerating the Crisis*. Camp reminds us of the importance of attending to dissent from below mounted by those who lived in the communities ravaged by the counterinsurgent law-and-order platform that gave rise to the neoliberal carceral state.

6   Detention Watch Network, "Mandatory Detention."

7   B. Hing, *Deporting Our Souls*, 63–64.

8   See Zheng, "Prison-to-Leadership Pipeline." Prison activist Eddy Zheng corrects a common misperception that Asian Americans are not targeted by law enforcement by making Asian American prisoners visible and connecting Asian American experiences to mass incarceration. Zheng chronicles Asian American activism to establish Asian American studies in San Quentin State Prison and Solano State Prison. He documents the creation of the Asian Prisoner Support Committee (APSC). For the continuing work of APSC and the recent resistance of Oakland's Cambodian community to ICE raids, see Dinh, "'When We Fight, We Win.'"

9   For one exception, see Escudero, "Federal Immigration Laws and U.S. Empire."

10 Hawai'i Appleseed Center for Law and Economic Justice, *Broken Promises, Shattered Lives*.

11 Hong, *Death beyond Disavowal*.

12 Speed, *Incarcerated Stories*.

13 Macías-Rojas, *From Deportation to Prison*.

14 See Mijente et al., *Who's behind ICE?* The report documents the scale and scope of the technology infrastructure being built to accelerate deportations through biometric data sharing and the relationship of tech companies with Congress and federal government agencies.

15 Manisha Vaze, interview with the author, July 10, 2009, New York City.

16 CBP can arrest a person within one hundred miles of the US border.

17 Detention Watch Network et al., *Deportation 101*, 61. While the person in police custody has the right to remain silent and the right to an interpreter,

the refusal to provide these agents with one's citizenship status comes with the consequence of remaining in jail until the judge makes a determination on the criminal custody. At this stage, the person does not have the right to legal counsel.

18 Immigrant Defense Project and Cardozo Law, "New York City New Detainer Discretion Law Chart and Practice Advisory"; Immigrant Defense Project, "Detainers."

19 Center for Constitutional Rights, "Landmark Decision."

20 NYU School of Law Immigrant Rights Clinic and Families for Freedom, *Justice Detained, Justice Denied*, 9, 11.

21 Schneiderman, "Guidance concerning Local Authority Participation in Immigration Enforcement and Model Sanctuary Provisions."

22 ACLU of New York, "Court Rules NY Law Enforcement Cannot Detain Immigrants for ICE."

23 California Assembly Bill 4: An Act to Add Chapter 17.1 (Commencing with Section 7282) to Division 7 of Title 1 of the Government Code, Relating to State Government (passed October 5, 2013), accessed February 23, 2024, at LegiScan, https://legiscan.com/CA/text/AB4/id/670300.

24 NYU School of Law Immigrant Rights Clinic and Families for Freedom, *Justice Detained, Justice Denied*; Immigrant Legal Resource Center, "California Post-conviction Relief Vehicles." The Immigrant Legal Resource Center infographic was explained and discussed at the 2017 IYC youth empowerment summit I attended.

25 Detention Watch Network et al., *Deportation 101*, 71.

26 Alexander, *New Jim Crow*, 87–89.

27 Immigrant Legal Resource Center, "ICE's Criminal Alien Program (CAP)."

28 The review of this literature is beyond the scope of the chapter. Throughout, I cite specific scholarly works that I have found helpful in understanding the localized effects of these developments.

29 Macías-Rojas, *From Deportation to Prison*, 135.

30 Capps et al., *From Control to Crisis*.

31 Rozensky, "Biden Administration Routinely Separates Immigrant Families."

32 For an analysis of the relationship between race, space, and crime, see Cacho, *Social Death*.

33 Muñiz, *Police, Power*.

34 Muñiz, *Police, Power*, 60.

35 Siegel, "Gangs and the Law," 223–26.

36 Zilberg, *Space of Detention*.

37 US Congress, "18 U.S. Code § 521"; Offices of the United States Attorneys, "1457. Criminal Street Gangs Statute."

38 In *Space of Detention*, Zilberg gives us an account of the impact of the Violent Gang Task Force on Los Angeles' Salvadoran, and, more broadly, Latino youth in the wake of the 1992 Los Angeles uprising.

39 Zilberg, *Space of Detention*, 38.

40 For the racial politics of California's Proposition 21, see Cacho, *Social Death*, 35–60.

41 US Immigration and Customs Enforcement, "Operation Community Shield."

42 CounterVortex, "Massachusetts: ICE 'Gang' Sweeps Protested." I learned about the increased law enforcement surveillance of Lowell's Southeast Asian youth, their profiling as gang members, and the OCS raid from Deported Diaspora's Dimple Rana and Sandy Wright.

43 Cacho, *Social Death*, 61–96. Cacho discusses Ma's case in depth. She argues that Ma's criminalization as a refugee and gang member is contingent on notions of contagion and incapacity, associations that make his body legible and punishable.

44 Pages, "Indefinite Detention," 1225, quoting the *Zadvydas* Supreme Court case.

45 Office of the Solicitor General, "Reno v. Ma-Petition."

46 A House of Representatives bill was reintroduced in 2023 to halt the deportation of refugees who had arrived in the United States before 2008 from Cambodia, Laos, and Vietnam and had final orders of removal. See US House, Southeast Asian Deportation Relief Act of 2023. The Southeast Asia Resource Action Center and the Southeast Asia Freedom Network supported the bill. Southeast Asia Resource Action Center, "SEARC, SEAFN Celebrate House Reintroduction."

47 Office of the Solicitor General, "Reno v. Ma-Petition."

48 1Love Movement, "40 Years Later."

49 Fernandes, *Targeted*, 73–109.

50 Boundaoui, *Feeling of Being Watched*.

51 Shiu-Ming Cheer, interview with the author, February 28, 2009, Los Angeles; Hamid Khan, interview with the author, April 29, 2009, Artesia, California; Manisha Vaze, interview with the author, July 10, 2009, New York City.

52 South Asian Network, *From Displacement to Internment*, 24–28.

53 Khan, interview.

54 South Asian Americans Leading Together, National Action Agenda, 38.

55 South Asian Network et al., "Grassroots Immigrant Rights Organizations."

56 For a nuanced discussion of the differences in political priorities that surfaced among various immigrant rights groups in the wake of the 2006 mega marches and the subsequent formulation of a comprehensive immigration reform platform, see Cho, "Beyond the Day without an Immigrant."

57 South Asian Network et al., "Grassroots Immigrant Rights Organizations."

58 National Immigration Law Center, *Untangling the Immigration Enforcement Web*. The information about these programs in this section comes from the trainings I have taken as well as innumerable conversations with activists and lawyers.

59 National Immigration Law Center, "Justice Dep. Contemplates Extending Immigration Enforcement."

60 Gehi, "Gendered (In)Security."

61 See Mijente et al., *Who's behind ICE?*, 4.

62 US Immigration and Customs Enforcement, "Secure Communities."

63 Executive Office of the President, EO 13768; Biden, "Executive Order on the Revision of Civil Immigration Enforcement."

64 Anti-violence Advocates against Deportation, "Building Truly Secure Communities," May 2012.

65 Law, "Against Carceral Feminism."

66 Aizeki, "Mass Deportation under the Homeland Security State"; see Gehi, "Gendered (In)Security." Pooja Gehi, at the time the litigation and advocacy director at the Sylvia Rivera Law Project in New York City, participated in the AVA meetings with feminist academic and antiviolence activist Soniya Munshi. They asked the coalition to examine the carceral approaches to addressing gender- and sexuality-based violence by accounting for the experiences of queer and trans immigrants of color with law enforcement. In her article, Gehi offers a trenchant critique of the political gaps between the immigrant rights movement and LGBTQ rights advocacy. It spells out the multiple ways in which criminal and immigration enforcement harms gender nonconforming and transgender immigrants living in poverty. On the work of New York City–based Queer Detainee Empowerment Project, see Hammami, "Bridging Immigration Justice and Prison Abolition."

67 Das Gupta and Munshi, "Turning Points." We analyze AVA's evolving position on differential impacts of carceral solutions to domestic violence.

68 For a discussion of the problems with the victim-perpetrator distinction in addressing gender-based violence, see Survived and Punished, "S and P Analysis and Vision."

69 Gorman, "Cities and Counties Rely on U.S. Immigrant Detention Fees"; Steinhauer, "To Cut Costs, States Relax Prison Policies."

70 Steinhauer, "Bipartisan Push Builds to Relax Sentencing Laws"; P. Barker, "Obama, in Oklahoma, Takes Reform Message to Prison Cell Block"; Eilperin, "Obama Tells NAACP That Justice Reform Is Long Overdue."

71 Aizeki, "Mass Deportation"; Chishti, Pierce, and Bolter, "Obama Record on Deportations."

72 *New York Times*, "Lost in the Immigration Frenzy"; US House, *Sanctuary Cities: A Threat to Public Safety Hearing.*

73 Transactional Records Access Clearing House (TRAC), "ICE Detainees."

74 Macías-Rojas, *From Deportation to Prison*, 74–76.

75 The data are from Detention Watch Network, *Toxic Relationship*. See also Detention Watch Network and Center for Constitutional Rights, *Banking on Detention.*

76 Detention Watch Network. "Detention Quotas." ICE contracts with local or state governments are known as Intergovernmental Service Agreements.

Local or state detention for ICE is one of the three categories of detention facilities.

77   Detention Watch Network, *Toxic Relationship*, 3.

78   Hobson and Raphelson, "California Bans Private Prisons and Immigrant Detention Centers."

79   Community Initiatives for Visiting Immigrants in Confinement (CIVIC) and Immigrant Rights Clinic at NYU School of Law, "Prolonged Detention Stories." This website is a repository of stories from immigrants in detention. Historian and Soros Justice Fellow Kristina Shull, herself impacted by deportation, started the storytelling project with CIVIC.

80   Kim, "Feinstein under Fire."

81   Edwards and Ortega, "Economic Contribution of Unauthorized Workers"; Goodman, "Illegal Immigrants Benefit the U.S. Economy"; Zong et al., "Profile of Current DACA Recipients by Education, Industry, and Occupation."

82   Cuauhtémoc García Hernández, "Migrant Detention, Corporate Profit."

83   Gilmore, *Golden Gulag*.

84   Davis, "Masked Racism."

85   *Laura Flanders Show*, "What Is a Sanctuary with Jails?"

86   Ritchie and Morris, *Centering Black Women, Girls, Gender Nonconforming People and Fem(Me)s*."

87   As prisons and detention centers became hotspots for the spread of COVID-19, it was clear that confinement had become a death sentence, strengthening the alliances across those social justice movements pressing for decarcaration.

88   Hernández, *City of Inmates*, 64–91.

89   Hernández, *City of Inmates*, 64.

90   Alexander, *New Jim Crow*, 59–74.

91   The police department is incentivized through the fines it collects for the impounded cars, which are seized and sold when the detained or deported owners cannot return to claim them. Activists in the Inland Empire have campaigned to stop the police practice of impounding cars of undocumented migrants. The IYC chapter in San Gabriel Valley has confronted this form of anti-immigrant economic injustice. See also M. Rodriguez, "Pomona Council Votes Down Proposal to Halt Vehicle Impounds." California's AB 60 has allowed undocumented migrants to get driver's licenses since 2015, but undocumented immigrants continue to face harassment and economic penalty.

92   See INCITE!, "Quality of Life Policing."

93   Foucault, *Society Must Be Defended*. Queer studies scholar Roderick Ferguson reminds us that Foucault's rendition of the transition from household to the biopolitical production of a population "does not nullify the gendered and eroticized tactics associated with the domestic model of governmentality." Ferguson, "Of Our Normative Strivings," 90.

94 Yazzie, "Abolition and Abundance"; Yazzie, "Organizing an End to Violence against Native Peoples in Border Towns."

95 Estes et al., *Red Nation Rising*, 5–7.

CHAPTER 2 "IT IS OUR MORAL RESPONSIBILITY TO DISOBEY UNJUST LAWS"

1 Feminist and queer activists started to use "Tod@s Som@s Arizona" in the last few months of 2010. Others continued to use "TsAZ." I use "Tod@s" throughout this chapter.

2 Coalition for Humane Immigrant Rights in Los Angeles (CHIRLA), "Local Law Enforcement and Immigration: The 287(g) Program in Southern California," handout in the author's possession. I picked up the handout during one of my visits to CHIRLA's office in the MacArthur Park–West Lake area in spring 2009. See chapter 1 for 287(g) programs.

3 Though a federal judge issued injunctions on some SB 1070 provisions, such as the authorization of state law officers to determine immigration status during any lawful stop, other parts went into effect on July 29, 2010. Demanding the repeal of the law in its entirety and pointing to twenty-one other states discussing similar laws, Tod@s maintained that "justice cannot be partial" at the press conference held at the Wilshire Boulevard and Highland Avenue action on July 29.

4 Naazneen Diwan and Patricia Torres, interview with the author, April 9, 2016, Los Angeles.

5 Winton, "33 Charged with Blocking L.A. City Streets during Immigration Protests."

6 State of Arizona Senate, Senate Bill 1070. The bill's "Intent" section stated, "The provisions of this act are intended to work together to discourage and deter the unlawful entry and presence of aliens and economic activity by persons unlawfully present in the United States."

7 Exemplary works on organizing and protest in the wake of SB 1070 in Arizona include Freeman, "Neocolonial Biopolitics of Southern Arizona"; Fuller, "Creating Resistance on the Border"; Marquez, "Tod@s Somos Arizona"; Mendez and Cabrera, "Targets but Not Victims"; Oliver, "Civil Disobedience"; Riedel, "Phoenix Rising." Marquez's research on Tod@s Somos Arizona in Arizona analyzes the decentralized organizing by Comités en Defensa del Barrio, which loosely connected various localities across Arizona to defend against many state propositions and SB 1070 by encouraging migrants to reclaim Indigeneity as a way to emplace themselves in Arizona. Comités encouraged revitalizing values of communitarianism and reciprocity. Marquez recognizes the problematic dimensions of a romantic resuscitation of North American Indigenous presence through associations with Aztec/Mexica, such as those circulated by La Danza Azteca, adopted

and popularized in the United States during the Chicano movement in the 1970s. Marquez argues that the comités indigenized notions of identity of the migrants being targeted by these Arizona policies as well as notions of citizenship.

8   Tohono O'odham Legislative Council, "Resolution of the Tohono O'odham Legislative Council." The resolution stated that the enhanced local police powers would "expose Arizona tribal members to arrest if they are suspected of being illegal aliens and cannot document their citizenship and presence in the United States and, whereas SB 1070 provides that a tribal member who can show a tribal enrollment card or other tribal identification will be 'presumed' not to be an illegal alien, but the Nation opposes any law requirement that members carry proof under threat of arrest, that they are lawfully present within their aboriginal homelands."

9   Yazzie, "Solidarity with Palestine from Diné Bikéyah." Yazzie powerfully articulates why solidarity with Palestine is central to anticolonial politics by stating, "Palestinian liberation requires the liberation of Indigenous and other oppressed peoples from occupation by Israel's collaborator and guarantor, the United States" (1007).

10   For gendercide as a Spanish colonial tool in California, see Miranda, "Extermination of *Joyas*." See also Finley, "Decolonizing the Queer Native Body," 33–37; Driskill, *Asegi Stories*; J. Barker, "Introduction: Critically Sovereign," 14–21; Lee-Oliver et al., "Imperialism, Settler Colonialism, and Indigeneity," particularly the contributions to the conversation by Fobear and Lee-Oliver. For a discussion of contemporary carceral-colonial violence against Indigenous women in Mexico as part of the "war on drugs," see Hernández Castillo, "Prison as Colonial Enclave."

11   On care work in radical movements, especially in direct action and nonhierarchical organizing, see Hobart and Kneese, "Radical Care."

12   Torres and Diwan, "Moving from the Flesh," 19.

13   In non-Indigenous-led movements, Black Lives Matter, BYP 100, and the Asian American Feminist Collective are contemporary exceptions. Queer and feminist politics are intrinsic their movement building. See also Khan-Cullors and bandele, *When They Call You a Terrorist*, 111–232; Garza, *Purpose of Power*.

14   In the two years when Tod@s was most active, at least thirty-five organizers worked tirelessly on multiple projects that took on prison divestment and immigrant detention. Many organizers identified as queer, feminist, and/or nonbinary. Those who identified as feminists spanned all genders. I did not formally interview these organizers, other than Naazneen and Patricia; thus, they are not mentioned by name, even as I incorporate their insights in the chapter. My many conversations with Hamid outside of the organizing space were crucial in understanding SB 1070, Tod@s's framing of the legislation, and abolition.

15 Diwan and Torres, interview; Mariella Saba, interview with the author, April 12, 2016, Los Angeles. All quotes are drawn from these interviews unless otherwise noted.

16 On internal insurgencies to shift heterosexist, classist and masculinist power dynamics within social justice movements, see Blackwell, ¡Chicana Power!, 42.

17 King, "Letter from Birmingham Jail." Our chant, "It is our moral responsibility to disobey unjust laws," was drawn from this part of the letter: "The answer lies in the fact that there are two types of laws: just and unjust. I would be the first to advocate obeying just laws. One has not only a legal but a moral responsibility to obey just laws. Conversely, one has a moral responsibility to disobey unjust laws. I would agree with St. Augustine that 'an unjust law is no law at all.'"

18 In 2007, Senator Dick Durbin proposed the provisions of the DREAM Act as an amendment to the 2008 Department of Defense Authorization Bill (S. 2919). It included the military service option. If college was out of reach for DREAMers, they could join the military and get credit for their service. Those who wrote the amendment took out proposed language that would have eliminated an Illegal Immigration Reform and Immigration Responsibility Act restriction that barred states from granting in-state college tuition to undocumented residents. Eliminating the restriction would have made college relatively affordable. For a brilliant analysis of the liberal egalitarian state that ties the promise of equality to violence, in this case, the military and national defense, see Reddy, *Freedom with Violence*. Reddy formulates freedom and violence as a conjunction rather than a contradiction that comes with the liberal state's formal protection of a legally vulnerable group.

19 Cho, "Beyond the Day without an Immigrant"; Flores-Gonzáles and Gutiérrez, "Taking the Public Square"; Fink, "Labor Joins La Marcha."

20 Gehi, "Gendered (In)Security." Pooja Gehi points out that mainstream LGBTQ groups opposed SB 1070 without having to dedicate resources or reformulate their platforms to account for the criminalization of survival activities of queer and trans people of color. Todos Somos Arizona, "Anticipated Questions and Talking Points." This handout was prepared for those who took part in the July 29, 2010, civil disobedience as part of the education and outreach packet. The handout is in the author's possession.

21 Torres and Diwan, "Moving from the Flesh," 20.

22 See Thuma, *All Our Trials*. Thuma instructs us on the centrality of institutional and interpersonal gender-based and sexual violence in the analysis developed in the 1970s by antiracist, queer, and feminist organizers against police and prisons. There is a through line between that period and the antiviolence work of Critical Resistance, which inspired Tod@s feminists.

23 Diwan and Torres, interview.

24 Saba, interview.

25 S.I.N. Collective, "Students Informing Now (S.I.N.)," 74.

26 Popular and scholarly debates have emerged over media characterizations of the mega marches of 2006 as the "new civil rights movement" and
the subsequent analogies between the lawful exclusionary treatment of
undocumented migrants residing in the United States and the legalization
of segregation in the Jim Crow era. Usually reduced to a Black and Latinx
conflict, political figures in Black communities have objected to the appropriation of civil rights imagery, language, and strategies in the immigrant
rights movement. See Cacho, *Social Death*, 115–45. Lisa Marie Cacho draws
our attention to the racialized and gendered deployment of respectability,
illegality, and criminality in framing Black and Latino "conflicts." See also
Cachón, "Civil Rights, Immigrants' Rights, and Human Rights." Jennifer
Cachón finds merit in the parallels between the two movements and the way
law operates for immigrants and African Americans to obscure systemic injustices. She argues that Martin Luther King Jr.'s call to disobey unjust laws,
his internationalist politics, and the impact of surveillance on his life shed
light on similarities between the struggle for civil rights and that for immigrant rights. Cacho and Cachón offer nuanced analyses of the particularities
of laws that criminalize migrants and those that discriminate against African
Americans. Tod@s drew inspiration from MLK to disobey unjust laws. It
mixed MLK's message with Black radical insights into the state's investment
in carcerality as a mode of differentially governing subordinate groups. It
demanded the abolition of structures that deny full social membership to
Black people and people of color. Those who had trained at the International
Center for Nonviolent Conflict knew of the many nonviolent traditions of
civil disobedience across the globe and their transnational circulation. Simultaneously, they were aware of the long and unfinished struggle for civil
rights waged by African American and Chicanx communities.

27 Payán, "Paulina González Uses Story Telling as a Tool of Civil Resistance."
I met Paulina in 2009 when she was working at UNITE HERE! Local 11. In
2010, she was the executive director of Strategic Actions for a Just Economy.

28 Sam Pullen, interview with the author, March 17, 2009, Los Angeles. Subsequent quotes are drawn from this interview.

29 Immigration Prof, "Hunger Strike for Immigrant Rights at Placita Olvera."
On the significance of La Placita Olvera, see Pulido, Barrraclough, and
Cheng, *People's Guide to Los Angeles*, 52–53; Hernández, *City of Inmates*,
208. A Tongva village, Yaanga, was located in downtown Los Angeles. The
plaza around La Placita church was built downtown with convict labor in
the 1930s. Historically, it has been a meeting ground for Indigenous people
living in the area, Mexican and Chinese immigrants, and African Americans
fleeing the Jim Crow South. It developed as a place of worship, commerce,
leisure, and protest. During the 1980s, it served as a Sanctuary Movement
hub for Central American refugees.

30 Therisemovement, *Fast for Our Future*, October 1, 2008, YouTube video, 8:27, https://www.youtube.com/watch?v=ISnaY4njlWo; Rebeldeyo, "The Fast for Our Future to Re-ignite the Immigrant Rights Movement." The website documents the first twelve days of the fast. For frequently asked questions about the fast, see Immigration Prof, "Hunger Strike for Immigrant Rights at Placita Olvera."

31 Pullen, interview.

32 Pullen, interview.

33 Shiu-Ming Cheer, interview with the author, March 24, 2016, Los Angeles. Shiu-Ming was referring to Frances Fox Piven and Richard Cloward's classic, *Poor People's Movements*. Subsequent references are drawn from this interview. Betty Hung, a legal trainer and observer for Tod@s, refers to such lawyering as rebellious. Hung, "Movement Lawyering as Rebellious Lawyering."

34 Bose and Lyons, "Introduction: Toward a Critical Corporate Studies," 9–10; Todos Somos Arizona distributed a flyer entitled "G4S Wackenhut: Profiting from the Criminalization of People and Communities of Color" at the action and produced "Anticipated Questions and Talking Points" for the collective members to answer questions from the press and the public on the day of the action. Both handouts are in the author's possession.

35 See Freeman, "Neocolonial Biopolitics of Southern Arizona." Freeman frames SB 1070 as an economic revitalization plan for Arizona and, more broadly, the US Southwest economy by expanding the prison industrial complex and its revenue flow.

36 Todos Somos Arizona, "G4S Wackenhut."

37 Sullivan, "Prison Economics Helped Drive Ariz. Immigration Law"; Sullivan, "Shaping State Laws with Little Scrutiny."

38 Boycott Divestment and Sanctions, "G4S." In 2010, BDS was laying the groundwork for its campaign #StopG4S, which launched in 2012.

39 Todos Somos Arizona, "G4S Wackenhut."

40 For Neidi Dominguez Zamorano's role as a strategist in inspiring direct action among undocumented youth, see Gonzalez, "Winning the Dream"; Hung, "Movement Lawyering as Rebellious Lawyering."

41 Pulido, Barrraclough, and Cheng, *People's Guide to Los Angeles*, 110.

42 Lipsitz, "Learning from Los Angeles." For the organizing work of the Bus Riders Union, see 514–17.

43 Saba, interview.

44 Cheer, interview.

45 Rath, "Todos Somos Arizona."

46 Onyekwere, "How Cash Bail Works."

47 Diwan and Torres, interview. My emphasis.

48 Torres and Diwan, "Moving from the Flesh," 22.

49 Torres and Diwan, "Moving from the Flesh," 24–25.

50   Diwan and Torres, interview.

51   Torres and Diwan, 21. Emphasis in original.

52   For "Pensamiento Serpentino," see Valdez, *Early Works*, 70–199; for Teatro Campesino, see Gómez-Quiñones and Vásquez, *Making Aztlán*, 262–63.

53   Diwan and Torres, interview.

54   These observations are based on my July 29, 2010, experience at police precincts and conversations with Tod@s members.

55   Winton, "33 Charged with Blocking L.A. City Streets during Immigration Protests."

56   Cheer, interview.

57   cbs Los Angeles, "LA Immigration Protesters"; *Pacific Progressive*, "LA City Attorney Carmen Trutanich's Crackdown on Activists Protested."

58   Cheer, interview.

59   Linthicum and Blankstein, "Los Angeles Gets Tough with Political Protestors"; Watt, "Protesters Demand LA Protest Charges Be Dropped."

60   Email communication, September 23, 2010.

61   Saba, interview.

62   Saba, interview.

63   dtla, "About Us."

64   Hamid Khan, email message to author, July 29, 2011.

65   Diwan and Torres, interview.

66   Zamorano et al., "dream Activists." The article, written by undocumented organizers, presents their position and discussions about the dream Act's military option. In the article, the authors noted that at first, they listened and responded thoughtfully to the criticism of the military option in the proposed legislation. But over time, they came to this conclusion: "Our so-called allies need to realize that they are not undocumented and, as such, do not have the right to say what undocumented youth need or want. Our progressive allies insist in imposing their paternalistic stand to oppose the dream Act and tell us that this is not the 'right' choice for us to acquire 'legal' status in this country."

67   Saba, interview.

68   Sundial Cal State University Northridge (csun) YouTube Channel, "Jose Gomez on Walkout and Arrest," March 9, 2010, YouTube video, 1:50, https://www.youtube.com/watch?v=ohdJheBQcdk; Gordon, Rivera, and Santa Cruz, "Thousands Protest California Education Cuts"; *Pacific Progressive*, "LA City Attorney Carmen Trutanich's Crackdown on Activists Protested."

69   To learn about the current day rebellious work of the Youth Justice Coalition and lacan, see Hernández, *City of Inmates*, 195–220. For the Youth Justice Coalition's work on gang injunctions, see Muñiz, *Police, Power*, 78–111.

70   Diwan and Torres, interview.

71 Diwan and Torres, interview.

72 Diwan and Torres, interview.

73 Linthicum, "L.A. Drops Charges against Westwood Protesters Who Supported DREAM Act."

74 Several Tod@s members joined the 2014 BLM action that shut down the 101 freeway to protest the police slaughter of Michael Brown in Ferguson. The city and police treated BLMLA activists severely. Seven were brought to trial for charges similar to those leveled at Tod@s members—blocking a thoroughfare and refusing to disperse. The case against BLM dragged on for two years. Naazneen, who regularly attended the trial as part of a court solidarity team in 2016, noted the city's anti-Black prosecutorial practices. See Ceasar, "Black Lives Matter Protestors Who Blocked L.A. Freeway Are 'Vessels of Change,' Lawyer Tells Jury." For LA area "Undocumented, Unafraid" organizing, see chapter 5 of this book.

75 Saba, interview.

CHAPTER 3 "DON'T DEPORT OUR DADDIES"

An earlier version of this chapter was published as Monisha Das Gupta, "'Don't Deport Our Daddies': Gendering State Deportation Practices and Immigrant Organizing," *Gender and Society* 28, no. 1 (2014): 83–109.

1 Hipsman and Chishti, "Fierce Opposition, Court Rulings Place Future of Family Immigration Detention in Doubt."

2 Office of Inspector General, *Separated Children Placed in Office of Refugee Resettlement Care*. Between May and June of 2018, the Department of Homeland Security separated 2,737 children from parents. The parents were taken into custody by US Marshals and jailed to be criminally prosecuted for immigration violations. The Office of Inspector General report revealed that in 2017 federal immigration agents separated thousands more children from their parents before the administration announced the formal policy. The media coverage of crying children being torn away from parents—and the subsequent public outcry—led to an end of the policy in June 2018. The Trump administration's zero tolerance policy turbocharged these practices to horrific effect. A class action lawsuit was filed against ICE in February 2018 to stop the separation of children from their parents. The justice department rescinded the policy in January 2021.

3 Lang, "Activists Marvel as Calls for Immigrant Rights Enter the Mainstream"; Yoon-Hendricks and Greenberg, "Protests across U.S. Call for End to Migrant Family Separations"; Ember and Herndon, "How 'Abolish ICE' Went from Social Media to Progressive Candidates' Rallying Cry."

4 FFF consciously uses "deported," "detained," "deportee," and "detainee" to describe impacted members. Until recently, those at risk of deportation and their loved ones comprised FFF. As the organization has grown, it has

included those who have witnessed the harmful effects of immigration enforcement but have not directly experienced it. Some activist-scholars like Asian Amercanist Tavleen Kaur, who volunteered at detention centers in California, prefer to use "detained individuals." Kaur does so to retain the individuality of those she assisted because they appeared in the official record as case numbers. See Kaur, "Ungovernable and Inviolable."

5   According to an *Axios* report, Texas bused approximately 18,500 migrants to New York City between April 2022 and October 2023. Kight, "Texas Surpasses 50,000 Migrants Bused to Major Cities." By the end of 2023, New York City was estimated to have processed 161,500 asylum seekers. Chen and Mays, "To Avoid New York Rules, Hundreds of Migrants Dropped Off in New Jersey."

6   See Thuma, *All Our Trials*, 15–54. Thuma traces the emergence of the call "Free Them All" to the 1970s grassroots feminist BIPOC antiviolence campaigns to rally for women incarcerated for defending themselves against abusers. The campaigns connected gender-based violence to racialized criminalization and birthed "a nascent politics of prison abolition" (18). Today's calls resonate with this history.

7   Wayne Gardine was incarcerated for twenty-eight years for a crime he did not commit. Since his release from prison in April 2022, he has been incarcerated in a federal detention center. For details, see Families for Freedom, "Free Wayne Gardine."

8   For the Roxroy campaign, see Das Gupta, "'Don't Deport Our Daddies.'"

9   Glenn, "Settler Colonialism as Structure."

10 Thobani, "Navigating Colonial Pitfalls"; Thobani, *Exalted Subjects.*

11 For my discussion of the reservation scholars have expressed about the appeal to family in advocating immigrant rights, see Das Gupta, "'Don't Deport Our Daddies,'" 85–86. In the article, I use a queer of color framework to understand FFF's deployment of families.

12 Pallares, *Family Activism*; R. Rodríguez, *Next of Kin.*

13 Briggs, *How All Politics Became Reproductive Politics.*

14 For the regulation of biological reproduction in immigrant communities see Chavez, *Latino Threat*; Glenn, *Unequal Freedom*; Ordover, *American Eugenics*; M. Ramírez, "Making of Mexican Illegality."

15 Balderrama and Rodríguez, *Decade of Betrayal.*

16 Ong, *Neoliberalism as Exception.*

17 Uncle Malik's story was told by Aarti Shahani. Families for Freedom, "Uncle Malik."

18 Families For Freedom, "FFF History."

19 NYU School of Law Immigrant Rights Clinic, Immigrant Defense Project, and Families for Freedom, *Insecure Communities, Devastated Families*, 2–3, 5, 7, and 10.

20　Janay "Jani" Cauthen, interview with the author, May 25, 2023, Zoom.

21　Locally, the organization has long-term connections with a network of progressive religious groups, which used to be part of the New Sanctuary Movement. It is allied with the Northern Manhattan Coalition for Immigrant Rights (now renamed Coalition for Immigrant Freedom). It also has strong ties with the Immigrant Defense Project, the Black Alliance for Just Immigration, and Mekong NYC, which addresses the toll of deportation on the city's Southeast Asian communities. Early on, it seeded organizations like Deported Diaspora in Lowell, Massachusetts, and supported Homies Unidos in Los Angeles at a time when the immigrant rights movement avoided defending gang-involved youth or those accused or convicted of violent crimes. See Northern Manhattan Coalition for Immigrant Rights, *Deportado, Dominicano, y Humano*. To learn about Mekong NYC, see Tang, *Unsettled*. To learn about Homies Unidos, see Zilberg, *Space of Detention*.

22　Krawczyk, "Felons Have Families Too."

23　Families for Freedom, "Free Michael Santiago"; Cauthen, interview.

24　Families for Freedom, "FFF History." See the section "Grassroots Leadership and Community Organizing."

25　Detention Watch Network, *Expose and Close*.

26　istandwithravi, "Justice for Ravi Ragbir"; *Democracy Now!*, "Facing Possible Deportation, Immigrant Activist Ravi Ragbir Speaks Out before ICE Check-In"; *New York Times*, "ICE Tried to Deport an Immigration Activist"; Families for Freedom, "#KeepJeanHome." Ravi continues to live with the threat of deportation since his removal was deferred for only three years in 2022.

27　For FFF's recent effort to demand that Congress vote against billions of dollars of supplemental funding for ICE and Customs and Border Protection, see Families for Freedom, "Thank You Detention Watch Network NYC Dissenters and United We Dream." Between 2009 and 2014, FFF was part of the New York State Working Group against Deportation and worked closely with the Immigrant Defense Project on ending the ICE presence at Rikers and against the Secure Communities and Priority Enforcement Program. Immigrant Defense Project, "Ending Police Collaboration with Mass Deportation Programs." For archived campaign materials see, New York State Working Group against Deportation, "Stop 'Secure Communities' in New York"; Anti-violence Advocates against Deportation, "Anti-violence Advocates Condemn City Efforts."

28　NYU School of Law Immigrant Rights Clinic and Families for Freedom, *Justice Detained, Justice Denied*, 14–18.

29　Fortune Society, "One Day to Protect New Yorkers."

30　Families for Freedom, "Clemency Justice Act" (click on the petition to see the changes that activists demand for a fair and transparent clemency application process); Clemency Coalition of New York, "Who We Are."

31   Families for Freedom redesigned its website. The testimonies carried on the first version of FFF's website are no longer accessible through the current website. The old website page with the names of the families whose stories FFF gathered and blurbed can be found at Archive.org.

32   See Beverley, *Testimonio*. For debates over the veracity of *testimonios* and their usefulness in the social sciences, see Das Gupta, "'Don't Deport Our Daddies,'" 89–91.

33   Speed, *Incarcerated Stories*; Blackwell, *¡Chicana Power!*, 6, 14–42.

34   Berlant, *Female Complaint*, 3.

35   Cohen, "Deviance as Resistance"; Ferguson, *Aberrations in Black*; Luibhéid, "Heteronormativity and Immigration Scholarship." Immigration scholarship, in lamenting family separation, tends to reinscribe heteronormative conjugality. This chapter joins the body of scholarship critical of this type of analysis.

36   Puar, *Terrorist Assemblages*, 146.

37   Manisha Vaze, interview with the author, July 10, 2009, New York City. All subsequent quotes are drawn from this interview.

38   Golash-Boza and Hondagneu-Sotelo, "Latino Men and the Deportation Crisis"; M. Ramírez, "Making of Mexican Illegality." For the breakdown of arrests, detention, and deportation by gender, see Capps et al., *Revving up the Deportation Machinery*, 29; Ryo and Peacock, "Landscape of Immigration Detention in the United States"; Transactional Records Access Clearinghouse, "ICE Deportations: Gender, Age, and Country of Citizenship." TRAC obtained the data on gender under the Freedom of Information Act. The 2021 DHS yearbook does not break down the data on immigration enforcement actions in the interior by gender.

39   Pallares, *Family Activism*, 38–51.

40   For a review of the literature that analyzes transnational mothering and family unity, see Das Gupta, "'Don't Deport Our Daddies,'" 91–92.

41   Schaffer and Smith, *Human Rights and Narrated Lives*, 162, 183.

42   Berlant, *Female Complaint*, 2.

43   Families for Freedom, "Josh and Kathy." I am using the story with FFF's permission.

44   For media critiques leveled at women like Arellano for involving children in activism, see Pallares, *Family Activism*, 48–49.

45   Families for Freedom, "Barbara and Howard." I am using the story with FFF's permission. Kremer, Moccio, and Hammell, "Severing a Lifeline," 81–97.

46   Families for Freedom, "Joe and Mei." I am using the story with FFF's permission.

47   Wessler, "Double Punishment."

48   Janis Rosheuvel, interview by phone with Author, July 28, 2010. All subsequent quotes are drawn from this interview.

49   Families for Freedom, "#KeepJeanHome"; for details of the legal strategy to reunite Jean with his children, see Families for Freedom, "Immigrant Rights Activist Jean Montrevil's Case to Be Reopened for a New Hearing"; *Democracy Now!*, "Ending 30-Year Saga."

50   Families for Freedom, "Jean and Jani."

51   Cauthen, interview.

52   Pallares, *Family Activism*, 23–37. Pallares observes that antideportation activism has foregrounded citizens' right to family and the human right to family for noncitizens even though, technically, US courts do not recognize these as rights except in the increasingly rare case of cancellation or deferral on the grounds of extreme hardship the deportation would create for citizens. See also Kremer, Moccio, and Hammell, "Severing a Lifeline."

53   Beverley, *Testimonio*, 34–48.

54   Rosheuvel, interview.

55   Melamed, "Racial Capitalism."

56   Krawczyk, "Felons Have Families Too."

57   Rosheuvel, interview.

58   Gilmore, *Golden Gulag*, 194–96, 222–23.

59   Pallares, "Representing 'La Familia,'" 219, 229–30.

60   Ngai, *Impossible Subjects*, 75–90.

61   Vaze, interview. My emphasis.

62   Buff, "Deportation Terror." Over the years, many FFF members fighting their deportation have garnered media attention.

63   As I will discuss in chapter 5, Walter Nicholls attributes the emergence and power of DREAMers—undocumented youth—as influential social movement actors to their disciplined messaging through telling their migration and assimilation stories. He also documents the growing dissatisfaction among DREAMers with that discipline and the increasingly formulaic expectations about how the story needed to be told. Nicholls, *DREAMers*.

64   Rosheuvel, interview.

65   NYU School of Law Immigrant Rights Clinic and Families for Freedom, *Justice Detained, Justice Denied*," 10–11. For the infographic presenting the effects of New York City Police Department's stop-and-frisk program on the city's immigrants, see 11. The infographic shows that people of color are stopped and arrested at nine times the rate of white people and one out of nine adults in the city have been convicted of a crime between 2004 and 2014. A federal court found the NYPD's stop-and-frisk program to be racially discriminatory and unconstitutional in 2013.

66   Families for Freedom, "New Way Forward Act"; Office of Congresswoman Ayanna Pressley, "Pressley, García, Casar Re-introduce the New Way Forward Act."

67   Freedom for Immigrants, "Our Storytelling Archive." Freedom for Immigrants was formerly known as Community Initiatives for Visiting Immigrants in Confinement.

68   Speed, *Incarcerated Stories*, 6–7.

69   US Immigration and Customs Enforcement, "ERO FY 2020."

CHAPTER 4. "DEPORTATION = GENOCIDE"

Portions of this chapter were published as Monisha Das Gupta, "'KNOw History / KNOw Self': Khmer Youth Organizing for Justice in Long Beach," *Amerasia Journal* 45, no. 2 (2019): 137–56.

1   Echeverry, "Public Forum Exposes Cambodian Community's Deportation Challenges"; Yanga and Sagn, "Fight to Keep Them Home."

2   The civil rights organization Asian Americans Advancing Justice filed a class action suit in November 2017 challenging the arrests and redetention, putting the brakes on the removal process. On December 15, 2017, a federal judge temporarily halted the deportations, and on January 26, 2018, the judge ruled to block the deportation of ninety-two Cambodian refugees. However, in early April 2018, the forty-three who were not able to reopen their cases were deported. Southeast Asia Resource Action Center, "Southeast Asian American Community Responds to the ICE Roundup"; J. Hing, "How a Group of Immigration Attorneys Stopped a Deportation Flight to Cambodia"; Magagnini and Chabria, "Federal Judge Stops Trump Administration"; Levine and Rosenberg, "U.S. Judge Blocks Prompt Deportation of Cambodians"; Yam, "U.S. Just Quietly Deported the Largest Group of Cambodians Ever."

3   Gov, "Cambodian Community Comes Together."

4   For Oakland's Asian and Pacific Islander Youth Promoting Advocacy and Leadership (AYPAL) campaigns against the deportation of Cambodian refugees, see Kwon, *Uncivil Youth*, 95–119. Like AYPAL members, KGA organizers learn to challenge institutional violence and, thus, elude neoliberal governance aimed at managing at-risk youth.

5   Lian Cheun, interview with the author, April 4, 2016, Long Beach. All subsequent quotes are drawn from this interview.

6   Espiritu, *Body Counts*; Espiritu, "Toward a Critical Refugee Study"; Schlund-Vials, *War, Genocide, and Justice*; Schlund-Vials, "Subjects of 1975"; Nguyen, *Gift of Freedom*; Um, *From the Land of Shadows*.

7   Chan, *Survivors*, 4–12, 64–80; Kiernan, "American Bombardment of Kampuchea, 1969–1973"; Owen and Kiernan, "Bombs over Cambodia"; Tang, *Unsettled*; Um, *From the Land of Shadows*; Dao, "Refugee Representation," 90–92.

8   Bishaw and Fontenot, "Poverty 2012–2013," 4. According to an analysis of the 2007–11 American Community Survey (ACS) five-year estimates, the poverty rate among Asians in Cambodia Town was 33 percent—substantially

higher than Los Angeles County. Unemployment was 12 percent among Cambodia Town Asians. The census did not present disaggregated data for the Asian category. UCLA Asian American Studies Center, Asian Pacific Policy and Planning Council, and UCLA Department of Urban Planning, *State of Cambodia Town*, 11–13.

9 KGA's 2014–15 newsletter states, "From war, bombings and refugee camps to displacement, poverty, incarceration and deportation, we've reflected on the institutional root causes that have shaped our family's experiences." Hard copies of the newsletter were available at the KGA office during my 2016 fieldwork in Long Beach. Ashley Uyeda, interview with the author, March 18, 2016, Long Beach. All subsequent quotes are drawn from this interview. Ashley transitioned out of KGA in 2017.

10 On the racialization and spatialization of Southeast Asian gang violence, see Cacho, *Social Death*, 61–96.

11 Rios, *Punished*.

12 B. Hing, *Deporting Our Souls*; Walter Leitner International Human Rights Clinic, Returnee Integration Support Center, and Deported Diaspora, *Removing Refugees*; Newnham and Grabias, *Sentenced Home*.

13 Prime Minister Hun Sen maintained his and the Cambodian People's Party's grip for over thirty years by repressing opposition parties and freedom of speech and assembly. A Khmer Rouge commander who broke rank, Hun Sen, in his role as prime minister, has used lethal violence against political dissidents and trade union leaders and has obstructed the prosecution of Khmer Rouge leaders for war crimes. In 2023, Hun Sen stepped down, handing over the position to his son, Hun Manet, who continues to repress opposition parties. See Human Rights Watch, "30 Years of Hun Sen"; Human Rights Watch, "Cambodia: Events of 2016"; Human Rights Watch, "Cambodia: New Prime Minister." Cathy Schlund-Vials discusses Hun Sen's efforts to induce genocide amnesia. Schlund-Vials, *War, Genocide, and Justice*.

14 Asian Americans Advancing Justice, "Resources"; National Coalition for Asian Pacific American Community Development, "Our Neighborhoods," 32. A House bill reintroduced in 2023 to provide deportation relief for Southeast Asians puts the number of Cambodians deported since 2002 at one thousand. US House, Southeast Asian Deportation Relief Act of 2023.

15 Schlund-Vials, *War, Genocide, and Justice*. Ethnic studies scholars who study Cambodia and Cambodian Americans as well as Cambodian American community-based organizations prefer the term "genocide" instead of "auto-genocide" to characterize the mass killings and atrocities committed by the Khmer Rouge. See Schlund-Vials, *War, Genocide, and Justice*, loc. 173 of 5027; Um, *From the Land of the Shadows*, 4–5.

16 Between 1964 and 1975, the United States dropped 2,756,941 ordnance on Cambodia, affecting 113,716 sites. See Owen and Kiernan, "Bombs over Cambodia."

17 As self-descriptors, Tongva also use Gabrielino/Tongva, Gabrielino or Gabrieleño. Following Jurmain and McCawley, *O, My Ancestor*, I use Tongva in this chapter. On the Ancestor Walk on October 7, 2017, elders used Tongva to name themselves and the land.

18 KGA director Lian Cheun talked about seeking resources, including funding, to put the local Cambodian community in conversation with Indigenous and non-Indigenous groups impacted by genocide. She expressed the value of such exchanges and wished KGA was better resourced. Chhaya Chhoum of Mekong NYC and the Southeast Asian Freedom Network drew parallels, not congruence, between Cambodian refugee efforts to assert their identity and culture against all odds and Native American cultural revitalization. Addressing the limits of the single-issue frame of immigration reform, Chhoum pointed out that Khmer refugee efforts at cultural recovery are intrinsic to all efforts to build power in the community, just as Native American self-determination cannot be delinked from reclaiming culture and identity. Chhaya Chhoum, interview with the author, July 8, 2009, New York City.

19 Espiritu, *Body Counts*, 21.

20 Torres et al., "Perspectives on a Selection of Gabrieleño/Tongva Places." An alternative spelling of Povuu'ngna is Puvungna, which is how the site is named in a guide to the Ancestor Walk route. Indian Voices, "Ancestor Walk."

21 Leong and Carpio, "Carceral States," vii–xviii.

22 Uyeda, interview. The details here about KGA's structure and leadership development are drawn from this interview.

23 For an in-depth discussion of this first-year curriculum, see Das Gupta, "'KNOw History / KNOw Self.'"

24 Uyeda, interview.

25 Cheun, interview.

26 Muñiz, *Police*, 78–111.

27 The heading for this section, "Step into Long Beach," comes from a 2011 KGA report based on youth participatory action research. KGA youth leaders surveyed five hundred peers in Long Beach to produce the report. See Khmer Girls in Action, "Step into Long Beach." For the research design and findings, see Sangalang, Ngouy, and Lau, "Using Community-Based Participatory Research." One of the coauthors, Suely Ngouy, was the executive director of KGA when I visited the organization in 2009. She was part of the team that guided the participatory action research conducted by KGA youth.

28 Chhoum, interview.

29 Needham and Quintiliani, "Cambodians in Long Beach"; Needham and Quintiliani, "Why Long Beach?"; Asian Pacific Policy and Planning Council, UCLA Asian American Studies Center, and UCLA Department of Urban Planning, *State of Cambodia Town*, 9. Recent research shows that urban

redevelopment in Long Beach since 2015 is displacing the city's long-term immigrant residents, most of whom are renters, exacerbating housing instability and overcrowding. Trendy cafes and chains are pushing out immigrant-owned businesses. López et al., "Walking to Build a Critical Community-Engaged Project."

30   Chan, *Survivors*, 66.

31   Interview with the former executive director of KGA, Suely Ngouy, February 23, 2009, Long Beach.

32   Cheun, interview.

33   Camp, *Incarcerating the Crisis.* Jordan Camp, tracing the neoliberalization of the carceral apparatus, reminds us that the expansion of incarceration in the neoliberal era did not start or stop with Ronald Reagan but was a bipartisan agreement to pour resources into police, prisons, military, antiterrorism measures, and domestic counterinsurgency targeting liberation movements. The strategy fostered a "commonsense" about the necessity of the apparatus.

34   Needham and Quintiliani, "Cambodians in Long Beach," 39–43.

35   McCawley, introduction to *O, My Ancestor*, xxi–xxvi.

36   McCawley, "Enduring Vision", 199.

37   B. Hing, *Deporting Our Souls*; Walter Leitner International Human Rights Clinic, Returnee Integration Support Center, and Deported Diaspora, *Removing Refugees.* Neither touch on the developments in criminal law. The Leitner report makes recommendations to the State Department and raises the violations of refugee protections under international law (4–6).

38   For the legal development of gang injunctions, see Muñiz, *Police, Power.* For the impact of California and federal legislation governing gangs, see Zilberg, *Space of Detention.*

39   For a detailed discussion of the "Every Student Matters" campaign, see Das Gupta, "'KNOw History / KNOw Self,'" 145–48.

40   Rios, *Punished.*

41   Building Healthy Communities Long Beach, "Every Student Matters!," 1.

42   Building Healthy Communities Long Beach, "Every Student Matters: Profile; Long Beach Unified School District (LBUSD)," 8.

43   Khmer Girls in Action, "Step into Long Beach," 3, 10, 11.

44   Khmer Girls in Action, "Step into Long Beach," 5.

45   Khmer Girls in Action, "Step into Long Beach," 11.

46   Zilberg, *Space of Detention*, 25–35, 38; Menjívar, "Central American Immigrant Workers and Legal Violence in Phoenix, Arizona," 235–37. The foreign policy context sets refugees from Cambodia, Vietnam, and Laos apart from Central American refugees, who were similarly criminalized as gang members and deported. The United States was far more reluctant to grant Salvadorans and Guatemalans refugee status because of its overt and covert role of military support for counterrevolutionary forces throughout Central America during the 1980s. Less than 3 percent of Salvadorans and Guate-

malans were granted political asylum in the 1980s. When they were allowed
to reapply for refugee status in 1990 after a class action suit, the acceptance
rate went up minimally: 28 percent for Salvadorans and 18 percent for
Guatemalans. Nicaraguans, in contrast, were more readily granted refugee
status because the United States considered them to be fleeing a communist
regime.

47 Chan, *Survivors*, 64–66.

48 Section 4 of a House of Representatives bill reintroduced in 2023 proposes
the reopening of immigration cases of persons deported. US House, Southeast Asian Deportation Relief Act of 2023.

49 Southeast Asian Freedom Network, "SEAFN Campaign Solidarity Letter";
Smith, K., "Southeast Asian Community Members Vow to Fight."

50 Obama, "Remarks by the President in Address to the Nation on Immigra-
tion." Neither an expansion of Deferred Action for Childhood Arrivals nor
DAPA by the Obama administration could be implemented because the
US Supreme Court was tied and could not reach a majority decision. The
Supreme Court ruling was issued on June 23, 2016. The lower court blocks
on these two proposed programs remain in place. In 2017, the Department
of Homeland Security under the Trump administration rescinded the 2014
Obama administration memorandum. National Immigration Law Center,
"United States v. Texas"; I. Rodriguez, "What Does the DAPA Rescission
Mean?"

51 Um, *From the Land of Shadows*.

52 Chan, *Survivors*, 32–80.

53 The vast scholarship on genocide underlines the equally horrific efforts at
cultural extermination that work in tandem with physical extermination.

54 Schlund-Vials, *War, Genocide, and Justice*, 13.

55 Poeuv, *New Year Baby*.

56 Even as I make this comparison, it is essential to remember that the Department of Homeland Security and CoreCivic (formerly, the Corrections
Corporation of America) do not have a revolutionary goal, unlike the Khmer
Rouge. Khatharya Um rightly warns us that to forget that "flawed as it was,
the Khmer Rouge did have a vision of change that they pursued with blind
resoluteness, one that was not incubated in isolation but 'within the ruins
and ruinations' of empire" runs the risk of placing the regime outside of history, rendering its violence irrational. Um, *From the Land of Shadows*, 3.

57 In July 2023, Hun Sen announced that he would hand over power to his son
Hun Manet. Reuters, "Cambodian PM Hun Sen to Hand Over Power to
Son Next Month."

58 Human Rights Watch, "30 Years of Hun Sen"; Ruiz, "Cambodian Community
Calls on City Leaders"; Ruiz, "After Public Backlash, Hun Manet Says He
Won't Attend Long Beach Cambodian New Year Parade"; Dulaney, "Cambo-
dian Military Leader Not Invited to Cambodia Town Culture Festival."

59   KhmerTV, "Khmer Protest Long Beach City Hall," April 8, 2016, YouTube
     video, 1:02:01. https://www.youtube.com/watch?v=rvGh4JJ4PrI.

60   Sophya Chhiv, interview with the author, April 7, 2016, Long Beach. All
     subsequent references are drawn from this interview.

61   Ngouy, interview.

62   This story, unlike the Families for Freedom public *testimonios* or the Im-
     migrant Youth Coalition's "Undocumented, Unafraid" stories, was shared
     unelicited during the interview.

63   Chhiv, interview.

64   Alexander, *New Jim Crow.*

65   Abrego, "On Silences."

66   I am often asked if I have thought about Audra Simpson's concept of refusal
     in the context of refugee refusal. The two types of refusals are not analogous,
     though they both advance critiques of state-sponsored violence. Audra
     Simpson frames the refusal of Mohawks of Kahnawà:ke and, more broadly,
     Indigenous peoples of North America as an assertion of self-determination
     and an alternative to political recognition offered by the United States, the
     occupying foreign power. I argue throughout that grasping the distinction
     between the conditions of racialized minorities and Indigenous sovereignty
     and nationhood is crucial for migration scholars. For the multiple registers
     of resistance in the form of survivors' silence about the atrocities of the Pol
     Pot regime, see Um, *From the Land of Shadows*, 193–98.

67   I participated in the Twentieth Annual Pilgrimage of "Tongva & Acjache-
     men people, carrying prayers for our ancestors and future generations" on
     October 7, 2017. For a map and description of the sacred sites, see Indian
     Voices, "Ancestor Walk." We visited the same sites on the 2020 map during
     the 2017 walk. At each of the eight ancient sites we visited, organizers of
     the pilgrimage shared stories of desecration as a result of development for
     residential as well as commercial use.

68   Jurmain, preface to *O, My Ancestor*; McCawley, introduction to *O, My An-
     cestor*; Ti'at Society, "A Conversation." See also Torres et al., "Perspectives on
     a Selection of Gabrieleño/Tongva Places."

69   Jurmain, preface to *O, My Ancestor*, xv.

70   Ti'at Society, "A Conversation," 127–36, 141–43, 145–46. I was honored to
     meet Tongva elder, poet, and writer Gloria Arellanes during the 2017 Ances-
     tor Walk. She taught us the significance of Bolsa Chica and other sites that
     Tongva have struggled to protect.

71   Indian Vision, "Ancestor Walk."

72   McCawley, "Enduring Vision," 197–214.

73   Blackhawk, *Violence over the Land.*

74   Aikau et al., "Indigenous Feminisms Roundtable," 87. Aikau elaborates on
     the Hawaiian concept of kuleana (responsibility, authority, and obligation)
     as central to the terms on which Kanaka ʻŌiwi, First Nations, and non-

Indigenous students engage with place, Indigenous politics, and ethics in Hawai'i.

75 Byrd, *Transit of Empire*, 53.

76 Simpson, *Mohawk Interruptus*.

CHAPTER 5 NOT DREAMING

1 Johnathan has aged out of "youth" organizing but continued to be closely involved with the Immigrant Youth Coalition, mentoring youth to take collective and transformative action until 2018. The IYC started to disband by late 2018. Many members continue to support each other and organize with one another in other political formations in the Los Angeles area.

2 Hall, "Which of These Things Is Not Like the Other"; Teves and Arvin, "Decolonizing API"; Okamura, "Race and/or Ethnicity in Hawai'i"; Darrah-Okike, "Theorizing Race in Hawai'i"; Kamaka et al., "Addressing Native Hawaiian and Pacific Islander Data Deficiencies."

3 Hauʻofa, "Our Sea of Islands."

4 Trask, "Color of Violence," 10–11.

5 Goodyear-Kaʻōpua, introduction to *Nation Rising*, 3–7. Goodyear-Kaʻōpua reminds us that though ea is often used to declare political sovereignty, its three registers—life, breath, sovereignty—are inseparable.

6 Office of Hawaiian Affairs, *Disparate Treatment of Native Hawaiians in the Criminal Justice System*; Irwin and Umemoto, *Jacked Up and Unjust*, 105–25; Das Gupta and Haglund, "Mexican Migration to Hawai'i and US Settler Colonialism," 469–73.

7 DREAMer storytelling, especially in the early years when adults controlled the narrative, promotes the dominant understanding of youth as would-be citizens and ideal workers whose potential needed to be tapped. For a transnational approach to youth studies that moves away from developmental theories, see Maira, *Missing*, 15–21; for a review of critical youth studies, see Irwin and Umemoto, *Jacked Up and Unjust*, 13–15. Irwin and Umemoto shift their research from the crime and deviance literature's focus on "at-risk" youth. Instead, they attend to the intersecting injustices that constitute their experience, resilience, and resistance.

8 Chávez, *Queer Migration Politics*, 2368–2514 of 5401; Escudero, *Organizing While Undocumented*; Abrego and Negrón-Gonzales, *We Are Not Dreamers*; Pallares, *Family Activism*, 97–130; Ramirez Solórzano, "Welcome to Cuban Miami."

9 On the strategic use of the term "Micronesian," see Joakim "Jojo" Peter in Lyons and Tengan, "COFA Complex," 665–66.

10 Tengan, "Hoa." Tengan explicates the noun and verb forms of hoa. As a noun, it refers to a companion; as a verb, it refers to tying or lashing with braided cordage made from coconut husk. In other works, Tengan concep-

tualizes the related concept of ʻaha, usually used to refer to a gathering or assembly. He expands on the word's other meanings. ʻAha also refers to the braided cordage used in a hoa lashing. He elaborates on ʻaha as a measuring, gauging, marking, and recalibrating practice that ensures architectural stability. His interpretation points to the construction of new Indigenous solidarities and connectivities that lend integrity, mana (sacred power), and balance to these formations. The cord's hoa (lashing) function in build-ing canoes for voyaging also activates genealogical connections to places, people, and spiritual forces across Moana Nui (Oceania). Tengan, "Mana of Kū," 68–71; Tengan, Kaʻili, and Fonoti, "Genealogies."

11   Lyons and Tengan, "cofa Complex"; Tengan, "Hoa"; Lā Hoʻi Hoʻi Ea Ho-nolulu, "Together We Rise Solidarity Panel," July 26, 2021, Facebook video, 1:30:21, https://www.facebook.com/lahoihoiea/videos/810562566318437/; Fujimori, "hpd Shootings Questioned in Wake of Chauvin Verdict."

12   The United States tested sixty-seven hydrogen and atomic bombs on Eniwetok and Bikini in the Marshall Islands between 1946 and 1958. The Bravo nuclear test conducted on March 1, 1954, was one thousand times more powerful than the bomb the United States dropped on Hiroshima. The Bravo test released radioactive debris that scattered over seven thousand square miles of ocean and inhabited land. The effects of the nuclear fallout is associated with twenty-two types of cancer. Hawaiʻi Appleseed Center for Law and Economic Justice, *Broken Promises, Shattered Lives*; Genz et al., *Militarism and Nuclear Testing in the Pacific*, 12–25; Geminiani, "Case for Justice for Micronesians in Hawaii"; Letman, "Micronesians in Hawaii Face Uncertain Future"; Department of Busi-ness, Economic Development, and Tourism, cofa *Migrants in Hawaii*.

13   On the importance of place-specific processes of racialization in undocuqueer organizing, see Ramirez Solórzano, "Welcome to Cuban Miami."

14   I have heard Johnathan tell his story several times. Here, I present a compos-ite. The direct quotes are taken from a presentation to students in one of my courses on February 24, 2012. In the chapter, I also draw on two interviews with Johnathan. Perez, interview with the author, November 8, 2014, Los Angeles; Perez, interview with the author, July 23, 2022, Zoom.

15   Perez, interview, July 23, 2022. Johnathan, detailing the growth of the iyc, said that it established six chapters over time, starting in 2010. The SGV, LA, and San Fernando Valley chapters had the same governing structure. The other iyc chapters were independent and determined their local platforms. All chapters convened from time to time and coordinated statewide actions. In Orange County, the iyc supported the formation of Resilience OC to develop the capacity of youth to bring about systemic change. See also Flores, "#iyc Immigrant Youth Coalition."

16   I am quoting from the November 18, 2017, San Gabriel Valley iyc Youth Empowerment Summit program. The summit was held in Baldwin Park. In the "Overview and Purpose" section of the program, the iyc used "Trans*

and Queer youth" to describe its members. A hard copy of the program is in the author's possession. The ɪʏᴄ's focus on undocuqueer and undocuBlack leadership was clear to me from attending an ɪʏᴄ Coming Out of the Shadows event in Boyle Heights on March 25, 2016, and the Baldwin Park Youth Empowerment Summit.

17 Cheng, *Changs Next Door to the Díazes*. In her study of the majority Asian and Latinx in San Gabriel Valley, Wendy Cheng documents a place-specific suburban racial and political consciousness that emerged from mundane codes of coexistence.

18 On the metaphor, shadows, and the coalitional possibilities of migrant youth adopting the rhetoric of "coming out" from ʟɢʙᴛǫ visibility politics, see K. Chávez, *Queer Migration Politics*, 2028–2141 of 5401.

19 K. Chávez, *Queer Migration Politics*, 2141–2276 of 5401. See also Escudero, *Organizing While Undocumented*, 77–104; Pallares, *Family Activism*, 97–131.

20 Perez, interview, November 8, 2014.

21 For Neidi Dominguez Zamorano's role in the campaign for ᴅᴀᴄᴀ, see Hung, "Movement Lawyering as Rebellious Lawyering."

22 Zamorano et al., "ᴅʀᴇᴀᴍ Activists."

23 On the efforts by national organizations to harness grassroots energies to pass comprehensive immigration reform, see Nicholls, *DREAMers*, 43–45. On the rifts between these mainstream immigrant rights coalitions and DREAMers, see Nicholls, *DREAMers*, 74–98. On the disruption of heteropatriarchal structures and culture in the immigrant rights movement by the Trail of Dreams undocumented queer of color youth and nontraditional leaders, see Ramirez Solórzano, "Trail of Dreams." Risking detention and deportation, they walked 1,500 miles across the South to make the struggles of undocumented people visible and call for action.

24 Zamorano et al., "ᴅʀᴇᴀᴍ Activists."

25 Ransby, *Ella Baker and the Black Freedom Movement*, 239–64. On the pivotal role youth played in sit-ins in the US South starting in 1960, and, more broadly, in the Black freedom movement, see also Harding and Ikeda, *America Will Be!*, 103–16.

26 Zamorano et al., "ᴅʀᴇᴀᴍ Activists."

27 Perez, interview, November 8, 2014.

28 Nicholls, *DREAMers*, see 130–42.

29 Immigrant Youth Coalition Leaders, interview with the author, April 13, 2016, Los Angeles. All subsequent references are to this interview. My emphasis. Four ɪʏᴄ leaders joined me that day for a group interview. Marcela and Claudia were among the four.

30 Perez, interview, November 8, 2014. Johnathan discussed the parallels between ɴᴀꜰᴛᴀ and the Obama administration's Trans-Pacific Partnership pushed at the 2011 Asia-Pacific Economic Cooperation forum held in Honolulu in 2011. The Moana Nui conference, held as a parallel event, put forth

an alternative vision of trans-Pacific relations and economic integration. See
Moana Nui, "Moana Nui Statement."

31 Immigrant Youth Coalition Leaders, interview.

32 Perez, interview, July 23, 2022.

33 Perez, interview, July 23, 2022. For Valeria's story, see Zonkel, "Transgender
    Activist Valeria De La Luz Ramos."

34 Perez, interview, November 8, 2014.

35 Perez, interview, November 8, 2014.

36 Immigrant Youth Coalition Leaders, interview.

37 Perez, interview, November 8, 2014.

38 Perez, interview, November 8, 2014.

39 By 2016, California provided health care for undocumented children under
    nineteen living in low-income families. California Legislative Information,
    "SB-4 Health Care Coverage"; California made undocumented migrants
    twenty-five and under eligible for the state's Medicaid program in 2019; see
    Allyn, "California is 1st State to Offer Health Benefits." In 2021, California
    extended Medi-Cal to low-income adults aged fifty years and older, regard-
    less of their immigration status; see Office of Governor Gavin Newsom,
    "Governor Newsom Signs Into Law First-in-the-Nation Expansion." In 2022,
    the California Assembly introduced a universal health care bill. See Califor-
    nia Legislative Information, "AB-1400 Guaranteed Health Care for All."

40 See Office of Hawaiian Affairs, *Disparate Treatment of Native Hawaiians
    in the Criminal Justice System*. The report is visually organized around
    the planting and harvesting of kalo (taro), the plant that grew out of the
    stillborn child of Wākea (Sky father) and Hoʻohōkūkalani. They had a
    second child, considered to be the first kanaka (human). Kalo, named
    Hāloanakalaukapalili, is the elder sibling of this first human, Hāloa. The
    creation story emphasizes the genealogical connection between kalo and
    Native Hawaiians and the interdependency of land and people. Humans
    have a responsibility to care for kalo. The report emphasizes all the ways in
    which incarceration disconnects Native Hawaiians from the ʻāina (land and
    water bodies), their extended family, and their community and recommends
    that the kind of care that allows kalo to flourish be extended to Native Ha-
    waiian prisoners (paʻahao) in their reintegration. It is an excellent resource
    for culturally grounded responses to Native Hawaiians under correctional
    control and their families. For a feminist reading of the mating of Wākea and
    Hoʻohōkūkalani, see Goodyear-Kaʻōpua, "Kuleana Lāhui," 147–50.

41 For the evolution of a colonial system of punishment in the nineteenth-
    century Hawaiian Kingdom, during the tumultuous years following the
    overthrow and the territorial period, see Sonoda, "Nation Incarcerated,"
    99–103; Keahiolalo-Karasuda, "Genealogy of Punishment in Hawaiʻi"; Stan-
    nard, *Honor Killing*; Okamura, *Raced to Death in 1920s Hawaiʻi*, 29–36. For
    the overwhelming number of Native Hawaiians arrested and incarcerated

and the explosion of prisoners in Hawaiʻi, see Office of Hawaiian Affairs, *Disparate Treatment of Native Hawaiians in the Criminal Justice System*; Chesney-Lind and Merce, "Toward a Smaller, Smarter Correctional System for Hawaiʻi."

42   Labrador, "'I No Eat Dog K,'" 73.

43   Tengan, "Hoa," 281; Kahapeʻa, "Sailing the Ancestral Bridges of Oceanic Knowledge"; Kānehūnāmoku Voyaging Academy, "Kānehūnāmoku Voyaging Academy"; We Are Oceania, "Youth Empowerment Center"; Kōkua Kalihi Valley, "History"; Kōkua Kalihi Valley, "Pacific Voices."

44   The Community Alliance on Prisons, cofounded by Kat Brady, who attended several YES events, is a watchdog body that tracks prison expansion legislation and policy in Hawaiʻi. During this time, it was raising awareness about the state government's contracts with private prisons in Arizona and Oklahoma.

45   Sonoda, "Nation Incarcerated," 107–10. Sonoda uses the term "deporation" to drive home the relocation of Native Hawaiians from the Hawaiian Nation to the US continent. This characterization, which I find appropriate, should not be confused with my critique in the introduction of the analogy between Indian removal and deportation. For the treatment of Native Hawaiians under the US legal system, see Kauanui, *Hawaiian Blood*.

46   US Immigration and Customs Enforcement and Hawaii Criminal Justice Data Center, *Memorandum of Agreement*.

47   Das Gupta and Haglund, "Mexican Migration to Hawaiʻi and US Settler Colonialism."

48   A decade-plus fight ensued against Hawaiʻi state's removal of COFA citizens from the state's Medicaid program (QUEST). The policy shift increased Micronesian mortality rates. The move was instigated by federal laws, which made Micronesians along with undocumented migrants and unqualified legal permanent residents ineligible for Medicaid. The community-based organizing against the elimination was successful in getting Congress to restore Medicaid to COFA residents in 2020. For the impact of federal and state policies on the access of COFA residents to health care, see Riklon et al., "'Compact Impact' in Hawaiʻi"; McElfish et al., "Compact of Free Association Migrants and Health Insurance Policies." For Hawaiʻi's community responses, see Peter, Tanaka, and Yamashiro, "Reconnecting Our Roots." For the health status of Hawaiʻi's Micronesians, see Pobutsky, Krupitsky, and Yamada, "Micronesian Migrant Health Issues in Hawaii." For higher mortality rates among COFA residents resulting from curtailed health care, see Ng Kamstra, Molina, and Halliday, "Compact for Care." For the restoration of Medicaid to COFA citizens by Congress, see Young, "Over 20 Years Later."

49   Sound-Kikku, interview with author, July 1, 2022, Zoom. The direct quotes are drawn from this interview. Other references to her community-building work and youth mentorship are based on my many conversations with her

over the years. To get a sense of Sound-Kikku's resolute work of cultural revitalization in the face of vicious discrimination Micronesians face in Hawai'i, see Sound-Kikku, "I Am of Oceania."

50 See Peter, Tanaka, and Yamashiro, "Reconnecting Our Roots," 198.

51 Transactional Records Access Clearinghouse, "ICE Deportations by Country of Citizenship: FY 2012–FY 2013"; US Immigration and Customs Enforcement, *U.S. Immigration and Customs Enforcement Fiscal Year 2020 Enforcement and Removal Operations Report*, 30–31. The numbers declined in 2020, in keeping with an overall decline in removals and criminal ICE arrests that year.

52 Office of Hawaiian Affairs, *Disparate Treatment of Native Hawaiians in the Criminal Justice System*, 29.

53 Irwin and Umemoto, *Jacked Up and Unjust*, 115.

54 Prison Policy Initiative, "Hawaii Profile"; Jedra and Hofschneider, "'Significant' Disparity in Use of Force"; Hill, "HPD's Use of Lethal Force Is Near the US Average."

55 Maria shared her participation in civil disobedience during an interview aired on O'ahu's public access television. *Equally Speaking*, "Undocumented and Unafraid." A DVD of the program is in the author's possession.

56 Johnathan, Isabel, and Maria shared these experiences at multiple events during the IYC visit to Honolulu between February 23 and 29, 2012.

57 National Immigrant Youth Alliance, "Youth Empowerment Summit (YES Training): Leadership Workshop Guide," 15. The manual was published October 2011 in California. The manual was shared with the author in preparation for the training. It was not made available online.

58 Irwin and Umemoto, *Jacked Up and Unjust*, 89.

59 Sound-Kikku, interview. Lack of mental health support for Micronesian youth has become an increasing concern among community advocates. In 2022, suicides in Kalihi Valley, including by an eleven-year-old, have shaken the community. Innocenta raised the alarm, asking for more resources and spaces for youth to speak their mind.

60 US Commission on Civil Rights, "Micronesians in Hawaii," 34–36.

61 Hofschneider, "#BeingMicronesian in Hawaii Means Lots of Online Hate"; Hofschneider, "Why Talking about Anti-Micronesian Hate Is Important"; Caparoso and Collins, "College Student Racial and Ethnic Stereotype-Based Humor as a Cultural Domain."

62 Lawrence, "Local Kine Implicit Bias," 460. In his analysis, Lawrence quotes in length a *Honolulu Star-Advertiser* report on the state appeals court's resentencing ruling because of the prosecutor's ethnically biased remarks asking the trial judge to impose a harsher sentence based on the accused man's ethnicity. Lawrence emphasized the text I quote.

63 Lawrence, "Local Kine Implicit Bias," 459–72.

64 Hawai'i Scholars for Education and Social Justice, *Racism and Discrimination against Micronesians in Hawai'i*, 11–12.

65   Hawaiʻi Scholars for Education and Social Justice, *Racism and Discrimination against Micronesians in Hawaiʻi*, 9–10.

66   On the disconnection of Hawaiʻi's Chuukese youth from their culture and language, see Lyons and Tengan, "COFA Complex," 673–75.

67   Sound-Kikku, interview.

68   The play was created by Leilani Chan and Ova Saopeng in collaboration with Innocenta Sound-Kikku and Kalihi-based Pacific Voices. Chan and Soaping have roots in Hawaiʻi. The play allowed them to return and develop a creative work with the community. They have lovingly named Innocenta a "cultural navigator." They describe their production company TeAda as "nomadic theatre of color" and the play as decolonizing theatre. See TeAda Productions, *Masters of the Currents*, to learn about the play and watch clips. For a conversation with the directors and cast, see USC Visions and Voices, "*Masters of the Currents*: A Conversation with the Creators and Cast," April 9, 2021, YouTube video, 1:10:55, https://www.youtube.com/watch?v=D1Lp7HvaoSs.

69   Hauʻofa, "Our Sea of Islands."

70   Futurity as a utopian impulse embedded in a collectivity has been taken up and elaborated by queer, Indigenous, and disability justice scholars. While a review of the literature is beyond the scope of this chapter, see Arvin, Tuck, and Morrill, "Decolonizing Feminism," 24–25, on futurity and decolonization.

71   Innocenta Sound-Kikku, personal communication, January 24, 2024.

72   Sound-Kikku, interview.

73   University of Hawaiʻi News, "Regents Approve Undocumented Immigrants Policy."

74   For a student-centered definition of education equity, see S.I.N. Collective, "Students Informing Now (S.I.N.) Challenge the Racial State." Members of the S.I.N collective, like Neidi Dominguez Zamorano and Mariella Saba, are comrades of IYC founders.

75   Okamura, *Ethnicity and Inequality in Hawaiʻi*, 85–88.

76   A fact sheet prepared by the students with the help of faculty stated that undocumented students would not become eligible for any of the financial assistance programs or tuition differentials reserved for Native Hawaiians and clarified that under federal law, undocumented students were not eligible for federal aid. The fact sheet was widely circulated inside and outside the university and was presented to the regents.

77   Kamaka et al., "Addressing Native Hawaiian and Pacific Islander Data Deficiencies."

78   Hawaiʻi Scholars for Education and Social Justice, *Racism and Discrimination against Micronesians in Hawaiʻi*, 8; Okamura, *Ethnicity and Inequality in Hawaiʻi*, 76–88.

79   Tengan, "Hoa," 281.

80   ho' omanawanui et al., "Teaching for Maunakea."

81   Boylan, "Family of Iremamber Sykap Sues City and Officers"; Boylan, "3 Honolulu Police Department Officers Are Charged."

82   Yamaga, "Pull Down Barriers That Cause Mistrust of 'Other' Communities."

83   Jedra, "Honolulu Officers Will Not Be Tried in Sykap Killing, Judge Rules."

84   USC Visions and Voices, *Masters of the Currents.*

CONCLUSION JAILBREAK

1   Yalamarty, "Lessons from 'No Ban on Stolen Land.'" Yalamarty gives several examples to demonstrate that the ban broadly targeted Muslims entering the United States, regardless of their citizenship, passport, or visa.

2   Yalamarty, "Lessons from 'No Ban on Stolen Land'"; Lee-Oliver et al., "Imperialism, Settler Colonialism, and Indigeneity"; Walia, *Undoing Border Imperialism.* In the last chapter, Walia signposts organizing strategies to undo border imperialism.

3   Kaba, *We Do This 'Til We Free Us,* 66.

4   I am grateful to Ty Kāwika Tengan for sharing his account of the ceremony and explaining the layered meanings of 'aha and hoa. See Lyons and Tengan, "COFA Complex," 675–77; Tengan, "Mana of Kū," 68–71; Tengan, "Hoa."

BIBLIOGRAPHY

Abrego, Leisy. "On Silences: Salvadoran Refugees Then and Now." *Latino Studies* 15, no. 1 (2017): 73–85.

Abrego, Leisy, and Genevieve Negrón-Gonzales. *We Are Not Dreamers: Undocumented Scholars Theorize Undocumented Life in the United States.* Durham, NC: Duke University Press, 2020.

ACLU of New York. "Court Rules NY Law Enforcement Cannot Detain Immigrants for ICE." November 14, 2018. https://www.nyclu.org/en/press-releases/court -rules-ny-law-enforcement-cannot-detain-immigrants-ice.

Agarwal, Nina. "Black Lives Matter, Other Activists Protest to Stop Jail Expansion." *Los Angeles Times*, September 26, 2017. https://www.latimes.com/local/lanow /la-me-ln-black-lives-matter-protests-jail-expansion-20170926-story.html.

Aikau, Hokulani, Maile Arvin, Mishuana Goeman, and Scott Morgensen. "Indigenous Feminisms Roundtable." *Frontiers* 36, no. 3 (2015): 84–106.

Aizeki, Mizue. "Mass Deportation under the Homeland Security State: Anti-violence Advocates Join the Fight against Criminalization of Immigrants." *s and F Online* 15, no. 3 (2019). https://sfonline.barnard.edu/mass-deportation -under-the-homeland-security-state-anti-violence-advocates-join-the-fight -against-criminalization-of-immigrants/.

Alexander, Michelle. *The New Jim Crow: Mass Incarceration in the Age of Colorblindness.* New York: New Press, 2010.

Alianza Indígena Sin Fronteras and Christina Leza. *Handbook on Indigenous Peoples' Border Crossing Rights between the United States and Mexico.* Tucson: Alianza Indígena Sin Fronteras, 2019. https://www.ohchr.org /Documents/Issues/IPeoples/EMRIP/Call/IndigenousAllianceWithoutBorde rs.pdf.

Allyn, Bobby. "California is 1st State to Offer Health Benefits to Adult Undocumented Immigrants." NPR, July 10, 2019. https://www.npr.org/2019 /07/10/740147546/california-first-state-to-offer-health-benefits-to-adult -undocumented-immigrants.

Anti-violence Advocates against Deportation. "Anti-violence Advocates Condemn City's Efforts to Limit Harm of Secure Communities Program; Call for Further Protections." New York State Working Group against Deportation, January 25, 2013. https://newyorkagainstdeportation.files.wordpress.com/2019/05 /ava-press-statement-20130125-final.pdf.

Anti-violence Advocates against Deportation. "Building Truly Secure Communities." New York State Working Group against Deportation, May 2012. https://
newyorkagainstdeportation.files.wordpress.com/2011/04/ava-points-of-unity
-may-2012-v2.pdf.

Archuleta, Elizabeth. "'I Give You Back': Indigenous Women Writing to Survive."
Studies in American Indian Literatures 18 no. 4 (2006): 88–114.

Arvin, Maile, Eve Tuck, and Angie Morrill. "Decolonizing Feminism: Challenging
Connections between Settler Colonialism and Heteropatriarchy." *Feminist
Formations* 25, no. 1 (2013): 8–34.

Asian Americans Advancing Justice. "Resources for Southeast Asian Refugees Facing Deportation." Last updated November 10, 2022. https://www
.advancingjustice-alc.org/news-resources/guides-reports/resources-southeast
-asian-refugees-facing-deportation.

Audre Lorde Project (ALP). *Community at a Crossroads: U.S. Right Wing Policies
and Lesbian, Gay, Bisexual, Two Spirit and Transgender Immigrants for Color
in New York City*. New York: Audre Lorde Project, 2004.

Balderrama, Francisco E., and Raymond Rodríguez. *Decade of Betrayal: Mexican
Repatriation in the 1930s*. Rev. ed. Albuquerque: University of New Mexico
Press, 2006.

Barker, Joanne. "Indigenous Feminisms." In *The Oxford Handbook of Indigenous
People's Politics*, edited by José Antonio Lucero, Dale Turner, and Donna
Lee VanCott, 2015. Oxford: Oxford University Press. https://doi.org/10.1093
/oxfordhb/9780195386653.013.007.

Barker, Joanne. "Introduction: Critically Sovereign." In *Critically Sovereign: Indigenous Gender, Sexuality and Feminist Studies*, 1–44. Durham, NC: Duke
University Press, 2017.

Barker, Joanne. *Native Acts: Law, Recognition, and Cultural Authenticity*. Durham,
NC: Duke University Press, 2011.

Barker, Joanne, ed. *Sovereignty Matters: Locations of Contestation and Possibility in
Indigenous Struggles for Self-Determination*. Lincoln: University of Nebraska
Press, 2005.

Barker, Peter. "Obama, in Oklahoma, Takes Reform Message to Prison Cell Block."
New York Times, July 16, 2015. https://www.nytimes.com/2015/07/17/us
/obama-el-reno-oklahoma-prison.html.

Batalova, Jeanne, Monisha Das Gupta, and Sue Haglund. *Newcomers to the Aloha
State: Challenges and Prospects for Mexicans in Hawai'i*. Washington, DC:
Migration Policy Institute, 2013. https://www.migrationpolicy.org/research
/newcomers-aloha-state-challenges-and-prospects-mexicans-hawaii.

Berlant, Lauren. *The Female Complaint: The Unfinished Business of Sentimentality
in American Culture*. Durham, NC: Duke University Press, 2008.

Beverley, John. *Testimonio: On the Politics of Truth*. Minneapolis: University of
Minnesota Press, 2004.

Biden, Joseph. "Executive Order on the Revision of Civil Immigration Enforcement." White House, January 20, 2021. https://www.whitehouse.gov/briefing-room/presidential-actions/2021/01/20/executive-order-the-revision-of-civil-immigration-enforcement-policies-and-priorities/.

Bishaw, Alemayehu, and Kayla Fontenot. "Poverty 2012–2013." US Census Bureau, September 2014. https://www2.census.gov/library/publications/2014/acs/acsbr13-01.pdf.

Blackhawk, Ned. *Violence over the Land*. Cambridge, MA: Harvard University Press, 2006.

Blackwell, Maylei. *¡Chicana Power! Contested Histories of Feminism in the Chicano Movement*. Austin: University of Texas Press, 2011.

Blackwell, Maylei. "Geographies of Indigeneity: Indigenous Migrant Women's Organizing and Translocal Politics of Place." *Latino Studies* 15, no. 2 (2017): 156–81.

Blackwell, Maylei. "Líderes Campesinas: Nepantla Strategies and Grassroots Organizing at the Intersection of Gender and Globalization." *Aztlán: A Journal of Chicano Studies* 35, no. 1 (2010): 13–47.

Blackwell, Maylei, Floridalma Boj Lopez, and Luis Urrieta. "Introduction: Critical Latinx Indigeneities." *Latino Studies* 15, no. 2 (2017): 126–37.

Bose, Purnima, and Laura Lyons. "Introduction: Toward a Critical Corporate Studies." In *Cultural Critique and the Global Corporation*, edited by Purnima Bose and Laura Lyons, 1–27. Bloomington: Indiana University Press, 2010.

Boundaoui, Assia, dir. *The Feeling of Being Watched*. New York: Women Make Movies, 2018. Video, 87 mins. https://www.feelingofbeingwatched.com/.

Boycott Divestment and Sanctions. "G4S: Securing Israeli Apartheid." BDS Movement, April 12, 2016. https://bdsmovement.net/stop-g4s.

Boylan, Peter. "Family of Iremamber Sykap Sues City and Officers, Alleges Intimidation by Honolulu Police." *Honolulu Star-Advertiser*, May 21, 2021. https://www.staradvertiser.com/2021/05/21/breaking-news/family-of-iremamber-sykap-files-wrongful-death-lawsuit-against-city-alleges-police-intimidation/.

Boylan, Peter. "3 Honolulu Police Department Officers Are Charged in the Fatal Shooting of a 16-Year-Old Boy." *Honolulu Star-Advertiser*, June 16, 2021. https://www.staradvertiser.com/2021/06/16/hawaii-news/3-hpd-officers-are-charged-in-the-fatal-shooting-of-a-16-year-old-boy/.

Briggs, Laura. *How All Politics Became Reproductive Politics: From Welfare Reform to Foreclosure to Trump*. Oakland: University of California Press, 2017.

Browne, Simone. *Dark Matters: On the Surveillance of Blackness*. Durham, NC: Duke University Press, 2015.

Buff, Rachel Ida. *Against the Deportation Terror: Organizing for Immigrant Rights in the Twentieth Century*. Philadelphia: Temple University Press, 2017.

Buff, Rachel Ida. "The Deportation Terror." *American Quarterly* 60, no. 3 (2008): 523–51.

Buff, Rachel Ida, ed. *Immigrant Rights in the Shadows of Citizenship*. New York: New York University Press, 2008.

Buff, Rachel Ida. *Immigration and the Political Economy of Home: West Indian Brooklyn and American Indian Minneapolis, 1945–1992*. Berkeley: University of California Press, 2001.

Building Healthy Communities Long Beach. "Every Student Matters!" June 2013. https://kgalb.org/wp-content/uploads/2024/03/School-Discipline-and -Suspensions_ESM-2Page-Final-En-1.pdf.

Building Healthy Communities Long Beach. "Every Student Matters: Profile; Long Beach Unified School District (LBUSD)." July 9, 2014. https://kgalb.org/wp -content/uploads/2024/03/ESM-LB-Profile_7.9.14-FULL-REPORT-1.pdf.

Burns, Matt. "Leaked Palantir Doc Reveals Uses, Specific Functions and Key Clients." *Tech Crunch*, January 11, 2015.

Byrd, Jodi A. *The Transit of Empire: Indigenous Critiques of Colonialism*. Minneapolis: University of Minnesota Press, 2011.

Cacho, Lisa Marie. *Social Death: Racialized Rightlessness and the Criminalization of the Unprotected*. New York: New York University Press, 2012.

Cachón, Jennifer M. "Civil Rights, Immigrants' Rights, and Human Rights: Lessons from the Life and Works of Dr. Martin Luther King, Jr." *New York University Review of Law and Social Change* 32, no. 4 (2008): 465–84.

California Legislative Information. "AB-1400 Guaranteed Health Care for All." January 21, 2022. https://leginfo.legislature.ca.gov/faces/billNavClient.xhtml?bill _id=202120220AB1400.

California Legislative Information. "SB-4 Health Care Coverage: Immigration Status." October 9, 2015. https://leginfo.legislature.ca.gov/faces/billNavClient .xhtml?bill_id=201520160SB4.

Camacho, Alicia Schmidt. *Migrant Imaginaries: Latino Cultural Politics in the U. S.-Mexico Borderlands*. New York: New York University Press, 2008.

Camp, Jordan. *Incarcerating the Crisis: Freedom Struggles and the Rise of the Neoliberal State*. Oakland: University of California Press, 2016.

Canaday, Margot. *The Straight State: Sexuality and Citizenship in Twentieth-Century America*. Princeton, NJ: Princeton University Press, 2009.

Caparoso, Jenna, and Christopher Collins. "College Student Racial and Ethnic Stereotype-Based Humor as a Cultural Domain." *Power and Education*, 7, no. 2 (2015): 196–223.

Capps, Randy, Muzaffar Chishti, Julia Gelatt, Jessica Bolter, and Ariel G. Ruiz Soto. *Revving Up the Deportation Machinery: Enforcement and Pushback under Trump*. Washington, DC: Migration Policy Institute, 2018. https://www .migrationpolicy.org/sites/default/files/publications/ImmigrationEnforcement -FullReport-FINAL-WEB.pdf.

Capps, Randy, Doris Meissner, Ariel G. Ruiz Soto, Jessica Bolter, and Sarah Pierce. *From Control to Crisis: Changing Trends and Policies Reshaping U.S.-Mexico Border Enforcement*. Washington, DC: Migration Policy Institute, 2019.

https://www.migrationpolicy.org/research/changing-trends-policies
-reshaping-us-mexico-border-enforcement.

Castellanos, M. Bianet, Lourdes Gutiérrez Nájera, and Arturo J. Aldama, eds. *Comparative Indigeneities of the Américas: Toward a Hemispheric Approach.* Tucson: University of Arizona Press, 2012.

CBS Los Angeles. "ICE Arrests 101 People in LA Immigration Sweep." September 28, 2017. https://www.cbsnews.com/losangeles/news/ice-arrests-immigration -sweep/.

CBS Los Angeles. "LA Immigration Protesters: Trutanich Wants to Silence Dissent." January 18, 2011. https://www.cbsnews.com/losangeles/news/la-immigration -protesters-trutanich-wants-to-silence-dissent/.

Ceasar, Stephen. "Black Lives Matter Protestors Who Blocked L.A. Freeway Are 'Vessels of Change,' Lawyer Tells Jury." *Los Angeles Times*, March 17, 2016. https://www.latimes.com/local/california/la-me-black-lives-matter-trial -20160318-story.html.

Center for Constitutional Rights. "Landmark Decision: Judge Rules NYPD Stop and Frisk Practices Unconstitutional, Racially Discriminatory." August 12, 2013. https://ccrjustice.org/node/1269.

Chan, Sucheng. *Survivors: Cambodian Refugees in the United States.* Urbana: University of Illinois Press, 2004.

Chávez, Karma R. *Queer Migration Politics: Activist Rhetoric and Coalitional Possibilities.* Urbana: University of Illinois Press, 2013. Kindle.

Chávez, Karma R., and Eithne Luibhéid, eds. *Queer and Trans Migrations: Dynamics of Illegalization, Detention, and Deportation.* Urbana: University of Illinois Press, 2020.

Chavez, Leo R. *The Latino Threat: Constructing Immigrants, Citizens, and the Nation.* Stanford: Stanford University Press, 2008.

Chen, Stefanos, and Jeffery Mays. "To Avoid New York Rules, Hundreds of Migrants Dropped Off in New Jersey." *New York Times*, January 1, 2024. https:// www.nytimes.com/2024/01/01/nyregion/ny-nj-migrants-buses.html.

Cheng, Wendy. *The Changs Next Door to the Díazes: Remapping Race in Suburban California.* Minneapolis: University of Minnesota Press, 2013.

Chesney-Lind, Meda, and Robert Merce. "Toward a Smaller, Smarter Correctional System for Hawai'i." In *The Value of Hawai'i 3: Hulihia, the Turning*, edited by Noelani Goodyear-Ka'ōpua, Craig Howes, Jonathan Kay Kamakawiwo'ole Osorio, and Aiko Yamashiro, 115–18. Honolulu: University of Hawai'i Press, 2020.

Chishti, Muzaffar, Sarah Pierce, and Jessica Bolter. "The Obama Record on Deportations: Deporter in Chief or Not?" Washington, DC: Migration Policy Institute, January 25, 2017. https://www.migrationpolicy.org/article/obama -record-deportations-deporter-chief-or-not.

Cho, Eunice. "Beyond the Day without an Immigrant: Immigrant Communities Building a Sustainable Movement." In *Immigrant Rights in the Shadows of*

Citizenship, edited by Rachel Ida Buff, 94–121. New York: New York University Press, 2008.

Chomsky, Aviva. *Undocumented: How Immigration Became Illegal*. Boston: Beacon, 2014.

Clemency Coalition of New York. "Who We Are." Accessed February 28, 2024. https://www.clemencycoalitionny.org/ccny.

CNN Wire, Elizabeth Espinoza, Tracy Bloom, and Kareen Wynter. "LAPD Declares Unlawful Assembly after DACA Supporters Block Traffic on Wilshire Blvd. in Westwood; 9 Arrested." *KTLA 5*, October 5, 2017. https://ktla.com/news/local-news/immigration-rights-activists-blocking-traffic-on-wilshire-boulevard-in-westwood-as-daca-renewal-deadline-looms/.

Cohen, Cathy. "Deviance as Resistance: A New Research Agenda for the Study of Black Politics." *Du Bois Review* 1, no. 1 (2004): 27–45.

Coleman, Mathew. "Immigrant Il-Legality: Geopolitical and Legal Borders in the US, 1882–Present." *Geopolitics* 17 no. 2 (2012): 402–22.

Community Initiatives for Visiting Immigrants in Confinement (CIVIC) and Immigrant Rights Clinic at NYU School of Law. "Prolonged Detention Stories: Immigration Detention Exposed." Accessed June 28, 2020. https://www.prolongeddetentionstories.org/home.

Correctional News. "California Corrections Budget Continues to Increase." January 27, 2016. http://correctionalnews.com/2016/01/27/california-corrections-budget-continues-increase/.

CounterVortex. "Massachusetts: ICE 'Gang' Sweeps Protested." *CounterVortex*, August 18, 2008. http:/ww4report.com/node/5910.

Cruz, Pamela Lizette. "A Vulnerable Population: U.S. Citizen Minors Living in Mexico." Rice University's Baker Institute for Public Policy, March 19, 2018. https://www.bakerinstitute.org/media/files/research-document/3869bc0a/bi-brief-031918-mex-citizenminors.pdf.

Cuauhtémoc García Hernández, César. "Migrant Detention, Corporate Profit." American Bar Association, April 12, 2023. https://www.americanbar.org/groups/crsj/publications/human_rights_magazine_home/economic-issues-in-criminal-justice/migrant-detention-corporate-profit/.

Cvetkovich, Ann. "Public Feelings." *South Atlantic Quarterly* 106, no. 3 (2007): 459–68.

Dao, Loan. "Refugee Representation: Southeast Asian American Youth, Hip Hop, and Immigrant Rights." *Amerasia Journal* 40, no. 2 (2014): 88–109.

Darrah-Okike, Jennifer. "Theorizing Race in Hawai'i: Centering Place, Indigeneity, and Settler Colonialism." *Sociology Compass* 14, no. 7 (2020): 1–18. https://doi.org/10.1111/soc4.12791.

Das Gupta, Monisha. "'Don't Deport Our Daddies': Gendering State Deportation Practices and Immigrant Organizing." *Gender and Society* 28, no. 1 (2014): 83–109.

Das Gupta, Monisha. "'KNOw History / KNOw Self': Khmer Youth Organizing for Justice in Long Beach." *Amerasia Journal* 45, no. 2 (2019): 137–56.

Das Gupta, Monisha. "Of Hardship and Hostility: The Impact of 9/11 on New York City Taxi Drivers." In *Wounded City: The Social Impact of 9/11*, edited by Nancy Foner, 208–41. New York: Russell Sage Foundation, 2005.

Das Gupta, Monisha. "Rights in a Transnational Era." In *Immigrant Rights in the Shadows of Citizenship*, edited by Rachel Ida Buff, 402–25. New York: New York University Press, 2008.

Das Gupta, Monisha. "Shadowed Lives: Invisibility and Visibility of Mexicans in Hawai'i." In *Transpacific Americas: Encounters and Engagement with the Americas and South Pacific*, edited by Eveline Dürr and Philip Schorch, 42–63. London: Routledge, 2016.

Das Gupta, Monisha. *Unruly Immigrants: Rights, Activism, and Transnational South Asian Politics in the United States*. Durham, NC: Duke University Press, 2006.

Das Gupta, Monisha, and Sue Haglund. "Mexican Migration to Hawai'i and US Settler Colonialism." *Latino Studies* 13, no. 4 (2015): 455–80.

Das Gupta, Monisha, and Soniya Munshi. "Turning Points: South Asian Feminist Responses to Gender-Based Violence and Immigration Enforcement." In *Our Voices, Our Histories: Asian American and Pacific Islander Women*, edited by Shirley Hune and Gail Nomura, 338–54. New York: New York University Press, 2020.

Davis, Angela Y. *Are Prisons Obsolete?* New York: Seven Stories, 2003.

Davis, Angela Y. *Freedom Is a Constant Struggle: Ferguson, Palestine, and the Foundations of a Movement*. Chicago: Haymarket, 2016.

Davis, Angela Y. "Masked Racism: Reflections on the Prison Industrial Complex." *Colorlines*, September 10, 1998. https://www.colorlines.com/articles/masked-racism-reflections-prison-industrial-complex.

Davis, Angela Y. "Racialized Punishment and Prison Abolition." In *The Angela Y. Davis Reader*, edited by Joy James, 96–110. Malden, MA: Blackwell, 1998.

Deer, Sarah. *The Beginning and End of Rape: Confronting Sexual Violence in Native America*. Minneapolis: University of Minnesota Press, 2015.

De Genova, Nicholas. *Working the Boundaries: Race, Space, and "Illegality" in Mexican Chicago*. Durham, NC: Duke University Press, 2005.

Democracy Now! "Facing Possible Deportation, Immigrant Activist Ravi Ragbir Speaks Out before ICE Check-In." March 9, 2017. https://www.democracynow.org/2017/3/9/exclusive_facing_likely_deportation_immigrant_activist.

Democracy Now! "Ending 30-Year Saga, Judge Rules Haitian Activist Targeted by ICE Should Not Face Deportation Again." April 19, 2023. https://www.democracynow.org/2023/4/19/haitian_activist_jean_montrevil.

Department of Business, Economic Development and Tourism. *COFA Migrants in Hawaii*. Honolulu: Department of Business, Economic Development and Tourism Research and Economic Analysis Division, 2020. https://files.hawaii.gov/dbedt/economic/reports/COFA_Migrants_in_Hawaii_Final.pdf.

Detention Watch Network. "Detention and Deportation Consequences of Arizona Immigration Law (SB 1070)." Archived July 23, 2010, at Archive.org. https://

web.archive.org/web/20100723172245/http://detentionwatchnetwork.org
/SB1070_Talking_Points.

Detention Watch Network. "Detention Quotas." Accessed February 23, 2024.
https://www.detentionwatchnetwork.org/issues/detention-quotas.

Detention Watch Network. *Expose and Close: Etowah County Jail, Alabama.*
Washington, DC: Detention Watch Network, 2012. https://www.detention
watchnetwork.org/sites/default/files/reports/DWN%20Expose%20and%20
Close%20Etowah%20County.pdf.

Detention Watch Network. *The Influence of the Private Prison Industry in the Immigration Detention Business.* Washington, DC: Detention Watch Network,
2011. https://www.detentionwatchnetwork.org/pressroom/reports/2011
/private-prisons.

Detention Watch Network. "Mandatory Detention." Detention Watch Network,
February 8, 2016. https://www.detentionwatchnetwork.org/issues/mandatory
-detention.

Detention Watch Network. *A Toxic Relationship: Private Prisons and U.S. Immigration Detention.* Washington, DC: Detention Watch Network, 2016. https://
www.detentionwatchnetwork.org/sites/default/files/reports/A%20Toxic%20
Relationship_DWN.pdf.

Detention Watch Network and Center for Constitutional Rights. *Banking on Detention: 2016 Update.* Washington, DC: Detention Watch Network, 2016. https://
www.detentionwatchnetwork.org/sites/default/files/reports/Banking%20
on%20Detention%202016%20Update_DWN%2C%20CCR.pdf.

Detention Watch Network, Families for Freedom, Immigrant Defense Project,
and National Immigration Project of the National Lawyers Guild. *Deportation 101: A Community Resource on Anti-deportation Education and
Organizing.* Washington, DC: Detention Watch Network, 2010. https://
immigrantdefenseproject.org/wp-content/uploads/2011/02/Deportation101-1
-11HiRes.pdf.

Dinh, Thaomi Michelle. "'When We Fight, We Win': Time and Care in Asian
American Abolition Work." *Journal of Asian American Studies* 25, no. 3
(2022): 445–62.

Driskill, Qwo-Li. *Asegi Stories: Cherokee Queer and Two-Spirit Memory.* Tucson:
University of Arizona Press, 2016.

Driskill, Qwo-Li, Chris Finley, Brian J. Gilley, and Scott Lauria Morgensen, eds.
*Queer Indigenous Studies: Critical Interventions in Theory, Politics, and Liter-
ature.* Tucson: University of Arizona Press, 2011.

DTLA. "About Us: A Catalyst in the Revitalization of Downtown LA." Accessed
March 8, 2024. https://downtownla.com/dtla-alliance/about-us.

Dulaney, Josh. "Cambodian Military Leader Not Invited to Cambodia Town
Culture Festival." *Long Beach Press-Telegram*, March 23, 2016. http://www
.presstelegram.com/general-news/20160323/cambodian-military-leader-not
-invited-to-cambodia-town-culture-festival.

Echeverry, Sebastian. "Public Forum Exposes Cambodian Community's De-
    portation Challenges." *Signal Tribune* (blog), December 14, 2017. https://
    signaltribunenewspaper.com/36117/news/public-forum-exposes-cambodian
    -communitys-deportation-challenges/.
Edwards, Ryan, and Francesca Ortega. "The Economic Contribution of Unauthor-
    ized Workers: An Industry Analysis." Working paper, National Bureau of
    Economic Research, November 2016. https://doi.org/10.3386/w22834.
Eilperin, Juliette. "Obama Tells NAACP That Justice Reform is Long Overdue."
    Washington Post, July 14, 2015. https://www.washingtonpost.com/politics
    /obama-tells-naacp-that-justice-reform-is-long-overdue/2015/07/14/98c14e8a
    -2a52-11e5-a250-42bd812efc09_story.html.
Ember, Sydney, and Astead W. Herndon. "How 'Abolish ICE' Went from Social
    Media to Progressive Candidates' Rallying Cry." *New York Times*, June 29,
    2018. https://www.nytimes.com/2018/06/29/us/politics/abolish-ice-midterms
    -immigration.html.
Equally Speaking. "Undocumented and Unafraid." Honolulu: ʻŌlelo Community
    Media. Aired February 29, 2012. DVD, 26:59 min.
Escudero, Kevin. "Federal Immigration Laws and U.S. Empire: Tracing Immigration
    Lawmaking in the Mariana Islands." *Amerasia Journal* 46, no. 1 (2020): 63–78.
Escudero, Kevin. *Organizing While Undocumented: Immigrant Youth's Political
    Activism under the Law.* New York: New York University Press, 2020.
Espiritu, Yên Lê. *Body Counts: The Vietnam War and Militarized Refugees.* Berke-
    ley: University of California Press, 2014.
Espiritu, Yên Lê. *Home Bound: Filipino American Lives across Cultures, Communi-
    ties, and Countries.* Berkeley: University of California Press, 2003.
Espiritu, Yên Lê. "Toward a Critical Refugee Study: The Vietnamese Refugee
    Subject in US Scholarship." *Journal of Vietnamese Studies* 1, no. 1–2 (2006):
    410–33.
Estes, Nick, Melanie Yazzie, Jennifer Denetdale, and David Correia. *Red Nation Ris-
    ing: From Bordertown Violence to Native Liberation.* Oakland: PM, 2021.
Executive Office of the President. "Executive Order 13768, Enhancing Public Safety
    in the Interior of the United States." *Federal Register*, January 30, 2017. https://
    www.federalregister.gov/documents/2017/01/30/2017-02102/enhancing
    -public-safety-in-the-interior-of-the-united-states.
Families for Freedom. "Barbara and Howard." Archived June 7, 2008, at Archive.org.
    https://web.archive.org/web/20080607135534/http://www.familiesforfreedom
    .org/httpdocs/our_families/barbara_howard.html.
Families for Freedom. "Clemency Justice Act." Accessed February 28, 2024. https://
    familiesforfreedom.org/current-campaigns/clemencynow.
Families for Freedom. "FFF History." Accessed February 28, 2024. https://
    familiesforfreedom.org/about.
Families for Freedom. "Free Michael Santiago." Accessed February 28, 2024. https://
    familiesforfreedom.org/current-campaigns/free-michael-santiago.

Families for Freedom. "Free Wayne Gardine." Accessed February 28, 2024. https://familiesforfreedom.org/current-campaigns/freegardine.

Families for Freedom. "Immigrant Rights Activist Jean Montrevil's Case to Be Reopened for a New Hearing." January 24, 2022. https://familiesforfreedom.org/press-releases/jan-24-2022-immigrant-rights-activist-jean-montrevils-case-to-be-reopened-for-a-new-hearing.

Families for Freedom. "Jean and Jani." Archived July 24, 2010, at Archive.org. https://web.archive.org/web/20100724031014/http://www.familiesforfreedom.org/httpdocs/our_families/jean_jani.html.

Families for Freedom. "Joe and Mei." Archived July 22, 2007, at Archive.org. https://web.archive.org/web/20070722005239/http://familiesforfreedom.org/node/70.

Families for Freedom. "Josh and Kathy." Archived August 14, 2007, at Archive.org. https://web.archive.org/web/20070814191416/http://familiesforfreedom.org/node/81.

Families for Freedom. "#KeepJeanHome." Accessed February 28, 2024. https://familiesforfreedom.org/current-campaigns/keepjeanhome.

Families for Freedom. "New Way Forward Act." Accessed February 28, 2024. https://familiesforfreedom.org/current-campaigns/new-way-forward-act.

Families for Freedom. "Thank you Detention Watch Network NYC Dissenters and United We Dream for joining us at our Defund ICE & CBP End of the Year action yesterday." Facebook. December 13, 2023. https://www.facebook.com/families4freedom?_rdr.

Families for Freedom. "Uncle Malik." Archived June 7, 2008, at Archive.org. https://web.archive.org/web/20080607053824/http://www.familiesforfreedom.org/httpdocs/our_families/uncle_malik.html.

Ferguson, Roderick. *Aberrations in Black: Toward a Queer of Color Critique*. Minneapolis: University of Minnesota Press, 2004.

Ferguson, Roderick. "Of Our Normative Strivings: African American Studies and the Histories of Sexuality." *Social Text* 23, no. 3–4 (2005): 85–100.

Fernandes, Deepa. *Targeted: Homeland Security and the Business of Immigration*. New York: Seven Stories, 2007.

Fink, Leon. "Labor Joins La Marcha: How New Immigrant Activism Restored the Meaning of May Day." In *¡Marcha! Latino Chicago and the Immigrant Rights Movement*, edited by Amalia Pallares and Flores-González Nilda, 109–19. Urbana: University of Illinois Press, 2010.

Finley, Chris. "Decolonizing the Queer Native Body (and Recovering the Native Bull-Dyke): Bringing 'Sexy Back' and Out of Native Studies' Closet." In *Queer Indigenous Studies: Critical Interventions in Theory, Politics, and Literature*, edited by Qwo-Li Driskill, Chris Finley, Brian Joseph Gilley, and Scott Lauria Morgensen, 31–42. Tucson: University of Arizona Press, 2011.

Flores, Kevin. "#IYC Immigrant Youth Coalition." Kevin's Site (website). Accessed July 1, 2022. http://swiss1326.weebly.com/immigrant-youth-coalition.html.

Flores-Gonzáles, Nilda, and Elena Gutiérrez. "Taking the Public Square: The National Struggle for Immigrant Rights." In *¡Marcha! Latino Chicago and the Immigrant Rights Movement*, edited by Amalia Pallares and Flores-González Nilda, 3–25. Urbana: University of Illinois Press, 2010.

Fortune Society. "One Day to Protect New Yorkers." Accessed June 15, 2023. https://fortunesociety.org/one-day-to-protect-ny/.

Foucault, Michel. *Society Must Be Defended: Lectures at the Collège de France: 1975–1976*. Translated by David Macey. New York: Picador, 2003.

Franklin, Cynthia. *Narrating Humanity: Life Writing and Movement Politics from Palestine to Mauna Kea*. New York: Fordham University Press, 2023.

Franklin, Cynthia, Njoroge Njoroge, and Suzanna Reiss. "Tracing the Settler's Tools: A Forum on Patrick Wolfe's Life and Legacy." *American Quarterly* 69, no. 2 (2017): 235–47.

Freedom for Immigrants. "Detention by the Numbers." Accessed July 14, 2022. https://www.freedomforimmigrants.org/detention-statistics.

Freedom for Immigrants. "Our Storytelling Archive." Accessed May 21, 2019. https://www.freedomforimmigrants.org/storytelling-projects.

Freedom to Thrive. "Prison Industry Divestment Movement." Accessed May 19, 2019. https://prisondivest.com/.

Freeman, Katherine. "Neocolonial Biopolitics of Southern Arizona: Lessons Learned from the SB 1070 Boycott." *Feminist Formations* 28, no. 3 (2016): 222–43.

Fujikane, Candace. "Foregrounding Native Nationalisms: A Critique of Anti-nationalist Sentiment in Asian American Studies." In *Asian American Studies after Critical Mass*, edited by Kent A. Ono, 71–97. Malden, MA: Blackwell, 2005.

Fujikane, Candace. "Introduction: Asian Settler Colonialism in the U.S. Colony of Hawai'i." In *Asian Settler Colonialism: From Local Governance to the Habits of Everyday Life in Hawai'i*, edited by Candace Fujikane and Jonathan Okamura, 1–42. Honolulu: University of Hawai'i Press, 2008.

Fujikane, Candace, and Jonathan Okamura, eds. *Asian Settler Colonialism: From Local Governance to the Habits of Everyday Life in Hawai'i*. Honolulu: University of Hawai'i Press, 2008.

Fujimori, Leila. "HPD Shootings Questioned in Wake of Chauvin Verdict." *Honolulu Star-Advertiser*, April 21, 2021. https://www.staradvertiser.com/2021/04/21/hawaii-news/hpd-shootings-questioned-in-wake-of-chauvin-verdict/.

Fujiwara, Lynn. *Mothers without Citizenship: Asian Immigrant Families and the Consequences of Welfare Reform*. Minneapolis: University of Minnesota Press, 2008.

Fuller, Denise A. "Creating Resistance on the Border: Coalitions and Counternarratives to S.B. 1070." PhD diss., Ohio State University, 2017.

Garza, Alicia. *The Purpose of Power: How We Come Together When We Fall Apart*. New York: One World, 2020.

Gehi, Pooja. "Gendered (In)Security: Migration and Criminalization in the Security State." *Harvard Journal of Law and Gender* 35, no. 2 (2012): 357–98.

Geminiani, Victor. "The Case for Justice for Micronesians in Hawaii." *Honolulu Civil Beat*, February 1, 2012. https://www.civilbeat.org/2012/02/14768-the-case-for -justice-for-micronesians-in-hawaii/.

Genz, Joseph, Noelani Goodyear-Kaʻōpua, Monica Briola, Alexander Mawyer, Elicita Morei, and John Rosa. *Militarism and Nuclear Testing in the Pacific.* Teaching Oceania. Honolulu: Center for Pacific Islands Studies, University of Hawaiʻi at Mānoa, 2019.

Gilmore, Ruth Wilson. *Golden Gulag: Prisons, Surplus Crisis, and Opposition in Globalizing California.* Berkeley: University of California Press, 2007.

Glenn, Evelyn Nakano. "Settler Colonialism as Structure: A Framework for Comparative Studies of U.S. Race and Gender Formation." *Sociology of Race and Ethnicity* 1, no. 1 (2015): 52–72.

Glenn, Evelyn Nakano. *Unequal Freedom: How Race and Gender Shaped American Citizenship and Labor.* Cambridge, MA: Harvard University Press, 2002.

Goeman, Mishuana. *Mark My Words: Native Women Mapping Our Nations.* Minneapolis: University of Minnesota Press, 2013.

Golash-Boza, Tanya Maria, and Pierrette Hondagneu-Sotelo. "Latino Men and the Deportation Crisis: A Gendered Racial Removal Program." *Latino Studies* 11, no. 3 (2013): 271–92.

Gómez-Quiñones, Juan, and Irene Vásquez. *Making Aztlán: Ideology and Culture of the Chicana and Chicano Movement, 1966–1977.* Albuquerque: University of New Mexico Press, 2014.

Gonzalez, Paulina. "Winning the Dream: Part II." *Narco News Bulletin*, July 11, 2012. https://www.narconews.com/Issue67/article4608.html.

Goodman, H. A. "Illegal Immigrants Benefit the U.S. Economy." *Hill*, April 23, 2014. https://thehill.com/blogs/congress-blog/foreign-policy/203984-illegal-immigrants -benefit-the-us-economy/.

Goodyear-Kaʻōpua, Noelani. Introduction to *A Nation Rising: Hawaiian Movements for Life, Land and Sovereignty*, edited by Noelani Goodyear-Kaʻōpua, Erin Kahunawaikaʻala Wright, and Ikaika Hussey, 1–34. Durham, NC: Duke University Press, 2014.

Goodyear-Kaʻōpua, Noelani. "Kuleana Lāhui: Collective Responsibility for Hawaiian Nationhood in Activists' Praxis." *Affinities: A Journal of Radical Theory, Culture, and Action* 5, no. 1 (2011): 130–63.

Goodyear-Kaʻōpua, Noelani. *Seeds We Planted: Portrait of a Native Hawaiian Charter School.* Minneapolis: University of Minnesota Press, 2013.

Gordon, Larry, Carla Rivera, and Nicole Santa Cruz. "Thousands Protest California Education Cuts." *Los Angeles Times*, March 5, 2010. https://www.latimes.com /archives/la-xpm-2010-mar-05-la-me-protests5-2010mar05-story.html.

Gorman, Anna. "Cities and Counties Rely on U.S. Immigrant Detention Fees." *Los Angeles Times*, March 17, 2009. https://www.latimes.com/archives/la-xpm -2009-mar-17-me-immigjail17-story.html.

Gov, Jenny. "Cambodian Community Comes Together over Concerns." *Press-Telegram*, December 19, 2017. https://www.presstelegram.com/2017/12/19/cambodian-community-comes-together-over-concerns/.

Gutiérrez, David, and Pierrette Hondagneu-Sotelo, eds. *Nation and Migration: Past and Future*. Baltimore: Johns Hopkins University Press, 2009.

Haley, Sarah. *No Mercy Here: Gender, Punishment, and the Making of Jim Crow Modernity*. Chapel Hill: University of North Carolina Press, 2016.

Hall, Lisa Kahaleole. "Which of These Things Is Not Like the Other: Hawaiians and Other Pacific Islanders Are Not Asian Americans, and All Pacific Islanders Are Not Hawaiian." *American Quarterly* 67, no. 3 (2015): 727–47.

Hammami, Jamila. "Bridging Immigration Justice." In *Queer and Trans Migrations: Dynamics of Illegalization, Detention, and Deportation*, edited by Karma R. Chávez and Eithne Luibhéid, 133–36. Urbana: University of Illinois Press, 2020.

Harding, Vincent, and Daisaku Ikeda. *America Will Be! Conversations on Hope, Freedom, and Democracy*. Cambridge, MA: Dialog Path, 2013.

Hauʻofa, Epeli. "Our Sea of Islands." *Contemporary Pacific* 6, no. 1 (1994): 147–61.

Hawaiʻi Appleseed Center for Law and Economic Justice. *Broken Promises, Shattered Lives: The Case for Justice for Micronesians in Hawaiʻi*. Honolulu: Hawaiʻi Appleseed Center for Law and Economic Justice, 2011. https://hiappleseed.org/publications/broken-promises-shattered-lives.

Hawaiʻi Scholars for Education and Social Justice. *Racism and Discrimination against Micronesians in Hawaiʻi: Issues of Educational Inequity*. May 1, 2022. http://hawaiischolars.weebly.com/uploads/1/3/5/6/135637363/hsesj_2022_final_may_12__with_signatories_.pdf.

Hernández Castillo, R. Aída. "Prison as Colonial Enclave: Incarcerated Indigenous Women Resisting Multiple Violence." In *Indigenous Women and Violence: Feminist Activist Research in Heightened States of Injustice*, edited by Lynn Stephen and Shannon Speed, 43–73. Tucson: University of Arizona Press, 2021.

Hernández, Kelly Lytle. *City of Inmates: Conquest, Rebellion, and the Rise of Human Caging in Los Angeles, 1771–1965*. Chapel Hill: University of North Carolina Press, 2017.

Hill, John. "HPD's Use Of Lethal Force Is Near the US Average. But There's Far More to the Story." *Honolulu Civil Beat*, June 1, 2021. https://www.civilbeat.org/2021/06/hpds-use-of-lethal-force-is-near-the-us-average-but-theres-far-more-to-the-story/.

Hing, Bill Ong. *Deporting Our Souls: Values, Morality, and Immigration Policy*. New York: Cambridge University Press, 2006.

Hing, Julianne. "How a Group of Immigration Attorneys Stopped a Deportation Flight to Cambodia." *Nation*, December 19, 2017. https://www.thenation.com/article/archive/how-a-group-of-immigration-attorneys-stopped-a-deportation-flight-to-cambodia/.

Hipsman, Faye, and Muzaffar Chishti. "Fierce Opposition, Court Rulings Place Future of Family Immigration Detention in Doubt." Washington, DC: Migration Policy Institute, September 15, 2015. https://www.migrationpolicy.org /article/fierce-opposition-court-rulings-place-future-family-immigration -detention-doubt.

Hobart, Hiʻilei, and Tamara Kneese. "Radical Care: Survival Strategies for Uncertain Times." *Social Text* 38, no. 1 (2020): 1–16.

Hobson, Jeremy, and Samantha Raphelson. "California Bans Private Prisons and Immigrant Detention Centers." *Here and Now*, WBUR, October 11, 2019. https://www.wbur.org/hereandnow/2019/10/11/california-set-to-ban-private -prisons.

Hofschneider, Anita. "#BeingMicronesian in Hawaii Means Lots of Online Hate." *Honolulu Civil Beat*, September 19, 2018. https://www.civilbeat.org/2018/09 /beingmicronesian-in-hawaii-means-lots-of-online-hate/.

Hofschneider, Anita. "Why Talking about Anti-Micronesian Hate Is Important." *Honolulu Civil Beat*, September 24, 2018. https://www.civilbeat.org/2018/09 /why-talking-about-anti-micronesian-hate-is-important/.

Hondagneu-Sotelo, Pierrette. *God's Heart Has No Borders: How Religious Activists Are Working for Immigrant Rights.* Berkeley: University of California Press, 2008.

Hong, Grace K. *Death beyond Disavowal: The Impossible Politics of Difference.* Minneapolis: University of Minnesota Press, 2015.

Hong, Grace K., and Roderick Ferguson, eds. *Strange Affinities: The Gender and Sexual Politics of Comparative Racialization.* Durham, NC: Duke University Press, 2011.

hoʻomanawanui, kuʻualoha, Candace Fujikane, Aurora Kagawa-Viviani, Kerry K. Long, and Kekailoa Perry. "Teaching for Maunakea: Kiaʻi Perspectives." *Amerasia Journal* 45, no. 2 (2019): 271–76.

Human Rights Watch. "Cambodia: Events of 2016." January 12, 2017. https://www .hrw.org/world-report/2017/country-chapters/cambodia.

Human Rights Watch. "Cambodia: New Prime Minister But No Improvements." January 11, 2024. https://www.hrw.org/news/2024/01/11/cambodia-new -prime-minister-no-improvements.

Human Rights Watch. "30 Years of Hun Sen: Violence, Repression, and Corruption in Cambodia." January 12, 2015. https://www.hrw.org/report/2015/01/12/30 -years-hun-sen/violence-repression-and-corruption-cambodia#page.

Human Rights Watch. "US: Poor Medical Care, Deaths, in Immigrant Detention." June 20, 2018. https://www.hrw.org/news/2018/06/20/us-poor-medical-care -deaths-immigrant-detention.

Hung, Betty. "Movement Lawyering as Rebellious Lawyering: Advocating with Humility, Love and Courage." *Clinical Law Review* 23, no. 2 (2017): 663–69.

Immigrant Defense Project. "Detainers." August 2017. https://www.immigrantdefense project.org/wp-content/uploads/IDP-Detainer-Resource-Full-Version.pdf.

Immigrant Defense Project. "Ending Police Collaboration with Mass Deportation Programs: PEP, ICE Out of Rikers, and Ending s-Comm." Accessed February 28, 2024. https://www.immigrantdefenseproject.org/campaign-to-end-secure-communities/.

Immigrant Defense Project and Cardozo Law. "New York City New Detainer Discretion Law Chart and Practice Advisory," 2014. https://www.immigrantdefenseproject.org/wp-content/uploads/2013/09/Practice-Advisory-2014-Detainer-Discretion-Law-PEP.pdf.

Immigrant Legal Resource Center. "California Post-conviction Relief Vehicles." Infographic. Immigrant Legal Resource Center, June 14, 2017. https://www.ilrc.org/sites/default/files/resources/capostconviction-one_pager.pdf.

Immigrant Legal Resource Center. "ICE's Criminal Alien Program (CAP): Dismantling the Biggest Jail to Deportation Pipeline." Last modified July 29, 2016. https://www.ilrc.org/sites/default/files/resources/cap_guide_final.pdf.

Immigration Prof. "Hunger Strike for Immigrant Rights at Placita Olvera (Los Angeles)." *ImmigrationProf Blog*, October 22, 2008. https://lawprofessors.typepad.com/immigration/2008/10/hunger-strike-f.html.

INCITE! "Quality of Life Policing." August 1, 2018. https://incite-national.org/quality-of-life-policing/.

Indian Voices. "Ancestor Walk." October 3, 2020. https://www.indianvoices.net/archives/130-call-to-action-news-happening-now/1918-ancestor-walk-2020.

Irwin, Katherine, and Karen Umemoto. *Jacked Up and Unjust: Pacific Islander Teens Confront Violent Legacies*. Berkeley: University of California Press, 2016.

istandwithravi. "Justice for Ravi Ragbir." January 8, 2024. https://istandwithravi.org/.

Jedra, Christina. "Honolulu Officers Will Not Be Tried in Sykap Killing, Judge Rules." *Honolulu Civil Beat*, August 18, 2021. https://www.civilbeat.org/2021/08/honolulu-officers-will-not-be-tried-in-sykap-killing-judge-rules/.

Jedra, Christina, and Anita Hofschneider. "'Significant' Disparity in Use of Force Questioned by Honolulu Police Commission." *Honolulu Civil Beat*, February 3, 2021. https://www.civilbeat.org/2021/02/significant-disparity-in-use-of-force-against-some-groups-questioned-by-honolulu-police-commission/.

Jurmain, Claudia. Preface to *O, My Ancestor: Recognition and Renewal for the Gabrielino-Tongva People of the Los Angeles Area*, edited by Claudia Jurmain and William McCawley, xv–xix. Berkeley: Heyday Books and Rancho Alamitos Foundation, 2009.

Jurmain, Claudia, and William McCawley. *O, My Ancestor: Recognition and Renewal for the Gabrielino-Tongva People of the Los Angeles Area*. Berkeley, CA: Heyday Books and Rancho Alamitos Foundation, 2009.

Kaba, Mariame. *We Do This 'Til We Free Us: Abolitionist Organizing and Transforming Justice*. Chicago: Haymarket, 2021.

Kahapeʻa, Bonnie. "Sailing the Ancestral Bridges of Oceanic Knowledge." In *Value of Hawaiʻi 2*, edited by Aiko Yamashiro and Noelani Goodyear-Kaʻōpua, 173–80. Honolulu: University of Hawaiʻi Press, 2014.

Kamaka, Martina Leialoha, Lisa Watkins-Victorino, Awapuhi Lee, Sharde Mersberg Freitas, Kara Wong Ramsey, Joshua Quint, Tercia L. Ku, Kauʻionalani Nishizaki, and Joseph Keaweʻaimoku Kaholokula. "Addressing Native Hawaiian and Pacific Islander Data Deficiencies through a Community-Based Collaborative Response to the COVID-19 Pandemic." *Hawaiʻi Journal of Health and Social Welfare* 80, no. 10, s2 (October 2021): 36–45.

Kānehūnāmoku Voyaging Academy. "Kānehūnāmoku Voyaging Academy." Accessed July 23, 2022. http://www.kanehunamoku.org/.

Kanstroom, Daniel. *Deportation Nation: Outsiders in American History.* Cambridge, MA: Harvard University Press, 2007.

Kaplan, Amy. "Manifest Domesticity." *American Literature* 70, no. 3 (1998): 581–606.

Kauanui, J. Kēhaulani. *Hawaiian Blood: Colonialism and the Politics of Sovereignty and Indigeneity.* Durham, NC: Duke University Press, 2008.

Kauanui, J. Kēhaulani. "Indigenous Hawaiian Sexuality and the Politics of Nationalist Decolonization." In *Critically Sovereign: Indigenous Gender, Sexuality and Feminist Studies*, edited by Joanne Barker, 45–68. Durham, NC: Duke University Press, 2017.

Kaur, Tavleen. "Ungovernable and Inviolable: Acts of Resistance in and against Immigrant Detention." *Amerasia Journal* 46, no.1 (2020): 101–6.

Keahiolalo-Karasuda, RaeDeen. "A Genealogy of Punishment in Hawaiʻi: The Public Hanging of Chief Kamanawa II." *Hūlili: Multidisciplinary Research on Hawaiian Well-Being* 6 (2010): 147–67.

Kerber, Linda K. "Toward a History of Statelessness in America." *American Quarterly* 57, no. 3 (2005): 727–49.

Khan-Cullors, Patrisse. *An Abolitionist's Handbook: 12 Steps to Changing Yourself and the World.* New York: St. Martin's, 2022.

Khan-Cullors, Patrisse, and asha bandele. *When They Call You a Terrorist: A Black Lives Matter Memoir.* New York: St. Martin's, 2018.

Khmer Girls in Action. "Step into Long Beach: Exposing How Cambodian Youth Are Under Resourced, Over Policed and Fighting Back for Their Wellness." November 2011. https://kgalb.org/wp-content/uploads/2024/03/Step-Into-Long-Beach-PAR-Report_11.2011-1.pdf.

Kiernan, Ben. "The American Bombardment of Kampuchea, 1969–1973." *Vietnam Generation* 1, no. 1 (1989): 4–41.

Kight, Stef. "Texas Surpasses 50,000 Migrants Bused to Major Cities." *Axios*, October 10, 2023. https://www.axios.com/2023/10/10/texas-migrant-buses-major-cities-numbers.

Kim, Seung Min. "Feinstein under Fire from Immigration Advocates." *Politico*, August 8, 2015. https://www.politico.com/story/2015/08/feinstein-under-fire-from-immigration-advocates-120911.

King, Martin Luther, Jr. "Letter from Birmingham Jail." April 16, 1963. https://kinginstitute.stanford.edu/letter-birmingham-jail.

Kōkua Kalihi Valley. "History." Accessed March 7, 2024. https://www.kkv.net/history.

Kōkua Kalihi Valley. "Pacific Voices." Accessed March 7, 2024. https://www.kkv.net/pac-voices.

Krawczyk, Dawid. "Felons Have Families Too." January 29, 2016, *Political Critique*. http://politicalcritique.org/world/usa/2016/felons-have-families-too/.

Kremer, James D., Kathleen A. Moccio, and Joseph Hammell. "Severing a Lifeline: The Neglect of Citizen Children in America's Immigration Enforcement Policy." Minneapolis: Dorsey and Whitney LLP, 2009.

Krogstad, Jens Manuel, Mark Hugo Lopez, and Jeffrey Passel. "Majority of Americans Say Immigrants Mostly Fill Jobs U.S. Citizens Do Not Want." Pew Research Center, June 10, 2020. https://www.pewresearch.org/short-reads/2020/06/10/a-majority-of-americans-say-immigrants-mostly-fill-jobs-u-s-citizens-do-not-want/.

Kwon, Soo Ah. *Uncivil Youth: Race, Activism, and Affirmative Governmentality.* Durham, NC: Duke University Press, 2013.

Labrador, Roderick. "'I No Eat Dog K': Humor, Hazing, and Multicultural Settler Colonialism." In *Beyond Ethnicity: New Politics of Race in Hawaiʻi*, edited by Camilla Fojas, Rudy P. Guevarra, and Nitasha T. Sharma, 65–81. Honolulu: University of Hawaiʻi Press, 2018.

Lang, Marissa. "Activists Marvel as Calls for Immigrant Rights Enter the Mainstream." *Savannah Morning News*, July 8, 2018. https://www.savannahnow.com/news/20180708/activists-marvel-as-calls-for-immigrant-rights-enter-mainstream.

Laura Flanders Show, The. "What Is a Sanctuary with Jails? Interview with Hamid Khan and Jennicet Gutiérrez." July 11, 2017. Video, 26:39. https://lauraflanders.org/2017/07/whats-a-sanctuary-with-jails-hamid-khan-and-jennicet-gutierrez/.

Law, Victoria. "Against Carceral Feminism." *Jacobin*, October 17, 2014. https://jacobin.com/2014/10/against-carceral-feminism/.

Lawrence, Charles, III. "Local Kine Implicit Bias: Unconscious Racism Revisited (Yet Again)." *University of Hawaiʻi Law Review* 37 (2015): 457–500.

Lee, Erika. "Exclusion Acts: Chinese Women during the Chinese Exclusion Era, 1882–1943." In *Asian/Pacific Islander Women: A Historical Anthology*, edited by Shirley Hune and Gail M. Nomura, 77–89. New York: New York University Press, 2003.

Lee-Oliver, Leece, Monisha Das Gupta, Katherine Fobear, and Edward Ou Jin Lee. "Imperialism, Settler Colonialism, and Indigeneity: A Queer Migration Roundtable." In *Queer and Trans Migrations: Dynamics of Illegalization, Detention, and Deportation*, edited by Eithne Luibhéid and Karma R. Chávez, 226–55. Urbana: University of Illinois Press, 2020.

Legislative Analyst's Office. "The 2017–18 Budget: California Department of Corrections and Rehabilitation." March 1, 2017. https://lao.ca.gov/Publications/Report/3595.

Leong, Karen, and Myla Vincenti Carpio. "Carceral States: Converging Indigenous and Asian Experiences in the Americas." *Amerasia Journal* 42, no. 1 (2016): vii–xviii.

Letman, Jon. "Micronesians in Hawaii Face Uncertain Future." *Al Jazeera*, October 3, 2013. https://www.aljazeera.com/news/2013/10/3/micronesians-in-hawaii-face-uncertain-future.

Levine, Dan, and Mica Rosenberg. "U.S. Judge Blocks Prompt Deportation of Cambodians." *Reuters*, January 26, 2018. https://www.reuters.com/article/us-usa-immigration-ruling/u-s-judge-blocks-prompt-deportation-of-cambodians-idUSKBN1FF2QO/.

Linthicum, Kate. "L.A. Drops Charges against Westwood Protesters Who Supported DREAM Act." *Los Angeles Times*, March 4, 2011. https://www.latimes.com/local/la-xpm-2011-mar-04-la-me-protesters-20110304-story.html.

Linthicum, Kate, and Andrew Blankstein. "Los Angeles Gets Tough with Political Protestors." *Los Angeles Times*, February 11, 2011. https://www.latimes.com/local/la-xpm-2011-feb-11-la-me-protester-prosecution-20110211-story.html.

Lipsitz, George. "Learning from Los Angeles: Another One Rides the Bus." *American Quarterly* 56, no. 3 (2004): 511–29.

López, Claudia, Varisa Patraporn, Kelliana Lim, and Kylee Khan. "Walking to Build a Critical Community-Engaged Project: Collaborative Observations of Neighborhood Change in Long Beach, California." *Social Sciences* 11, no. 2 (2022). https://doi.org/10.3390/socsci11050183.

Luibhéid, Eithne. "Heteronormativity and Immigration Scholarship: A Call for Change." *GLQ: A Journal of Lesbian and Gay Studies* 10, no. 2 (2004): 227–35.

Luibhéid, Eithne. *Pregnant on Arrival: Making the Illegal Immigrant*. Minneapolis: University of Minnesota Press, 2013.

Luibhéid, Eithne, and Lionel Cantú, eds. *Queer Migrations: Sexuality, U.S. Citizenship, and Border Crossings*. Minneapolis: University of Minnesota Press, 2005.

Lyons, Laura. "Dole, Hawai'i, and the Question of Land under Globalization." In *Cultural Critique and the Global Corporation*, edited by Purnima Bose and Laura Lyons, 64–101. Bloomington: Indiana University Press, 2010.

Lyons, Paul, and Ty P. Kāwika Tengan. "COFA Complex: A Conversation with Joakim 'Jojo' Peter." *American Quarterly* 67, no. 3 (2015): 663–79.

Macías-Rojas, Patrisia. *From Deportation to Prison: The Politics of Immigration Enforcement in Post–Civil Rights America*. New York: New York University Press, 2016.

Magagnini, Stephen, and Anita Chabria. "Federal Judge Stops Trump Administration from Deporting Scores of Cambodian Immigrants." *Sacramento Bee*, December 15, 2017. https://www.sacbee.com/news/local/article190035709.html.

Maira, Sunaina. *Missing: Youth, Citizenship, and Empire after 9/11*. Durham, NC: Duke University Press, 2009.

Marquez, Oscar. "Tod@s Somos Arizona: Indigenous Cultural Resistance and the Immigrant Rights Movement." Master's thesis, California State University, Los Angeles, 2012.

McCawley, William. "Enduring Vision: Recognition and Renewal." In *O, My Ancestor: Recognition and Renewal for the Gabrielino-Tongva People of the Los Angeles Area*, edited by Claudia Jurmain and William McCawley, 195–214. Berkeley: Heyday Books and Rancho Alamitos Foundation, 2009.

McCawley, William. Introduction to *O, My Ancestor: Recognition and Renewal for the Gabrielino-Tongva People of the Los Angeles Area*, edited by Claudia Jurmain and William McCawley, xxi–xxviii. Berkeley: Heyday Books and Rancho Alamitos Foundation, 2009.

McElfish, Pearl A., Rachel S. Purvis, Sheldon Riklon, and Seiji Yamada. "Compact of Free Association Migrants and Health Insurance Policies: Barriers and Solutions to Improve Health Equity." *INQUIRY: The Journal of Health Care Organization, Provision, and Financing* 56 (2019): 1–5.

Melamed, Jodi. "Racial Capitalism." *Critical Ethnic Studies* 1, no. 1 (2015): 76–85.

Mendez, Julian J., and Nolan L. Cabrera. "Targets but Not Victims: Latina/o College Students and Arizona's Racial Politics." *Journal of Hispanic Higher Education* 14, no. 4 (2015): 377–91.

Menjívar, Cecilia. "Central American Immigrant Workers and Legal Violence in Phoenix, Arizona." *Latino Studies* 11, no. 2 (2013): 228–52.

Menjívar, Cecilia. *Fragmented Ties: Salvadoran Immigrant Networks in America*. Berkeley: University of California Press, 2000.

Metzl, Jonathan. "Structural Competency." *American Quarterly* 64, no. 2 (2012): 213–18.

Mijente, National Immigration Project, and Immigration Defense Project. *Who's behind ICE? Tech and Data Companies Fueling Deportation*. October 2018. https://mijente.net/wp-content/uploads/2018/10/WHO%E2%80%99S-BEHIND -ICE_-The-Tech-and-Data-Companies-Fueling-Deportations-_v1.pdf.

Million, Dian. *Therapeutic Nations: Healing in an Age of Indigenous Human Rights*. Tucson: University of Arizona Press, 2013.

Million, Dian. "Felt Theory: An Indigenous Feminist Approach to Affect and History." *Wicazo Sa Review* 24 no. 2 (2009): 53–76.

Mingus, Mia. "Transformative Justice: A Brief Description." *Transform Harm*, January 11, 2019. https://transformharm.org/tj_resource/transformative-justice-a -brief-description/.

Miranda, Deborah. "Extermination of the *Joyas*: Gendercide in Spanish California." *GLQ* 16, no. 1–2 (2010): 253–84.

Moana Nui. "Moana Nui Statement." Accessed March 6, 2024. http://moananui2011 .org/.

Moreton-Robinson, Aileen. "Writing Off Treaties: White Possession in the United States Critical Whiteness Studies Literature." In *The White Possessive: Property, Power, and Indigenous Sovereignty*, edited by Aileen Moreton-Robinson, 47–63. Minneapolis: University of Minnesota Press, 2015.

Morgensen, Scott Lauria. *Spaces between Us: Queer Settler Colonialism and Indigenous Decolonization*. Minneapolis: University of Minnesota Press, 2011.

Morton, John. "Exercising Prosecutorial Discretion Consistent with the Civil Immigration Enforcement Priorities of the Agency for the Apprehension, Detention, and Removal of Aliens." US Department of Homeland Security memorandum, June 17, 2011. https://www.ice.gov/doclib/secure-communities/pdf/prosecutorial-discretion-memo.pdf.

Muñiz, Ana. *Police, Power, and the Production of Racial Boundaries*. New Brunswick, NJ: Rutgers University Press, 2015.

National Coalition for Asian Pacific American Community Development. "Our Neighborhoods: Asian American and Pacific Islander Anti-displacement Strategies." May 2016. https://nationalcapacd.org/sites/default/files/u19/anti_displacement_strategies_report.pdf.

National Immigration Law Center. "Justice Dep. Contemplates Extending Immigration Enforcement Responsibilities to State and Local Agencies." *Immigrants' Rights Update* 16, no. 2 (2002): 1–14. https://www.nilc.org/wp-content/uploads/2016/04/iru-2002-04-12.pdf.

National Immigration Law Center. "*United States v. Texas*: What Does the Supreme Court's Tie Vote Mean for DAPA and Expanded DACA?" June 24, 2016. https://www.nilc.org/wp-content/uploads/2016/06/DAPA-DACA-after-SCOTUS-US-v-TX-ruling-2016-06-24.pdf.

National Immigration Law Center. *Untangling the Immigration Enforcement Web: Basic Information for Advocates about Databases and Information Sharing among Federal, State, and Local Agencies*. Los Angeles: National Immigration Law Center, 2017. https://www.nilc.org/issues/immigration-enforcement/untangling-immigration-enforcement-web/.

NBC Los Angeles. "9 Arrested at DACA Protest in Westwood." October 5, 2017. https://www.nbclosangeles.com/news/daca-protest-westwood/25055/.

Needham, Susan, and Karen Quintiliani. "Cambodians in Long Beach, California: The Making of a Community." *Journal of Immigrant and Refugee Studies* 5, no. 1 (2007): 29–53.

Needham, Susan, and Karen Quintiliani. "Why Long Beach?" Cambodian Community History and Archive Project, May 2011. http://www.camchap.org/why-long-beach.

Nevins, Joseph. *Dying to Live: A Story of U.S. Immigration in an Age of Global Apartheid*. San Francisco: City Lights, 2009.

Nevins, Joseph. *Operation Gatekeeper and Beyond: The War on "Illegals" and the Remaking of the U.S.-Mexico Boundary*. 2nd ed. New York: Routledge, 2010.

Newnham, Nicole, and David Grabias, dirs. *Sentenced Home*. San Francisco: Center for Asian American Media, 2006. DVD, 73 min. https://caamedia.org/films /sentenced-home/.

New York State Working Group against Deportation. "Stop 'Secure Communities' in New York." Accessed February 28, 2024. https://newyorkagainstdeportation .wordpress.com/.

New York Times. "ICE Tried to Deport an Immigration Activist. That May Have Been Unconstitutional" (editorial). April 27, 2019. https://www.nytimes.com /2019/04/27/opinion/sunday/ice-deportation-activists.html.

New York Times. "Lost in the Immigration Frenzy" (editorial). July 13, 2015. https://www.nytimes.com/2015/07/13/opinion/lost-in-the-immigration -frenzy.html.

Ngai, Mae M. *Impossible Subjects: Illegal Aliens and the Making of Modern America*. Princeton, NJ: Princeton University Press, 2004.

Ng Kamstra, Joshua S., Teresa Molina, and Timothy Halliday. "Compact for Care: How the Affordable Care Act Marketplaces Fell Short for a Vulnerable Population in Hawaii." *BMJ Global Health* 6, no. 11 (November 2021): e007701. https://doi.org/10.1136/bmjgh-2021-007701.

Nguyen, Mimi Thi. *Gift of Freedom: War, Debt, and Other Refugee Passages*. Durham, NC: Duke University Press, 2012.

Nicholls, Walter. *The DREAMers: How the Undocumented Youth Movement Transformed the Immigrant Rights Debate*. Stanford: Stanford University Press, 2013.

Northern Manhattan Coalition for Immigrant Rights. *Deportado, Dominicano, y Humano: The Realities of Dominican Deportations and Related Policy Recommendations*. New York: Northern Manhattan Coalition for Immigrant Rights, 2009. https://www.law.nyu.edu/sites/default/files/upload_documents /Deportado%20Dominicano%20y%20Humano.pdf.

NYU School of Law Immigrant Rights Clinic and Families for Freedom. *Justice Detained, Justice Denied: Immigration and Customs Enforcement Prevents Immigrants from Fighting Unlawful Criminal Convictions*. New York: NYU School of Law Immigrant Rights Clinic and Families for Freedom, 2014. https://www.law.nyu.edu/sites/default/files/upload_documents/Justice%20 Detained%2C%20Justice%20Denied.pdf.

NYU School of Law Immigrant Rights Clinic, Immigrant Defense Project, and Families for Freedom. *Insecure Communities, Devastated Families: New Data on Immigrant Detention and Deportation Practices in New York City*. New ·York: Immigrant Defense Project, 2012. https://immigrantdefenseproject.org /wp-content/uploads/2012/07/NYC-FOIA-Report-2012-FINAL.pdf.

Obama, Barack. "Remarks by the President in Address to the Nation on Immigration." White House, November 20, 2014. https://www.whitehouse.gov/the -press-office/2014/11/20/remarks-president-address-nation-immigration.

Office of Congresswoman Ayanna Pressley. "Pressley, García, Casar Re-introduce the New Way Forward Act." March 29, 2023. https://pressley.house.gov/2023/03/29/pressley-garcia-casar-re-introduce-the-new-way-forward-act/.

Office of Governor Gavin Newsom. "Governor Newsom Signs into Law First-in-the-Nation Expansion of Medi-Cal to Undocumented Californians Age 50 and Over, Bold Initiatives to Advance More Equitable and Prevention-Focused Health Care." State of California, July 27, 2021. https://www.gov.ca.gov/2021/07/27/governor-newsom-signs-into-law-first-in-the-nation-expansion-of-medi-cal-to-undocumented-californians-age-50-and-over-bold-initiatives-to-advance-more-equitable-and-prevention-focused-health-care/.

Office of Hawaiian Affairs. *Disparate Treatment of Native Hawaiians in the Criminal Justice System.* Honolulu: Office of Hawaiian Affairs, 2010.

Office of Inspector General. *Separated Children Placed in Office of Refugee Resettlement Care.* US Department of Health and Human Services, 2019. https://oig.hhs.gov/oei/reports/oei-BL-18-00511.pdf.

Office of the Solicitor General. "*Reno v. Ma-Petition*: Brief." US Department of Justice, 2000. http://www.justice.gov/osg/brief/reno-v-ma-petition.

Offices of the United States Attorneys. "1457. Criminal Street Gangs Statute—18 U.S.C. 521, Department of Justice." Accessed May 24, 2017. https://www.justice.gov/usam/criminal-resource-manual-1457-criminal-street-gangs-statute-18-usc-521.

Okamura, Jonathan. *Ethnicity and Inequality in Hawai'i.* Philadelphia: Temple University Press, 2008.

Okamura, Jonathan. "Race and/or Ethnicity in Hawai'i: What's the Difference and What Difference Does It Make?" In *Beyond Ethnicity: New Politics of Race in Hawai'i*, edited by Camilla Fojas, Rudy P. Guevarra, and Nitasha Sharma, 97–116. Honolulu: University of Hawai'i Press, 2018.

Okamura, Jonathan. *Raced to Death in 1920s Hawai'i: Injustice and Revenge in the Fukunaga Case.* Urbana: University of Illinois Press, 2019.

Oliver, Veronica. "Civil Disobedience: Anti–sB 1070 Graffiti, Marginalized Voices, and Citizenship in a Politically Privatized Public Sphere." *Community Literacy Journal* 9, no. 1 (2014): 63–76.

Omi, Michael, and Howard Winant. *Racial Formation in the United States.* 3rd ed. New York: Routledge, 2014.

1Love Movement. "40 Years Later: US Human Rights Violations and the Deportation of Cambodian-American Refugees." March 18, 2015. https://1lovemovement.wordpress.com/2015/03/18/40-years-later-us-human-rights-violations-the-deportation-of-cambodian-american-refugees/.

Ong, Aihwa. *Neoliberalism as Exception: Mutations in Citizenship and Sovereignty.* Durham, NC: Duke University Press, 2006.

Onyekwere, Adureh. "How Cash Bail Works." Brennan Center for Justice, February 24, 2021. https://www.brennancenter.org/our-work/research-reports/how-cash-bail-works.

Ordover, Nancy. *American Eugenics: Race, Queer Anatomy, and the Science of Nationalism.* Minneapolis: University of Minnesota Press, 2003.

Owen, Taylor, and Ben Kiernan. "Bombs over Cambodia: New Light on US Air War." *Asia-Pacific Journal: Japan Focus* 5, no. 5 (2007). http://apjjf.org/-Taylor -Owen/2420/article.html.

Pacific Progressive. "LA City Attorney Carmen Trutanich's Crackdown on Activists Protested." January 18, 2011. https://www.pacificprogressive.com/immigration -reform/page/2/.

Pages, Myrna. "Indefinite Detention: Tipping the Scale toward the Liberty Interest of Freedom after *Zadvydas v. Davis.*" *Albany Law Review* 66 (2003): 1213–40.

Pallares, Amalia. *Family Activism: Immigrant Struggles and the Politics of Nonciti-zenship.* New Brunswick, NJ: Rutgers University Press, 2014.

Pallares, Amalia. "Representing 'La Familia': Family Separation and Immigration Activism." In *¡Marcha! Latino Chicago and the Immigrant Rights Movement,* edited by Amalia Pallares and Nilda Flores-Gonzáles, 215–36. Urbana: University of Illinois Press, 2010.

Park, John S. W. *Illegal Migrations and the Huckleberry Finn Problem.* Philadelphia: Temple University Press, 2013.

Payán, Ximena. "Paulina González Uses Story Telling as a Tool of Civil Resistance." *Narco News Bulletin,* June 4, 2013. https://www.narconews.com/Issue67 /article4699.html.

Peter, Joakim, Wayne Tanaka, and Aiko Yamashiro. "Reconnecting Our Roots: Navigating the Turbulent Waters of Health-Care Policy for Micronesians in Hawai'i." In *Beyond Ethnicity: New Politics of Race in Hawai'i,* edited by Camilla Fojas, Rudy P. Guevarra, and Nitasha T. Sharma, 194–211. Honolulu: University of Hawai'i Press, 2018.

Pobutsky, Ann, Dmitry Krupitsky, and Seiji Yamada. "Micronesian Migrant Health Issues in Hawaii: Part 2: An Assessment of Health, Language and Key Social Determinants of Health." *Californian Journal of Health Promotion* 7, no. 9 (2009): 32–55.

Poeuv, Socheata, dir. *New Year Baby.* New York: Broken English Productions, 2008. DVD, 74 mins. https://itvs.org/films/new-year-baby/.

Prashad, Vijay. *Karma of Brown Folk.* Minneapolis: University of Minnesota Press, 2000.

Prison Policy Initiative. "Hawaii Profile." Accessed July 4, 2022. https://www .prisonpolicy.org/profiles/HI.html.

Puar, Jasbir. *Terrorist Assemblages: Homonationalism in Queer Times.* Durham, NC: Duke University Press, 2007.

Pulido, Laura, Laura Barraclough, and Wendy Cheng. *A People's Guide to Los Ange-les.* Berkeley: University of California Press, 2012.

Ramírez, Marla Andrea. "The Making of Mexican Illegality: Immigration Exclu-sions Based on Race, Class Status, and Gender." *New Political Science* 40, no. 2 (2018): 317–35.

Ramirez, Reyna K. *Native Hubs: Culture, Community, and Belonging in Silicon Valley and Beyond.* Durham, NC: Duke University Press, 2007.

Ramirez Solórzano, Rafael. "The Trail of Dreams: Queering across the Fight for Migrant Rights." Master's thesis, University of California, Los Angeles, 2016.

Ramirez Solórzano, Rafael. "Welcome to Cuban Miami: Linking Place, Race, and Undocuqueer Youth Activism." In *Queer and Trans Migrations: Dynamics of Illegalization, Detention and Deportation*, edited by Eithne Luibhéid and Karma R. Chávez, 106–24. Urbana: University of Illinois Press, 2020.

Ransby, Barbara. *Ella Baker and the Black Freedom Movement: A Radical Democratic Vision.* Chapel Hill: University of North Carolina Press, 2003.

Rath, Rich. "Todos Somos Arizona." Soundcloud, November 27, 2021. https://soundcloud.com/richrath/todos-somos-arizona.

Rebeldeyo. "The Fast for Our Future to Re-ignite the Immigrant Rights Movement." *Fast For Our Future Day One* (blog), October 10, 2008. https://fastforourfuture.wordpress.com/2008/10/10/hello-world/.

Reddy, Chandan. *Freedom with Violence: Race, Sexuality, and the U.S. State.* Durham, NC: Duke University Press, 2011.

Reuters. "Cambodian PM Hun Sen to Hand Over Power to Son Next Month." Reuters, July 26, 2023. https://www.reuters.com/world/asia-pacific/cambodias-hun-sen-says-will-step-down-pm-speech-2023-07-26/.

Riedel, Ryan. "Phoenix Rising: Social Movement in an SB 1070 Arizona." Master's thesis, Tulane University, 2013.

Rifkin, Mark. "Around 1978: Family, Culture, and Race in the Federal Production of Indianness." In *Critically Sovereign: Indigenous Gender, Sexuality and Feminist Studies*, edited by Joanne Barker, 169–206. Durham, NC: Duke University Press, 2017.

Riklon, Sheldon, Wilfred Alik, Allen Hixon, and Neal Palafox. "The 'Compact Impact' in Hawai'i: Focus on Health Care." *Hawai'i Medical Journal* 69, no. 3 (2010): 7–12.

Rios, Victor M. *Punished: Policing the Lives of Black and Latino Boys.* New York: New York University Press, 2011.

Ritchie, Andrea, and Monique Morris. *Centering Black Women, Girls, Gender Nonconforming People and Fem(Me)s in Campaigns for Expanded Sanctuary and Freedom Cities.* National Black Women's Justice Institute, September 2017. https://forwomen.org/wp-content/uploads/2017/09/Centering-Black-women-final-draft6.pdf.

Robbins, Liz, and Annie Correal. "On a 'Day without Immigrants,' Workers Show Their Presence by Staying Home." *New York Times*, February 16, 2017.

Rodriguez, Ignacia. "What Does the DAPA Rescission Mean and What Implications Does It Have for DACA?" National Immigration Law Center, June 23, 2017. https://www.nilc.org/2017/06/23/dapa-rescission-mean-implications-daca/.

Rodriguez, Monica. "Pomona Council Votes Down Proposal to Halt Vehicle Impounds." *Daily Bulletin*, May 20, 2014. https://www.dailybulletin.com/2014/05/20/pomona-council-votes-down-proposal-to-halt-vehicle-impounds/.

Rodríguez, Richard T. *Next of Kin: Reconfiguring Family in Chicano/a Cultural Politics.* Durham, NC: Duke University Press, 2009.

Rozensky, Jordyn. "Biden Administration Routinely Separates Immigrant Families." National Immigrant Justice Center, January 19, 2022. https://immigrantjustice.org/staff/blog/biden-administration-routinely-separates-immigrant-families.

Ruiz, Jason. "After Public Backlash, Hun Manet Says He Won't Attend Long Beach Cambodian New Year Parade." *Long Beach Post*, March 28, 2016. https://lbpost.com/news/after-public-backlash-hun-manet-says-he-won-t-attend-cambodian-new-year-s-parade/.

Ruiz, Jason. "Cambodian Community Calls on City Leaders to Denounce Visit of Khmer Rouge Leader's Son." *Long Beach Post*, March 23, 2016. https://lbpost.com/news/cambodian-community-calls-on-city-leaders-to-denounce-visit-by-son-of-khmer-rouge-leader-to-annual-new-year-s-parade/.

Ryo, Emily, and Ian Peacock. "The Landscape of Immigration Detention in the United States." American Immigration Council, December 5, 2018. https://americanimmigrationcouncil.org/research/landscape-immigration-detention-united-states.

Sangalang, Cindy, Suely Ngouy, and Anna Lau. "Using Community-Based Participatory Research to Identify Health Issues for Cambodian American Youth." *Family and Community Health* 30 no. 1 (2015): 55–65.

Saranillio, Dean I. "Colliding Histories: Hawai'i Statehood at the Intersection of Asians 'Ineligible to Citizenship' and Hawaiians 'Unfit for Self-Government.'" *Journal of Asian American Studies* 13 no. 3 (2010): 238–309.

Saranillio, Dean I. "Why Asian Settler Colonialism Matters: A Thought Piece on Critiques, Debates, and Indigenous Difference." *Settler Colonial Studies* 3, no. 3–4 (2013): 280–94.

Schaeffer, Felicity Amaya. *Unsettled Borders: The Militarized Surveillance on Sacred Indigenous Land.* Durham, NC: Duke University Press, 2022.

Schaffer, Kay, and Sidonie Smith. *Human Rights and Narrated Lives: The Ethics of Recognition.* New York: Palgrave Macmillan, 2004.

Schlund-Vials, Cathy J. "Subjects of 1975: Delineating the Necessity of Critical Refugee Studies." *MELUS* 41, no. 3 (2016): 199–203.

Schlund-Vials, Cathy J. *War, Genocide, and Justice: Cambodian American Memory Work.* Minneapolis: University of Minnesota Press, 2012. Kindle.

Schneiderman, Eric. "Guidance concerning Local Authority Participation in Immigration Enforcement and Model Sanctuary Provisions." State of New York Office of the Attorney General, January 19, 2017. https://ag.ny.gov/sites/default/files/guidance_and_supplement_final3.12.17.pdf.

Shah, Nayan. *Stranger Intimacy: Contesting Race, Sexuality and the Law in the North American West.* Berkeley: University of California Press, 2011.

Sharma, Nandita. *Home Economics: Nationalism and the Making of "Migrant Workers" in Canada.* Toronto: University of Toronto Press, 2006.

Sharma, Nandita, and Cynthia Wright. "Decolonizing Resistance: Challenging Colonial States." *Social Justice* 35, no. 3 (2008–2009): 120–38.

Siegel, Loren. "Gangs and the Law." In *Gangs and Society,* edited by Louis Kontos, David Brotherton, and Luis Barrios, 213–27. New York: Columbia University Press, 2003.

Simpson, Audra. *Mohawk Interruptus: Political Life across the Borders of Settler States.* Durham, NC: Duke University Press, 2014.

S.I.N. Collective. "Students Informing Now (S.I.N.) Challenge the Racial State in California without Shame . . . *sin Vergüenza!*" *Journal of Educational Foundations* 21, nos. 1–2 (Winter–Spring 2007): 71–90.

Smith, Andrea. *Conquest: Sexual Violence and American Indian Genocide.* Cambridge, MA: South End, 2005.

Smith, Andrea. "Heteropatriarchy and the Three Pillars of White Supremacy: Rethinking Women of Color Organizing." In *The Color of Violence: The INCITE! Anthology,* edited by INCITE! Women of Color against Violence, 66–73. Cambridge, MA: South End, 2006.

Smith, Keeley. "Southeast Asian Community Members Vow to Fight against Unfair Deportation Policies." *Long Beach Post,* December 18, 2015. https://lbpost.com/news/in-long-beach-southeast-asian-community-members-vow-to-fight-for-better-policies-to-deter-deportations.

Sonoda, Healani. "A Nation Incarcerated." In *Asian Settler Colonialism: From Local Governance to the Habits of Everyday Life in Hawai'i,* edited by Candace Fujikane and Jonathan Okamura, 99–115. Honolulu: University of Hawai'i Press, 2008.

Sound-Kikku, Innocenta. "I Am of Oceania." In *The Value of Hawai'i 2,* edited by Aiko Yamashiro and Noelani Goodyear-Ka'ōpua, 144–45. Honolulu: University of Hawai'i Press.

South Asian Americans Leading Together. *National Action Agenda: Policy Recommendations to Empower South Asians in the United States.* Tacoma Park, MD: South Asian Americans Leading Together, 2008. https://saalt.org/wp-content/uploads/2012/09/National-Action-Agenda.pdf.

South Asian Network. *From Displacement to Internment: A Report of Human Rights Violations Experienced by L.A.'s South Asian Communities.* Artesia, CA: South Asian Network, 2010. https://www.saada.org/item/20160212-4555.

South Asian Network, Garment Workers Center, Homies Unidos, Youth Justice Coalition, Instituto de Educacion Popular del Sur de California, Khmer Girls in Action, and Coalicion de Derechos Humanos. "Grassroots Immigrant Rights Organizations Call for Speaking the Truth to Our Communities and Advancing Immigration Policies That Promote Healthy Communities and Protect Our Rights." 2007. https://www.saada.org/item/20160212-4556.

Southeast Asian Freedom Network. "SEAFN Campaign Solidarity Letter." Accessed
    August 25, 2016. https://docs.google.com/forms/d/e/1FAIpQLSd49FkHqVwTuk
    -O80XSVCPqgUQYwRVSg4Pl11RSoJ96UtUIFw/viewform.

Southeast Asia Resource Action Center. "SEARC, SEAFN Celebrate House Re-
    introduction of Southeast Asian Deportation Relief Act." August 22,
    2023. https://www.searac.org/immigration/searac-seafn-celebrate-house
    -reintroduction-of-southeast-asian-deportation-relief-act/.

Southeast Asia Resource Action Center. "Southeast Asian American Community
    Responds to the ICE Roundup of Cambodian and Vietnamese Americans."
    November 1, 2017. https://www.searac.org/our-voices/press-room/southeast
    -asian-american-community-responds-ice-roundup-cambodian-vietnamese
    -americans/.

Spade, Dean. "Impossibility Now." s and f Online, no. 11.1–11.2 (Fall 2012 / Spring
    2013). https://sfonline.barnard.edu/impossibility-now/.

Spade, Dean. Normal Life: Administrative Violence, Critical Transpolitics, and the
    Limits of Law. Durham, NC: Duke University Press, 2015.

Speed, Shannon. Incarcerated Stories: Indigenous Women Migrants and Violence in
    the Settler Capitalist State. Chapel Hill: University of North Carolina Press,
    2019.

Stanley, Eric A., Dean Spade, and Queer (In)justice. "Queering Prison Abolition,
    Now?" American Quarterly 64, no. 1 (2012): 115–27.

Stannard, David E. Honor Killing: Race, Rape, and Clarence Darrow's Spectacular
    Last Case. New York: Penguin, 2006.

State of Arizona Senate. Senate Bill 1070, Pub. L. No. SB 1070 (2010). www.azleg
    .gov/legtext/49leg/2r/bills/sb1070s.pdf.

Steinhauer, Jennifer. "Bipartisan Push Builds to Relax Sentencing Laws." New York
    Times, July 28, 2015. https://www.nytimes.com/2015/07/29/us/push-to-scale
    -back-sentencing-laws-gains-momentum.html.

Steinhauer, Jennifer. "To Cut Costs, States Relax Prison Policies." New York
    Times, March 24, 2009. https://www.nytimes.com/2009/03/25/us/25prisons
    .html.

Stephen, Lynn. Transborder Lives: Indigenous Oaxacans in Mexico, California, and
    Oregon. 2nd ed. Durham, NC: Duke University Press, 2007.

Survived and Punished. "s and p Analysis and Vision." 2016. https://survivedand
    punished.org/analysis/.

Sudbury, Julia, ed. Global Lockdown: Gender, Race and the Rise of the Prison Indus-
    trial Complex around the World. New York: Routledge, 2005.

Sullivan, Laura. "Prison Economics Helped Drive Ariz. Immigration Law." NPR, Oc-
    tober 28, 2010. https://www.npr.org/2010/10/28/130833741/prison-economics
    -help-drive-ariz-immigration-law.

Sullivan, Laura. "Shaping State Laws with Little Scrutiny." NPR, October 29, 2010.
    https://www.npr.org/2010/10/29/130891396/shaping-state-laws-with-little
    -scrutiny.

Tamez, Margo. "Indigenous Women's Rivered Refusals in El Calaboz." *Diálogo* 19, no. 1 (2016): 7–21.

Tamez, Margo. "Soveryempty: Narrative DeneNdé Poetics in Walled Home Lands." In *Indigenous Women and Violence: Feminist Activist Research in Heightened States of Injustice*, edited by Lynn Stephen and Shannon Speed, 209–42. Tucson: University of Arizona Press, 2021.

Tang, Eric. *Unsettled: Cambodian Refugees in the New York City Hyperghetto*. Philadelphia: Temple University Press, 2015.

TeAda Productions. *Masters of the Currents*. Accessed February 26, 2024. https://www.teada.org/masters-of-the-current-1.

Tengan, Ty P. Kāwika. "Hoa: On Being and Binding Relations." *Amerasia Journal* 46, no. 3 (2020): 280–83.

Tengan, Ty P. Kāwika. "The Mana of Kū: Indigenous Nationhood, Masculinity, and Authority in Hawai'i." In *New Mana: Transformations of a Classic Concept in Pacific Languages and Cultures*, edited by Matt Tomlinson and Ty P. Kāwika Tengan, 55–75. Canberra, Australia: ANU Press, 2016.

Tengan, Ty P. Kāwika, Tēvita O. Ka'ili, and Rochelle T. Fonoti. "Genealogies: Articulating Indigenous Anthropology in/of Oceania." *Pacific Studies; A Multidisciplinary Journal* 33, no. 2/3 (2010): 139–67.

Teves, Stephanie Nohelani. *Defiant Indigeneity: The Politics of Hawaiian Performance*. Chapel Hill: University of North Carolina Press, 2018.

Teves, Stephanie Nohelani, and Maile Arvin. "Decolonizing API: Centering Indigenous Pacific Islander Feminism." In *Asian American Feminisms and Women of Color Politics*, edited by Lynn Fujiwara and Shireen Roshanravan, 107–27. Seattle: University of Washington Press, 2018.

Thobani, Sunera. *Exalted Subjects: Studies in the Making of Race and Nation in Canada*. Toronto: University of Toronto Press, 2007.

Thobani, Sunera. "Navigating Colonial Pitfalls: Race, Citizenship and the Politics of 'South Asian Canadian' Feminism." In *Asian American Feminisms and Women of Color Politics*, edited by Lynn Fujiwara and Shireen Roshanravan, 155–75. Seattle: University of Washington Press, 2018.

Thuma, Emily L. *All Our Trials: Prisons, Policing, and the Feminist Fight to End Violence*. Urbana: University of Illinois Press, 2019.

Ti'at Society. "A Conversation." In *O, My Ancestor: Recognition and Renewal for the Gabrielino-Tongva People of the Los Angeles Area*, edited by Claudia Jurmain and William McCawley, 127–48. Berkeley: Heyday Books and Rancho Alamitos Foundation, 2009.

Tohono O'odham Legislative Council. "Resolution of the Tohono O'odham Legislative Council (Opposing Arizona Senate Bill 1070 as Discriminatory State Legislation)." Tohono O'odham Legislative Branch, May 18, 2010. https://www.tolc-nsn.gov/docs/Actions10/10184.pdf.

Torres, Craig, Cindi Alvitre, Allison Fischer-Olson, Mishuana Goeman, and Wendy Teeter. "Perspectives on a Selection of Gabrieleño/Tongva Places." Mapping

Indigenous LA, Los Angeles. Accessed March 6, 2024. https://www.arcgis.com
/apps/MapJournal/index.html?appid=4942348fa8bd427fae02f7e020e98764.

Torres, Patricia, and Naazneen Diwan. "Moving from the Flesh: Feminist and
Queer Thought and Action in LA Immigrant Rights Movements." *csw Update*, June 2011, 17–25.

Transactional Records Access Clearinghouse (TRAC). "ICE Deportations by Country of Citizenship: FY 2012–FY 2013." Syracuse University, 2014. https://trac
.syr.edu/immigration/reports/350/.

Transactional Records Access Clearing House (TRAC). "ICE Deportations: Gender,
Age, and Country of Citizenship." Syracuse University, April 9, 2014. https://
trac.syr.edu/immigration/reports/350/.

Transactional Records Access Clearing House (TRAC). "ICE Detainees." Syracuse
University. Accessed February 23, 2024. https://trac.syr.edu/immigration
/detentionstats/pop_agen_table.html.

Trask, Haunani-Kay. "The Color of Violence." *Social Justice* 31, no. 4 (2004): 8–16.

Trask, Haunani-Kay. *From a Native Daughter: Colonialism and Sovereignty in
Hawai'i*. Honolulu: University of Hawai'i Press, 1999.

Trask, Haunani-Kay. "Settlers of Color and 'Immigrant' Hegemony of 'Locals' in
Hawai'i." *Amerasia Journal* 26, no. 2 (2000): 1–24.

Tuck, Eve and Wayne K. Yang. "Decolonization Is Not a Metaphor." *Decolonization:
Indigeneity, Education & Society* 1 no.1 (2012): 1–40.

UCLA Asian American Studies Center, Asian Pacific Policy and Planning Council,
and UCLA Department of Urban Planning. *The State of Cambodia Town*. Los
Angeles: UCLA Asian American Studies Center, 2013. http://www.aasc.ucla
.edu/research/pdfs/cambodiatown.pdf.

Um, Khatharya. *From the Land of Shadows: War, Revolution, and the Making of the
Cambodian Diaspora*. New York: New York University Press, 2015.

University of Hawai'i News. "Regents Approve Undocumented Immigrant Policy."
February 26, 2013. https://www.hawaii.edu/news/2013/02/26/regents-approve
-undocumented-immigrant-policy/.

US Commission on Civil Rights. *Micronesians in Hawaii: Migrant Group Faces
Barriers to Equal Opportunity: A Report of the Hawaii Advisory Committee to
the U.S. Commission on Civil Rights*. March 2019. https://www.usccr.gov/files
/pubs/2019/08-13-Hawaii-Micronesian-Report.pdf.

US Congress. "18 U.S. Code § 521—Criminal Street Gangs." Legal Information Institute. Accessed May 24, 2017. https://www.law.cornell.edu/uscode/text/18/521.

US House. *Sanctuary Cities: A Threat to Public Safety Hearing; Hearing before
the Subcommittee on Immigration and Border Security*, 114th Cong. (2015).
https://judiciary.house.gov/sites/evo-subsites/judiciary.house.gov/files/2016
-02/114-34_95632.pdf.

US House. Southeast Asian Deportation Relief Act of 2023. H.R. 5248, 118th Cong.,
1st Sess. Introduced in the House August 22, 2023. https://www.congress.gov
/bill/118th-congress/house-bill/5248/text.

US Immigration and Customs Enforcement. "ERO FY 2020." Last updated October 29, 2021. https://www.ice.gov/features/ERO-2020.

US Immigration and Customs Enforcement. "Operation Community Shield." Last updated November 16, 2021. https://www.ice.gov/features/community-shield.

US Immigration and Customs Enforcement. "Secure Communities." Last updated February 9, 2021. https://www.ice.gov/secure-communities.

US Immigration and Customs Enforcement. *U.S. Immigration and Customs Enforcement Fiscal Year 2020 Enforcement and Removal Operations Report.* Last updated October 29, 2021. https://www.ice.gov/doclib/news/library/reports/annual-report/eroReportFY2020.pdf.

US Immigration and Customs Enforcement and Hawaii Criminal Justice Data Center. *Memorandum of Agreement between U.S. Department of Homeland Security, Immigration and Customs Enforcement and Hawaii Criminal Justice Data Center.* 2010. www.ice.gov/doclib/foia/secure_communities-moa/r_hawaii_4-18-10.pdf.

Valdez, Luis. *Early Works: Actos, Bernabe and Pensamiento Serpentino.* Houston: Arte Público, 1990.

Veracini, Lorenzo. *Settler Colonialism: A Theoretical Overview.* Basingstoke, UK: Palgrave Macmillan, 2010.

Vimalassery, Manu. "Antecedents of Imperial Incarceration: Fort Marion to Guantánamo." In *The Sun Never Sets: South Asian Migrants in an Age of U.S. Power,* edited by Vivek Bald, Miabi Chatterji, Sujani Reddy, and Manu Vimalassery, 350–74. New York: New York University Press, 2013.

Vimalassery, Manu. "The Prose of Counter-sovereignty." In *Formations of United States Colonialism,* edited by Alyosha Goldstein, 87–109. Durham, NC: Duke University Press, 2014.

Volpp, Leti. "The Indigenous as Alien." *UC Irvine Law Review* 5, no. 2 (2015): 289–325.

Walia, Harsha. *Undoing Border Imperialism.* Oakland, CA: AK, 2013. Kindle.

Walter Leitner International Human Rights Clinic, Returnee Integration Support Center, and Deported Diaspora. *Removing Refugees: U.S. Deportation Policy and the Cambodian-American Community.* New York: Leitner Center for International Law and Justice at Fordham Law School, 2010. http://www.leitnercenter.org/files/2010%20Cambodia%20Report_FINAL.pdf.

Watt, Brian. "Protesters Demand LA Protest Charges Be Dropped." Southern California Public Radio, February 14, 2011. https://laist.com/news/kpcc-archive/protesters-demand-la-protest-charges-be-dropped.

We Are Oceania. "Youth Empowerment Center." Accessed March 7, 2024. https://www.weareoceania.org/youth-empowerment-center/.

Wessler, Seth. "Double Punishment." *Colorlines,* October 9, 2009. https://colorlines.com/article/double-punishment/.

Wilkins, David E., and K. Tsianina Lomawaima. *Uneven Ground: American Indian Sovereignty and Federal Law.* Norman: University of Oklahoma Press, 2002.

Winton, Richard. "33 Charged with Blocking L.A. City Streets during Immigration Protests." *Los Angeles Times*, September 8, 2010. https://www.latimes.com /archives/la-xpm-2010-sep-08-la-me-immigration-crimes-20100908-story .html.

Wolfe, Patrick. "Settler Colonialism and the Elimination of the Native." *Journal of Genocide Research* 7, no. 2 (2006): 387–409.

Wolfe, Patrick. *Traces of History: Elementary Structures of Race.* London: Verso, 2016.

Yalamarty, Harshita. "Lessons from 'No Ban on Stolen Land.'" *Studies in Social Justice* 14, no. 2 (2020): 474–85.

Yam, Kimberly. "The U.S. Just Quietly Deported the Largest Group of Cambodians Ever." *Huffington Post*, April 6, 2018. https://www.huffingtonpost.com/entry /cambodians-deported-trump-immigration_us_5ac77dd9e4b07a3485e3da6c.

Yamada, Seiji, and Ann Pobutsky. "Micronesian Migrant Health Issues in Hawaii: Part 1: Background, Home Island Data, and Clinical Evidence." *California Journal of Health Promotion* 7, no. 2 (2009): 16–31.

Yamaga, Minda. "Pull Down Barriers That Cause Mistrust of 'Other' Communities." *Honolulu Star-Advertiser*, April 28, 2021. https://www.staradvertiser.com /2021/04/28/editorial/island-voices/column-pull-down-barriers-that-cause -mistrust-of-other-communities/.

Yanga, Joy, and Sinara Sagn. "The Fight to Keep Them Home." *Khmer Times* (blog), December 21, 2017. https://www.khmertimeskh.com/5097345/the-fight-to -keep-them-home/.

Yazzie, Melanie. "Abolition and Abundance: Living beyond Punishment." Paper presented at the annual meeting for the American Studies Conference, Honolulu, Hawai'i, November 7, 2019.

Yazzie, Melanie. "Organizing an End to Violence against Native Peoples in Border Towns." Paper presented at the annual meeting for the Native American and Indigenous Studies Association, Honolulu, Hawai'i, May 21, 2016.

Yazzie, Melanie. "Solidarity with Palestine from Diné Bikéyah." *American Quarterly* 67 no. 4 (2015): 1007–15.

Yoon-Hendricks, Alexandra, and Zoe Greenberg. "Protests across U.S. Call for End to Migrant Family Separations." *New York Times*, June 30, 2018. https://www .nytimes.com/2018/06/30/us/politics/trump-protests-family-separation.html.

Young, Jackie. "Over 20 Years Later, Expanded Medicaid Brings Affordable Health Care Back to Micronesian Patients." Hawai'i Public Radio, October 14, 2021. https://www.hawaiipublicradio.org/local-news/2021-10-14/over-20 -years-later-expanded-medicaid-brings-affordable-health-care-back-to -micronesian-patients.

Zamorano, Neidi Dominguez, Johnathan Perez, Nancy Meza, and Jorge Guitierrez. "DREAM Activists: Rejecting the Passivity of the Nonprofit, Industrial Complex." *Truthout*, September 21, 2010. https://truthout.org/articles/dream -activists-rejecting-the-passivity-of-the-nonprofit-industrial-complex/.

Zheng, Eddy. "Prison-to-Leadership Pipeline: Asian American Prisoner Activism." In *Contemporary Asian American Activism: Building Movements for Liberation*, edited by Diane Fujino and Robyn Magalit Rodriguez, 37–62. Seattle: University of Washington Press, 2022.

Zilberg, Elana. *Space of Detention: The Making of a Transnational Gang Crisis.* Durham, NC: Duke University Press, 2011.

Zong, Jie, Ariel G. Ruiz Soto, Jeanne Batalova, Julia Gelatt, and Randy Capps. "A Profile of Current DACA Recipients by Education, Industry, and Occupation." Washington, DC: Migration Policy Institute, November 2017. https://www.migrationpolicy.org/research/profile-current-daca-recipients-education-industry-and-occupation.

Zonkel, Phillip. "Transgender Activist Valeria De La Luz Ramos Fears Life in Mexico, Seeks U.S. Asylum." *Q Voice News*, March 23, 2017. https://qvoicenews.com/2017/03/22/transgender-activist-valeria-de-la-luz-ramos-fears-life-in-mexico-seeks-u-s-asylum/.

INDEX

AB 4 (California TRUST Act), 33, 151
AB 60, in California, 181n91
abolition: FFF on, 85, 106; IYC on, 141, 146; Native Hawaiian sovereignty movement and, 165–66; Tod@s Som@s Arizona exploring, 72–73
abolition antideportation organizing, 20–22
abolitionist commitments, antideportation organizing impacting, 52–53
abolitionist politics, 172n10
Abrego, Leisy, 130
ACS (American Community Survey), 193n8
Adebiyi, Christiana, 93
AEDPA (Antiterrorism and Effective Death Penalty Act), 30, 155–56
affect: affective labor of Tod@ feminists, 58; FFF mobilizing, 101; KGA appealing to families and, 124; sense of collectivity built through, 24; testimonios creating, 92–94
affective category, refugee as, 101
affective field of protest, by IYC, 149
African American communities: civil rights and, 185n26; criminal legal system controlling, 19; pitted against Latinos, 76
Agreements of Cooperation in Communities to Enhance Safety and Security, ICE (ICE ACCESS), 44–47
'aha (gathering), 170, 199n10
Aikau, Hōkūlani, 133, 198n74
Aizeki, Mizue, 46, 47
Alexander, Michelle, 19, 130
Alianza Indígena Sin Fronteras (organization), 177n4
Alien Criminal Apprehension Program (CAP), 31–35
Allies, the 43–44
Alva, Susan, 164
Alvitre, Cindi, 133
American Community Survey (ACS), 193n8
the Americas, Indigenous people migrating across, 8

Ancestor Walk, 119, 120, 198n67
anti-Black racism, 17, 27–28, 79, 84, 89, 138, 139–40, 188n74
anticolonial politics, Palestine and, 183n9
antideportation activists, 3, 7–8, 23, 47–48; crimmigration experienced by, xvii, 28; immigrant rights movement and, xiv; New Jim Crow and, 19–20; settler carcerality confronted by, 4–5; testimonies by, 24. See also Perez, Johnathan
antideportation movement, 4
antideportation organizers, vulnerability of, 23, 61, 68, 69
antideportation organizing, xi–xiv
Antiterrorism and Effective Death Penalty Act (AEDPA), 30, 155–56
Anti-violence Advocates (AVA), 46–47, 179nn66–67
Anzaldúa, Gloria, 145
APSC (Asian Prisoner Support Committee), 177n8
Arellanes, Gloria, 133
Arellano, Elvira, 95
Arizona, 43
Arizona Senate Bill 1070 (SB 1070), 19–20, 23, 29, 45, 54, 182n6; civil disobedience against, 48; feminist and queer activists against, 80; LGBTQ groups opposing, 184n20; racial profiling legitimized by, 56–57; Tod@s Som@s Arizona protesting, xviii, 5, 55, 66, 68, 144, 182n3; works on organizing and protest against, 182n7
Asian Americans, law enforcement targeting, 177n8
Asian Americans Advancing Justice, 193n2
Asian and Pacific Islander Youth Promoting Advocacy and Leadership (AYPAL), 193n4
Asian Prisoner Support Committee (APSC), 177n8
Asia-Pacific Economic Cooperation forum, 201n30

immigrant rights movement, xvii, 21, 86–87, 169; antideportation activism and, xiv; family separation decried by, 7; gender-based traumas and, 72; Obama reinvigorating, xiii

immigrant rights organizing, 4

"Immigrants for Sale" (video), 154

Immigrant Youth Coalition (IYC), x–xii, xix, 5; Black Lives Matter movement supported by, 165–66; civil disobedience by, ix, xii, 3–4, 29–30; Coming Out of the Shadows event by, 144, 150, 200n16; crimmigration critiqued by, 164; formation of, 141–45; "ICE Out of California" campaign by, 33; with National Youth Immigrant Alliance, 135; "New Jim Crow" circulated by, 175n60; political framework built by, 146; prison industrial complex prioritized by, 151; queer and abolitionist imagination of, 139; Resilience OC supported by, 200n15; undocuqueer leadership of, 146–51; YES organized by, 27, 151, 154, 155, 200n16; Youth Empowerment Summit organized by, 27

Immigrant Youth Justice League (IYJL), 144

immigration, labor and, 20–21

Immigration and Customs Enforcement (ICE), 23, 27, 34–35, 88, 177n14; Agreements of Cooperation in Communities to Enhance Safety and Security, 44–47; civil disobedience against, 49; direct action confronting, 149; Intergovernmental Service Agreements contracting with, 180n76; Micronesians targeted by, 156; Montrevil targeted by, 100; National Gang Unit of, 38; "Operation Safe City" by, x; prisons visited by, 32; Ragbir targeted by, 91

Immigration and Nationality Act, 21, 25

Immigration and Naturalization Services (INS), 31, 37

immigration control, as national security, 42–44

immigration enforcement, xiv; community formation targeted by, 23; criminal legal system mimicked by, 51–52; mass incarceration converging with, 169; in prisons, 31–35; under Trump, 50

Immigration Reform and Control Act (IRCA), 31

incarcerated immigrants, abuse faced by, 90–91

incarceration: mass, 16–17, 47, 169; of Native Hawaiians, 153; neoliberal era expanding, 196n33; settler power and, 16–25. See also prisons

INCITE!, 71

Indian Civil Rights Act, 20

Indian country, crime control in, 17

Indian removal, Chinese exclusion differentiating, 15

Indigenous Day Ancestor Walk, 119

Indigenous feminism, 10, 12, 173n24, 174n34; Barker defining, 25–26, 174n25

Indigenous Pacific Island youth, migration justice discussed by, 139–40

Indigenous people, 8, 11

Indigenous politics, migrant politics and, 11, 83, 113–14

Indigenous practices, gender and sexuality articulated in, 175n59

Indigenous self-determination, MCA impairing, 18

Indigenous sovereignty, 2, 10–14, 168

INS (Immigration and Naturalization Services), 31, 37

in-state policy, for undocumented applicants, 164

Instituto de Educación Popular del Sur de California (IDEPSCA), 67

Integrative Case Management (tool), 45

Intergovernmental Service Agreements, 180n76

internalities of power, 22

International Center for Nonviolent Conflict, 61

intimacy, publicity and, 20–25

IRCA (Immigration Reform and Control Act), 31

Irwin, Katherine, 158

Israel, 63–64, 79

IYC. See Immigrant Youth Coalition

IYC–National Immigrant Youth Alliance (IYC-NIYA), 136, 161, 165

IYJL (Immigrant Youth Justice League), 144

jail time, 70–74

James, Calvin, 96–98

James, Joshua, 96–98

Jesse Brewer Regional Headquarters (77th Precinct), 70

July 29 action, 62–66

Jurmain, Claudia, 118–19, 150

Justice LA, ix

Kaba, Mariame, 169
Kanaka 'Ōiwi, 165
Kanaka Maoli. *See* Native Hawaiians
Kanstroom, Daniel, 5, 13, 14–15
Kaplan, Amy, 173n11
Karma of Brown Folk (Prashad), 20
Kaur, Tavleen, 189n4
KGA. *See* Khmer Girls in Action
Khan, Hamid, xvii, 43, 50, 54, 63, 116, 183n14
Khmer community, 5, 111, 113, 124–26, 197n56
Khmer Girls in Action (KGA), xiv, xviii, 5, 36, 108, 110–11, 119–20; about, 114–16; coalition space organized by, 115–16; emotional safety at, 116–17; Every Student Matters campaign by, 121–22; Khmer New Year Parade not participated in by, 127; newsletter by, 194n9; "Not Home for the Holidays" led by, 109, 111; resettlement interrogated by, 113; resources lacked by, 195n18, 195n27; training by, 124–25; US imperialism implicated by, 132, 134
Khmer Justice Program (KJP), 115
Khmer New Year Parade, KGA not participating in, 127
Khmer Rouge, 111–12, 125–26, 127, 194n13
Khmer youth, criminalization of, 121
K'iche' Code of Conduct, 73
King, Martin Luther, Jr., 184n17, 185n26
KJP (Khmer Justice Program), 115
Kneese, Tamara, 176n73
Kobach, Kris, 63
Kong, Jocelyn, 110
Koreatown Immigrant Workers Alliance, 67
KRS-One (rapper), 69

LA. *See* Los Angeles, California
labor, immigration and, 20–21
LACAN (Los Angeles Community Action Network), 76
Landback movement, 174n28
land dispossession, Indigenous people experiencing, 8, 13–14, 140
LAPD. *See* Los Angeles Police Department
Latino youth, Violent Gang Task Force impacting, 178n38
law enforcement, 177n8, 179n42
Lawrence, Charles, III, 159, 166, 204n62
LBUSD (Long Beach Unified School District), 121–22

legal system, criminal. *See* criminal legal system
Leong, Karen, 3, 114, 171n6
"Letter from Birmingham Jail" (King), 184n17
Leza, Christina, 177n4
LGBTQ groups, SB 1070 opposed by, 184n20
Lomawaima, K. Tsianina, 14, 17, 18
Lone Wolf v. Hitchcock (US Supreme Court case), 18
Long Beach, California, 110, 115, 121–22, 125, 132–33; Cambodian refugees arriving in, 117–18; Cambodia Town in, 114, 117–18, 193n8; displacement and dispossession in, 116–19; gang injunctions instituted in, 38; refugee community in, xv. *See also* Khmer Girls in Action
Long Beach State College, 132
Long Beach Unified School District (LBUSD), 121–22
long-term legal permanent residents (LPRS), 30
Los Angeles, California (LA), ix; Cadillac-Corning in, 36; Freeway 101 in, 66; May Day protests in, xiii; Skid Row in, 76; Westwood Federal Building in, 61, 65; Yaanga in, 185n29. *See also* Immigrant Youth Coalition; Tod@s Som@s Arizona
Los Angeles Community Action Network (LACAN), 76
Los Angeles County, prison expansion in, ix–x
Los Angeles Police Department (LAPD), x, xvii, 56, 64–65, 74; communities of color swept by, 73; gang injunctions, 36–37; Tod@s Som@s Arizona members arrested by, 69–70
LPRS (long-term legal permanent residents), 30
Lyons, Laura, 9, 63

Ma, Kim Ho, 38–39, 179n43
Macías-Rojas, Patrisia, 6, 35
Major Crimes Act (MCA), 18
mandatory minimum prison sentences, 52
March 25 Coalition, 59
Marks, George, 93
Mark Twain Neighborhood Library, 118
Marquez, Oscar, 182n7
Marshall Islands, US bombing of, 200n12
mass incarceration, 16–17, 47, 169
Masters of the Currents (play), 161–62, 205n68

May Day protests, in Los Angeles, xiii
MCA (Major Crimes Act), 18
McArdle, Kathy, 96
McCain, John, 65, 144
McCawley, William, 118–19
Medicaid, COFA and, 203n48
mega marches, xiii, 185n26
methodology, xiv, 8, 83, 113
Mexican American Bar Association, 81
Micronesian Connections, 163–64
Micronesians, 152, 161; Hawai'i migrated to by, 138–39; Hawai'i state targeting, 153; ICE targeting, 156
Micronesian youth, 158–60, 161, 204n59
Micronesian Youth Leadership Conference (MYLC), 160–61
migrant justice activists, movement-building stories by, 21–22
migrant politics, Indigenous politics and, 11, 83, 113–14
migrant rights, in Hawai'i, xiii
migrants, economic value of, 49–50
migrants, Texas busing, 189n5
migrants of color, 83, 103
migration, root causes of, 147–48
migration justice, 3–4, 58–59, 139–40, 162, 169
Mijente (organizing space), 81, 177n14
Miranda, Deborah, 22
Moana Nui conference, 201n30
Mohawks of Kahnawà:ke, 198n66
Montrevil, Jean, 89, 99–101, 192n49
Mothers Reclaiming Our Children (ROC), 104
movement-building stories, 7–8, 21–22, 102–7, 142
Multi-ethnic Immigrant Worker Organizing Network, xv
Muñiz, Ana, 36
MYLC (Micronesian Youth Leadership Conference), 160–61

NAFTA (North American Free Trade Agreement), 8, 201n30
national belonging, 102, 173n16
National Gang Unit, of ICE, 38
National Immigrant Youth Alliance (NIYA), 136, 141
national security, immigration control as, 42–44
National Security Entry-Exit Registration System (NSEER) (Special Registration), 42–43, 88

National Youth Immigrant Alliance, 135
nation-state, 13
Native Americans, removal of, 13
Native American women, sexual violence against, 18–19
Native Hawaiians (Kanaka Maoli), 137–38, 165, 167–68, 202n40; deportations of, 203n45; incarceration of, 153; sovereignty movement of, 140, 165–66
Ndé lands, US appropriation of, 15
neoliberal era, incarceration expanding in, 196n33
New Jim Crow, 16–20
"New Jim Crow" (public discussion), IYC circulating, 175n60
New Sanctuary Movement, 91, 100, 190n21
Newsom, Gavin, 48
New Year Baby (documentary), 126–27
New York City, xiv, 189n5
New York City Police Department (NYPD), 33, 88, 192n65
New York State Working Group against Deportation, 46, 190n27
Ngai, Mae, 105
Ngouy, Suely, 116, 128, 195n27
Nicholls, Walter, 145, 146, 192n63
9/11, xiv, 42, 88
NIYA (National Immigrant Youth Alliance), 136, 141
Northam, Ralph (former Governor of Virginia), 101
North American Free Trade Agreement (NAFTA), 8, 201n30
"Not Home for the Holidays" (forum), 109, 111, 126
#Not1More, 49, 81
NSEER (National Security Entry-Exit Registration System), 42–43, 88
NYPD (New York City Police Department), 33, 88, 192n65
NYU School of Law, Immigrant Rights Clinic at, 181

Obama, Barack: DACA unveiled by, 123; immigrant rights movement reinvigorated by, xiii; S-Comm favored by, 154
OCS (Operation Community Shield), 38
Octopus of Oppression, 77–78
Octopus of Oppression and Transformation (installation), 75
Okamura, Jonathan, 164
1Love Movement, 40, 122–23
Ong, Aihwa, 88

Oparah, Julia Chinyere, 20
Operation Community Shield (OCS), by National Gang Unit, 38
"Operation Safe City," by ICE, x
oversentencing, 47

Pacific, settler carcerality in, 30–31
Pacific Islander youth, 153–54
Palantir (data-mining corporation), ix, 171n1
Palestine, 78–79, 183n9
Pallares, Amalia, 87, 95
Parker Center, 70–71
Pearce, Russell, 63
people of color, private sphere of, 96
PEP (Priority Enforcement Program), 45
Perez, Johnathan, xiv, 136–41, 142, 149, 199n1, 200nn14–15; civil disobedience impacting, 144; movement-building stories modeled by, 142; S-Comm impacting, 157
Piailug, Mau, 170
plenary power, 14–16, 18, 38–49. *See also* United States
Poeuv, Socheata, 126–27
police, cars impounded by, 191n91
police-immigration collaborations, 44–47
policing, racialized gender-sexual, 52
political coalition, Indigeneity in, 26
Polytechnic High School, 115
postconviction relief, 33–34, 91–92
Povuu'ngna, California, 114, 118–19, 132–33
Prashad, Vijay, 20
Priority Enforcement Program (PEP), 45
prison expansion, in Los Angeles County, ix–x
prison industrial complex, 89–90, 151
prisons, 203n44; COVID-19 spreading in, 181n87; detention centers connected to, 49; ICE visiting, 32; immigration enforcement in, 31–35
prison sentences, mandatory minimum, 52
private for-profit corporations, detention centers run by, 21
private sphere, of people of color, 96
profiling, of Cambodian youth, 112
Proposition 21, in California, 38
publicity, intimacy and, 20–25
Public Law 280, 18

QDEP (Queer Detainee Empowerment Project), 90
queer, trans, Black, Indigenous, people of color (QTBIPOC), 144

queer and feminist activists, 70–71; care in coalition introduced by, 57; political culture fostered by, 22; against SB 1070, 80
Queer Detainee Empowerment Project (QDEP), 90
queer migrant youth, DREAMers contrasted with, 145

race, space in relation to, 12
race-class-gender framework, 12
racialized gender-sexual policing, crimmigration embedding, 52
racial justice, FFF prioritizing, 89
racial minorities, Indigenous people contrasted with, 11–12
racial profiling, SB 1070 legitimized by, 56–57
Ragbir, Ravi, 91, 190n26
Ramos, Valeria De La Luz, 148
Rancho Los Alamitos, California, 132
Rath, Richard, 116
Reagan, Ronald, 117
Reddy, Chandan, 184n18
Red Nation Rising (Estes et al.), 53
refugee (term), 110–11
refugee community, in Long Beach, xv
refugee failure, criminality connected with, 134
refugee refusal, 198n66
refugees, as criminal aliens, 134
refugees, Cambodian. *See* Cambodian refugees
"Release Not Transfer" campaign, 33, 34
repatriation, 40–41, 123
reproductive politics, deportations as, 87, 131
resettlement, 110–14
Resilience OC, 200nn14–15
"Resolution of the Tohono O'odham Legislative Council" (Tohono O'odham Legislative Council), 183n8
respectability politics, families and, 96, 103–4
Rifkin, Mark, 12
Rios, Victor, 112
RISE Movement, 62
ROC (Mothers Reclaiming Our Children), 104
Rodríguez, Richard, 87
Rosheuvel, Janis, 99
rule of law, US exceptionalism and, 172n3

www.ingramcontent.com/pod-product-compliance
Lightning Source LLC
Chambersburg PA
CBHW071735270326
41928CB00013B/2680